Slumlords

A Story of Great Social and Political Import

Written by and based on the recollections of
Steve O

DEDICATION

This book is dedicated to Reverend Terry, the man who listened to my stories when no one else would and to my editor Wendy Bear for her love, encouragement and excellent punctuation skills.

Quadruple Disclaimer!!!!

This is a work of fiction. Names, characters, places and incidents either are products of the author's imagination, or are used fictitiously. Any resemblance to actual events or locales is purely coincidental.

Furthermore, all characters appearing in this work are definitely fictitious and any resemblance to real persons, living or dead is also purely coincidental.

Still furthermore, this is not a story based on historical fact, but on the fact that it is human nature to selfishly pursue one's own interest without regard for the interests or welfare of others.

As such, any similarities to actual events that you may have heard of or even remotely remember, involving city governments, apartment complexes, and the people who own them, are not only purely coincidental, but somewhat inevitable.

In addition; Warning! This work is not suitable for children as it contains adult themes; violence, explicit sex and coarse language and lots of other cool stuff that sells lots of copies of books.

As such, do not read it to your children as a bedtime story; and do not even think of suing us, as this would make us very upset and very, very, sad.

Prologue

I have come to take great comfort in the idea that in the world of cowboys, the brands which cattle come to bear say little about the cattle themselves and so much more about those doing the branding.

And it is with such a thought in mind that I offer up to you this cautionary tale about the ambitions of men and the caveats of wishes fulfilled.

It is a story which considers the notion that although no one deliberately sets out to be the villain, sometimes it just works out that way.

And this can be a good thing.

For sometimes amidst the most hideous of circumstances, when we find ourselves conscripted to play out the most villainous of roles, perhaps it is then that we may find redemption not in our fortunes, but in our misfortunes.

And at least for this we can be grateful.

"Steve my boy, this is not what we bargained for!"

"No indeed, Morty, not by a longshot!"

And in the end, this is all that could be said.

Chapter 1.1

Harold Bittlehauser Had Only One Lung

Woodcrest Apartments – El Paso, Texas – August 2000 - Exactly 24 hours and 14 minutes before the biggest gas explosion in Texas history

Harold Bittlehauser had only one lung. As he explained on numerous occasions, his physical abnormality was indirectly responsible for several DUI convictions which he had unjustly suffered in several states including Texas, Louisiana, Nevada, Arizona and New Mexico.

According to Harold, the fact that he only had one lung had caused the reading on his breathalyzer tests to erroneously double, seeing as that the alcohol only had one lung to exit from. It logically followed, according to Harold, that he was in fact, on all five occasions, at only 51 percent of the legal limit and as such he was the victim of shoddy police work and an unjust system of selective enforcement that didn't recognize the special needs of the handicapped, or the rights of hard-working *real* Americans like himself to relax a little at the end of the day, consume a six-pack or two and maybe a bottle of Jack, and then take a leisurely drive just to unwind.

Nonetheless, his personal opinions aside, during daylight hours Harold was a hard worker. As lead maintenance guy at the Woodcrest Apartments, a building Steve and his partners had owned for just about six months now, Harold was in charge of keeping 352 toilets, 352 stoves, 352 refrigerators, 704 sinks, 1,056 drains and 3,520 windows, in tip-top working order.

And at age 54, Harold knew just about everything there was to know about apartment maintenance – including plumbing, electric, heating and cooling, refrigeration, carpentry and construction.

With such a knowledgeable and talented guy around, at least according to Harold, Steve and The Boys were the luckiest God-damn apartment owners in all of the great state of Texas.

"Fuckin-A! You got that right! – With a guy like me on the team, those guys are covered. They don't need to hire none of those fancy licensed plumbers, or electricians, or heating and cooling guys. They got me, and no matter what goes wrong, I can fix it, no problem. All I need is the right parts, the right tools, a case of Bud Light, a pack of Marlboros and a couple of hours to put it all together."

And when fate came calling that hot Texas day in August Harold was there and he was ready – one man, one tool belt, one lung, and one day that will live in infamy in the annals of the El Paso Fire Department.

It was 12:00 noon that day and the temperature in the west parking lot of the apartments hovered at about 128 degrees. Fourteen minutes earlier the chiller system at the complex had mysteriously lost pressure and gone down.

And at first, no one really seemed to notice, but after about six minutes the temperature in the apartments began to climb and calls began flooding in to the office.

As Frank's mom Eileen – the new manager at "the Crest" – heard the tenants begin to complain about how hot it was getting in their apartments, she immediately concluded, being a religious woman, that the apocalypse, which she knew was likely to occur any day now, was indeed underway and that the entire neighborhood of Eastwood was in the process of being consumed by the fires of hell, thus explaining the sudden rise in temperature.

"I knew this would happen," she thought to herself.

Eileen, who had been the former manager of the Pinewood Villa Apartments, the first complex that Steve and The Boys had ever purchased in the El Paso area some eight years back, was no stranger to the property management game, nor was she a stranger to the evil ways of men with their lying and cheating and their thick, hard cocks which felt so good inside her but which, in the end, invariably left her feeling empty and alone.

And as she struggled for the last 23 years to raise her two children Frank and Jenny, stay away from the booze, and heal herself from a self-diagnosed tumor she was sure was growing inside her gall bladder, Eileen made a solemn vow to herself that she "would never again fall victim to the evil doings of men," and this didn't just include her drunk-ass ex-husband who had "gone out for cigarettes" some fifteen years back and had never returned. It included all men, even wealthy Jewish men who owned apartment complexes.

No, she had seen her share of their shenanigans and hung up the towel some eight years back when she quit as the manager of Pinewood, telling Steve at the time that if he wasn't going to let her have garage sales every Saturday on the front lawn of the apartments, and if he wasn't going to give her a Home Depot credit card, then he could take his job and go straight to the devil with it, which was kind of redundant in Eileen's mind because as a Jew he was going straight to the devil anyway.

So it was quite the surprise then, when just six months earlier Eileen had accepted the position of manager at Woodcrest, clearly and distinctly pointing out that her presence there in her new capacity was by no means a situation of her own choosing.

As a matter of fact, she emphatically insisted and repeated on numerous occasions that she had not accepted the job of Woodcrest manager because she wanted to manage the building or even because she needed the money.

No! She was there simply and solely because God, personally and in no uncertain terms, had commanded her to be there; her duty being to protect and defend the tenants of Woodcrest and the citizens of Eastwood against the evil influences of Satan and the minions of the non-believers, these minions being the new owners of the Woodcrest complex, Steve and his partners, a group of five wealthy investors who had come to be known in the El Paso area as the Beverly Hills Boys Back Home.

Chapter 2.1

Morty and Steve

Beverly Hills, California - August 1990 – Exactly ten years, 24 hours and 14 minutes before the biggest gas explosion in Texas history

Morton Simon Salt will always be remembered for three things: his vast wealth, his need to feel important and his enormous size-18 EEE feet.

"Morty," the organizer of the Beverly Hills Boys Back Home was a gaunt and jaundiced man in his late sixties. He had yellowish-grey skin, stood 6'4" tall, walked in a slightly hunched over manner and enthralled in the recitation of the phrase "they can just go pound sand," which he took great delight in repeating as often as possible when he was lucky enough to find an appropriate circumstance.

"They can just go pound sand," he would say referring to someone he didn't want to pay for some reason or another. (And there was always someone he didn't want to pay for some reason or another, not that he didn't have the money but he was just in love with the idea of getting something for nothing.) "They can just go pound sand," he would say when some republican candidate's office would solicit him for a campaign contribution (not that he didn't contribute to political campaigns, but he was a staunch supporter of the Democratic Party and despised republicans with a vengeance.) "They can just go pound sand," he would say when one of the many commercial tenants who inhabited one of his 300 shopping centers throughout the country would ask for some rent concession or improvement to their store space (not because he couldn't afford to grant concessions or make improvements to the properties but just because he firmly believed in the old adage "if it ain't broke, why fix it.")

His physical attributes and personality quirks aside, Morton Salt was a man who, despite the fact that he was a multi-multi-millionaire, fancied himself a man of learning – a stoic and meticulously-mannered individual. He spent much of his time studying for his PhD in psychoanalysis (a degree he wanted to receive so that people could call him Dr. Salt…he thought that was funny because it would be the opposite of Dr. Pepper), and collecting rare fabric swatches produced by ancient and medieval civilizations, the collection of which he displayed on the yellowish-grey walls which matched his yellowish-grey skin, in that gloomy crypt-like lair which Morty called his office on the fourth floor of that purposely non-descript brick building on Wilshire Boulevard in Beverly Hills, California.

But when he wasn't studying for his doctorate, collecting ancient fabric swatches or telling people to "pound sand," Morton Salt spent much of his time going through the motions of pursuing what he considered to be his obligation in life – the building of his own real estate empire, an empire he desperately needed to someday rival the accomplishments of his late father, the truly great Saul T. Salt.

You see Morty, a successful fellow by inheritance only, was a man of copious yet frustrated ambition; and as heir to the Fabric Frontier fortune, a company which had operated and owned over 300 fabric and craft stores throughout the U.S. until sometime in the early seventies, his "burden" in life was being able to prove that he was no Edsel Ford – that regardless of his vast inheritance, Morty's financial success would someday stand on its own merits.

Yes indeed, his father's legacy had left Morty with some pretty big shoes to fill.

The two billion-dollar empire that Morty had inherited was the sole product of his father's great business genius. Saul Theodore Salt (or *Saul T* as his friends called him) had not only built and operated the stores that comprised his fabric kingdom, he had also built the shopping centers that the stores were located in as well. Thus, he not only made money off the Fabric Frontier chain, he also made money off the other five or six stores that were tenants in each of his 300 or so Fabric Frontier Shopping Centers.

And the humble real estate that Saul Salt had amassed for $1000 an acre back in the 40s when he had begun his empire was now worth in excess of $1,000,000 an acre. When Saul died in 1985, his diligent yet clueless son Morton inherited one of the greatest personal real estate fortunes in U.S. history and became the proud owner of the nearly 300 shopping centers, an empire which stretched from Chappaqua, New York to Van Nuys, California.

Now as if Morty didn't already have enough money, in 1990 he married billionaire business woman and socialite Nicole Gamble, a Beverly Hills native 25 years his junior

and creator of a line of designer purses which were market-
ed under the brand name of *Nicki's Pouch*. In addition to
her own accomplishments in the purse industry, Nicki was
one of the heirs to a small business fortune of her own – a
little home products company founded by her great-great-
great-great-grandfather James.

Their combined net worth being estimated at somewhere
just over 2.5 billion dollars, the Salt-Gamble team was a
force to be reckoned with. They were acquaintances of Bill
and Hillary's, they were staunch supporters of the Democratic Party and had helped a mayor friend of theirs in her
bid for the U.S. Senate, they gave money to various chari-
ties and foundations and they were members of B'nai
B'rith. They were also members of both Sam's Club and
Costco since they liked to stock up on good bargains when
they had the chance.

Now the event which sets this whole story in motion was
the moment that Morton Salt met Steve Schafer.

Steve, an ambitious, young "up and comer" in the real
estate game was the individual who was to become the facilitator of Morty's dream – to rival the accomplishments of
his father, the late-great Saul T. Salt and to prove once and
for all to all his friends down at the Wilshire Golf and
Country Club that unlike them, his success would stand on
its own merits, and that just in general he was smarter and
better than they were.

An unlikely pairing to say the least, one could only conclude that Steve and Morty's partnership must have been
fate, because the likelihood of these two individuals ever
meeting in the first place, let alone becoming partners, was
one in two billion, two billion being the number of dollars
in Morty's bank account and one being the number of dollars in Steve's.

Morty was convinced upon meeting young Steve (for
just four and a half minutes) that Steve was the necessary

ingredient that had so far been missing in his plan to dominate the Beverly Hills' real estate investment scene and to prove to his friends that he was a financial genius.

It was a cloudy day in Los Angeles when the two met for the very first time at Morty's office in Beverly Hills. Tucked discretely away on the fourth floor of that nondescript five-story office building on Wilshire Boulevard, the entrance to his office had no sign on the door, no welcome mat and no doorbell.

The entrance was just two nine-foot high solid mahogany doors, each one with a single brass door knob. The doors were locked and the only way to summon anyone to open the door was to knock, which Steve did about five or six times before Dolores, a woman in her mid-sixties with a Brooklyn accent and a grey bouffant 50s' housewife hairdo, finally opened it and let Steve in.

As Steve walked in and looked around he thought to himself that walking into Morty's office was just like walking into a time capsule of the1950s. Polished wood furniture with uncomfortable fabric-covered cushions, yellowish-grey metal filing cabinets, and yellowish-grey metal desks filled the room; yellowish-grey striped fabric wallpaper covered the wall and ceiling of the entire office. As a matter of fact, the only thing that wasn't yellowish-grey and would have clued you in to the fact that it was 1990 was a large desktop computer and printer that sat on a wooden desk at the back of the entrance area.

Upon walking in, Dolores told Steve to sit on the couch and wait. She said Morty would be out in a few minutes and to "just make yourself comfortable," which was nearly impossible to do on that itchy, wooden-handled couch with the foam rubber stuffing.

She then returned to her own small work area in the back of the office which was sectioned off by a glass wall framed in a yellowish-grey wood partition.

Finally, after about 25 minutes, Morton Salt emerged from his own private section of the office and introduced himself to Steve. Steve stood up, shook Morty's hand, and began to make small talk – about the real estate business and about politics in general – knowing that Morty was a staunch supporter of the Democratic Party.

And with thirty seconds of chit-chat having been dispensed, and with still no invitation to join Morty in the inner sanctum of his office, it became clear to Steve that their entire meeting was going to take place right there, just five feet from the doorway where Steve had entered 25 minutes before.

Nevertheless, the moment that Morty and Steve met for that first time, the two of them immediately hit it off, and within two minutes of their first talking it became clear to both of them that not only was this a moment of divine destiny but an occurrence of extreme historical significance whose ramifications would not only effect generations to come but perhaps world history itself. (Morton Salt tended to take himself a little seriously.)

Now what always stuck in Steve's mind about their first meeting, besides Morty's grayish-yellow skin and his enormous feet, was both the brevity of the whole thing while at the same time the gravity of the whole thing.

You see the entire conversation, which was to become the basis of their partnership for the next ten years and which would come to effect the lives of so many people, lasted a total of just four short minutes.

And based on this one brief four-minute conversation, Steve, at least in his own mind anyway, immediately upon leaving Morty's office went from a bumbling young dreamer with two dollars in his pocket to a real estate tycoon with millions of dollars to spend, literally, in the blink of an eye.

It was a moment which, being the philosopher poet he was, inspired Steve to compose a bitter-sweet saying that from that day forward he would repeat to himself on numerous occasions when he was feeling reflective:

Ain't it funny how a moment can define who you are, and then simply just fade away.

But as they talked, ever so brief a conversation as it was, it became immediately clear that Steve and Morty had a lot in common.

Both Steve, at the tender age of 29, and Morty, at the tender age of 69, were just starting out in the world – looking to make their mark, build their empires, and conquer the unconquerable.

Both Steve and Morty were enthralled with the idea of negotiating the *killer* deal, the *home run*, the *Yes!* (Such a deal could be defined as buying a building listed for one million dollars, putting it in escrow at $875,000 and then incessantly and unrelentingly "grinding" the seller down, and beating the financial shit out of him until he finally handed over the keys for $150,000 begging you to "please just take it." Then only two hours after the sale was final, turning around and selling the very same building for two million dollars! Just talking about a deal like that was getting them high with excitement; it was like sex, only better.)

Both Steve and Morty took pride in their frugality, Steve boasting that not only did he "coupon shop" at the grocery store but that he averaged an impressive 50 percent off the total bill and had once even left the store with the checker *giving him* two cents after the coupons were deducted.

Morty retorted by telling Steve that he had been wearing the same pair of shoes for the last thirty years, explaining "if it ain't broke why fix it," the implications of which kind of scared Steve a little, bearing in mind that Morty owned over 300 shopping centers, surely somewhere, sometime, one of those shoes might have needed a little fixing even if it wasn't broke yet.

And perhaps the most striking commonality between the two was that they shared identical business philosophies which they had both formulated from reading the exact same book, Napoleon Hill's classic "success" treatise *Think and Grow Rich*.

The work, originally written sometime in the 1930s, chronicled and analyzed the successes of some of the great industrialists of the early twentieth century, including Andrew Carnegie, Thomas Edison and Henry Ford. It drew together the common themes which contributed to and allowed for the successes of these and other great men and it proposed a philosophy, or recipe, of success which if followed could take ordinary men like Morty and Steve and turn them into extraordinary men. As such, this book became the original blueprint which Morty and Steve used to begin their plan of attack on the unsuspecting real estate market.

Yes indeed, the two of them were about to embark on an extraordinary journey together.

And Morty, having the money to finance Steve's ambition of making it big in the apartment business, and Steve, having the street smarts to actually assemble a real estate empire that would rival the one built by Morty's father, well, it was clear that each of them were about to become the facilitator of each other's dreams.

But Steve and Morty's kinship went deeper than that. There was a certain dynamic to their relationship that one might say came not from their similarities but from their differences.

First of all, they did come from slightly different worlds. Morty's was one of wealth and privilege, his father being a business mogul. Steve's was one of educated poverty, his father being a school teacher.

Steve followed the rules. Morty was used to making his own rules.

Steve's behavior was subject to consequences. Morty's wasn't subject to consequences at all; when trouble arose in the past, Saul had simply "taken care of it."

Steve had to play the cards he was dealt. When Morty was dealt a bad hand, he simply got a new fucking deck of cards.

And finally, the most important difference between Steve Schaefer and Morton Salt – Steve was a pragmatist. He accepted things as they were and dealt with them as they came along. Morty was an "*im*pragmatist;" he lived in a world that *he* had created. He made up his own reality and then fit the facts in accordingly.

And so we come to the heart of the matter and that is this: the reason Morty and Steve hit it off so well was Morty was an expert at telling people what *he* wanted to hear, and Steve was an expert in telling people what *they* wanted to hear.

This dynamic – Morty wanting a certain reality and Steve providing it – was the basis of what could be referred to as "a match made in heaven, with possible repercussions made in hell."

And with Steve immediately empowered with an unlimited source of funds to buy any piece of real estate he so desired while at the same time armed with almost no experience whatsoever in buying and running large real estate empires, Steve, as long as he told Morty what Morty wanted to hear, was off to conquer the world.

And so in the time it would have taken to make a cup of coffee (not that Morton Salt ever made his own coffee), an undertaking that would cost hundreds of millions of dollars and affect the lives of thousands of people was launched right there in the reception area of Morty's office in Beverly Hills. It was founded on a *feeling*, just four and a half minutes after they had met, with absolutely no planning, no forethought and without the slightest consideration that neither one of them had any idea of what they were about to embark on, nor for that matter what they were doing.

And as it was Morty's habit to jot down the details of his plans in a little blue notebook that he kept in the left front pocket of his jacket, he began to list the major underpinnings of their ambitious plan, the plan being as follows:

1. Morton – Find investors to put up money. (O.P.M. – *Other People's Money*)

2. Steve – Find buildings to buy and run in El Paso, Texas. (The Savings & Loan Crisis of the early 80s had left a large amount of "cheap" buildings on the market in the El Paso area and both Morty and Steve both loved the idea of getting something "for cheap.")

CHAPTER 1.2

Like a Penny in a Cornfield

Woodcrest Apartments – El Paso, Texas - 24 hours and 8 minutes before the biggest gas explosion in the city's history

Now not only had God charged Eileen, in her new capacity as the manager of Woodcrest, with the ardent task of saving the inhabitants of the Eastwood neighborhood, he had also given her the extremely difficult job of saving Steve from himself, a feat she could only accomplish through constant prayer and by the diligent and systematic righting of the wrongs that Steve and his band of Beverly Hills "Christ Killers" had committed or had yet to commit upon the unsuspecting neighborhood.

And even though the job was hard she knew in her heart of hearts that eventually she would get Steve to see the error of his ways, to repent and to apologize not only for being a Jew but for being a man.

But now, with this whole rise in temperature thing and the whole chiller system being down situation, "God knows how long saving the neighborhood and saving Steve was going to take."

And regardless of the reason the chiller had gone down, and with all the complaints flooding into the office, it became clear that the situation required immediate attention, Eileen realizing that it would probably be a good idea, if not her duty, to call Steve and let him know what was going on.

But Eileen, being the shrewd thinker that she was, decided not to call Steve just yet, as she wasn't sure if Steve, being that he was definitely under the influence of the Prince of Darkness – if he wasn't indeed Satan himself – may have purposely sabotaged the system, hoping to give the poor tenants at "the Crest" a little taste of what it was going to be like when their immortal souls were finally cast into the furious fires of hell.

So she just decided to handle the problem on her own, at least for the moment, and called Harold to the office to see if there was anything he could do.

Now to fully appreciate the complexity of the problem it is important to understand how the chiller system at Woodcrest, or any chiller system for that matter, works.

The system itself was comprised of a giant compressor through which pressurized water would run through a series of radiator-like channels and be chilled to a temperature of about 38 degrees Fahrenheit.

The chilled water was then pumped through a series of underground pipes which stretched and turned for about four miles, just about six feet below the surface of the 7.8 acres on which the apartments were located.

These four miles of underground pipes in turn led to about six miles of above-ground pipes which ran into and out of the apartments and ran through cooling registers within the ceilings in each of those 352 apartments on the property.

Inside the cooling registers, fans would blow over the pipes containing the chilled water and cool the air inside the register. This cool air would then blow through the register and into the apartments, cooling the air inside the apartment and in turn cooling the residents who dwelled within.

The system had been installed using state of the art technology of its day. It was ingenious, it was efficient, and it was effective.

It was also forty-fucking years old(!) and as one might guess, eventually, inevitably, invariably and expectedly – somewhere, someday and for no particular reason – one of the pipes, somewhere along that ten-mile stretch, was going to spring a leak. And today was the day. And as a result of this leak, the system had lost pressure and the chiller had shut down.

Now as if the scope of the problem wasn't overwhelming enough, and just to give you an idea of the complexity of the whole situation – using state of the art technology at the time, it would probably have taken a NASA thermal imaging satellite about three hours at a cost of about twelve million dollars to scan the 7.8 acres and ten miles of piping at the property in order to locate and isolate the source of the leak in the system.

A leak large enough to depressurize the system and render it inoperative could be as small as an aspirin or maybe even a Tylenol or an Aleve or something like that, and the area covered by the apartments was approximately the size of eight football fields. So it was like finding a penny in a cornfield, or a needle in a haystack, or whatever other metaphor you feel like using.

Employing a less sophisticated method of running a small camera through the lines and visually observing the source of the leak, Roto-Rooter estimated it would take approximately twelve hours at a cost of about three thousand dollars to detect the leak and another three hours to excavate and repair the pipe at a cost of an additional two thousand dollars. But Harold, who said "a leak like that would not be that difficult to find," had a much simpler and less expensive plan.

Harold's half-nephew Andy, who had just come down from Arkansas with his wife Arlene and their two German Shepherds Rusty and Max, were all staying with Harold and his wife in their one-bedroom apartment at Woodcrest. Back home Andy had done some plumbing of his own and so Harold figured, since Andy was there anyway, and three lungs were better than one, they could work together on the chiller project.

Harold's ingenious plan was roughly as follows: he and Andy would use that new Ronco Super-Sensitive Micro-Phone Spy Device that Andy had bought at Eileen's Garage Sale (she sure did love to have garage sales) the previous weekend to "listen for" and to discover the leak.

Once located, they could dig up the pipe, go down to the plumbing supply warehouse to get the right size piece of replacement pipe and then return to the complex to install the new pipe section. Then once the system re-pressurized itself, they could reboot the chiller, flush out the condenser coils and before you knew it, the system would be up and running and as good as new.

And the best part about Harold's plan was that rather than telling anyone they had done the work themselves, they could say that Roto-Rooter had come and done the work; this way they could make up their own invoice for what Roto-Rooter would have charged, about $4800, keep what was left of the money themselves after paying the plumbing supply warehouse for supplies, with no one being the wiser and them being about $4500 richer!

The $4500 profit would then be split as follows: Harold to get $3,125.70 and Andy to get the rest, whatever that was because they didn't have a calculator with them when they figured out the split, and neither Harold nor Andy were really that good at math.

Of Harold's $3,125.70, three thousand could be used to pay off his most recent DUI fine and the remaining $125.70 could be used to pay the 90-day delinquent portion of his cable bill because the *Retro Weekend Sports Bonanza Featuring the Year 1955* was going to be on ESPN this coming Sunday and he didn't want to miss it. (As he had this kind of intuitive feeling that they were going to shut his cable off any day now.)

It was a plan of complexity in its undertaking and a plan of beauty in its simplicity and it all hinged on one magnificent technological marvel known as the Ronco Super-Sensitive Battery-Powered Micro-Phone Spy Device. It was the one advertised on TV and only available through a one-time special offer if you ordered before midnight tonight and which Eileen had purchased over the phone with the American Express Card which had come in the mail for Steve but which Eileen had neglected to tell Steve had arrived.

By calling the number on the TV screen and paying the unbelievably low price of only four payments of $9.99 while supplies lasted, not only did Eileen get the Micro-Phone Spy Device but she also got a free set of Ginzu steak knives and a complimentary one-year subscription to *Modern Espionage* magazine.

Her initial thought and her reason for buying the device in the first place was to use it to "listen in on" each and every one of the 352 apartments in the Woodcrest complex.

After listening to each of the tenants' conversations, she could then determine by the content of those conversations who was and who was not in league with Satan.

She could then compile a list of the tenants worthy of being saved in the upcoming apocalypse and a list of those who were to be condemned to the eternal fires of hell and she could then pass these lists on to God so that he would know who to condemn and who to save, and basically what to do when the time of judgment came.

"Good thing for God that I am around to help him," Eileen thought to herself.

Upon receiving the device though, she decided that the instructions on the back of the box for unscrewing the battery compartment and inserting and connecting the two six-volt batteries required to operate the machine were too complicated and so she never bothered to open the box.

She did, however, want to keep the free set of Ginzu steak knives and receive her complimentary issues of *Modern Espionage* so she decided not to return the device for a full refund to Steve's charge account, even though she wasn't "100 percent completely satisfied that the Micro-Phone Spy Device was the best listening spy device she had ever seen."

So after staring at the darn thing on her kitchen table for a couple of days, she finally decided to put it up for sale in one of her usual Saturday morning garage sales.

Andy, who had nothing to do that day since he was unemployed, decided to go over to the garage sale to kill a couple of hours, and picked it up for a cool two dollars and figured someday it might come in handy, especially if he ever got a job as a spy or a private detective or something like that.

With this "state of the art" technical marvel now in the expertly trained hands of Harold and Andy, they could find the leak by simply "listening for it" and once they could hear the leak, they would mark the spot on the ground where the leak was with a large red steel spike, another item Andy had picked up at the garage sale figuring it too might come in handy someday if he ever got a job as a mountain climber or an oil rigger or something like that.

Any other tools Harold and Andy needed, Andy said he could get from the tool shed over at the Juniper Apartments, another complex owned by Steve and The Boys. Andy pointed out that lately, he was always able to find a bunch of extra tools lying around at the Juniper including a ten-pound sledge hammer he had used just last weekend to try and bang out the dents in his recently demolished white Ford pick-up. Apparently Harold had accidentally run into it with the skid-steer while he was moving a load of cinder blocks he was using to fix the concrete wall outside the Woodcrest office.

(Just a quick note about that sledgehammer and the other *extra* tools that Andy had found over at the Juniper Apartments – they were indeed the very same tools that Norris, the ex-manager over at Juniper was looking for and the very ones which Norris swore that if he caught the son of a bitch who stole them he'd fucking kill 'em and then sue the thieving bastards for the full replacement value of the tools plus damages for psychological stress, entrusting the case to his friend and bowling league partner Stanley Parker, Attorney At Law.)

Sub-Chapter 1.2

Loss of Consortium – In Re: Those Tools Andy Just Happened to Find Lying Around on the Lawn at the Juniper Apartments

El Paso, Texas – June 2000 - The Juniper Apartments

He thrust his throbbing manhood into her warm wet honey-pot.

"Deeper, Deeper" she said, "fill me with every inch of your rock hard man rod." And as she felt his member explode inside her, spewing shot after shot of his hot thick man-juice, she screamed out, "YES! YES! YES! Fill Momma up and drive Momma home!"

Norris read on, but alas, it was to no avail. His once mighty turgid shaft was now as limp as the soft rubber air hose on his 362-piece pneumatic socket set, and try as he may, he just couldn't get it to stir.

The trouble had all started just a few weeks before with a surprise visit from Steve and his right hand man Buck. Steve and Buck had driven in from California, unannounced, to survey the situation at Steve and The Boys twenty-third and latest acquisition in the El Paso area, the Juniper Apartments.

The Juniper was a forty-unit building, located next to a cemetery, just three blocks away from Pinewood Villas – the first complex Steve and The Boys had ever purchased in Texas. Like "the Villas," the Juniper Apartments had a three-bedroom house located in front of the property, and like the Villas, the manager of Juniper Apartments, Norris Finch, lived in the house rent-free. His lovely wife, Anna Bell, who was unfortunately deaf, lived there with him.

As the story goes, when Steve and Buck arrived that afternoon, Norris was in the maintenance shed polishing his bowling ball for the semi-finals of the league tournament that was to take place that evening. He looked forward with great anticipation to the match because if they could win this one, it was almost a sure thing that they could win the finals coming up in Las Vegas the following week.

His friend, Stanley Parker, Attorney At Law, and his other friend Ron, a power tool salesman, comprised the three-man team that was the "sure on" favorite to take the trophy this year, and they were both grateful to Norris that he had shelled out the $575 entry fee for the tournament since they were both running a little short on cash this month. They did agree, however, that when they got some money, they would pay Norris back.

Having only owned the building for five days, Steve was excited to get down to business and learn as much as he could about running the Juniper Apartments. In light of the tremendous success of Pinewood Villas, and the fact that "the Villas" was only a few blocks away, Steve was under a little pressure to "turn the Juniper around" and to start making the same "gangbuster" profits that the Villas was turning out.

The Juniper, although it was almost fully occupied had, to date, turned in a lackluster performance. It did okay, but okay wasn't good enough for Steve and The Boys Back Home; they were looking to hit home runs, not singles.

So when Steve first met Norris, he introduced himself, asked Norris a little bit about Norris, pretended to listen, made a little small talk and then got down to business explaining to Norris that things were going to be a little different around there now that Steve and The Boys were the new owners.

Then he asked Norris the $27,500 question – was Norris up to the challenge of doing what needed to be done, which was to get the place back in tip-top shape and start making some real money at the Juniper?

You see the Juniper was looking a bit old and a bit tired and coincidentally Norris was looking a bit old and a bit tired too.

The truth was, Norris wasn't into all that ambitious, hit a home run, be Superman, stuff.

The truth was he *was* tired. And he just wanted to be left alone; to bowl, to drink a brewski (Bud Light of course), to watch some TV in his rent-free house and maybe once in a while putter in the maintenance shop, and since it was necessary, to collect the rents from the forty or so tenants that lived at the complex. And for him that was enough. And that's the way things had pretty much been for the last eleven years, when Mr. Peasdale had owned the place.

And so in light of how things had been for the last eleven years, you can imagine how Norris must have felt listening to Mr. Gung-ho Big City Businessman Steve, tell Norris his big plans to make the Juniper a shining star in the Beverly Hills Boys' "empire."

And as Norris listened to Steve spout off about big renovation plans, and increasing the rents, and lowering the utility bills, he quietly thought to himself, "this kid is full of shit, he doesn't know what he's talking about," and as Norris continued to listen to Steve he was beginning to feel a little shaken up, kind of like he was in a boat that had just been rocked, and then he started to feel kind of annoyed that Steve was trying to make all these changes, the kind of annoyed you feel when someone wakes you up from a nap, Norris's nap having lasted eleven years.

And so as he shook his head yes, saying that he was indeed up to the challenge, he thought to himself, "fuck you asshole!" and as he continued to shake his head yes, agreeing there was a lot that could be done around the Juniper to really make the place shine, he thought to himself, again, "fuck you, double asshole!" And as he was shaking his head yes and thinking fuck you, he quietly wondered to himself, "When was Steve going to finally shut the fuck up and just go away" so that he could go take a piss and then finally get back to polishing his bowling ball.

The inspection tour of the Juniper began with Steve asking Norris how many units were vacant and Norris telling him there was only one, unit #23. This was excellent news. The place was 97 percent occupied. Norris went on to tell Steve that he was in the process of re-doing the floors in unit #23 and so Steve and Buck couldn't get in there to see it right now, but it would probably be ready in about a week or so. By then, hopefully, the apartment would be rented.

With the occupancy rate squared away, Steve got down to the most important business at hand, picking up and accounting for the rents which Norris had collected for the month so far. This too turned out to be excellent news. Norris had collected the rents for all of the units, except of course for the vacant unit #23.

After taking the money that Norris had collected and putting it in the Bank of America money pouch they had just gotten when they had opened the new Juniper bank account, Steve and Buck were treated to a tour of the maintenance shed, which Norris was quick to point out was his pride and joy.

Norris had been at the Juniper for over eleven years, and over that time, had assembled a pretty impressive collection of power tools. Every month the old owner of Juniper, Harry Peasdale, had let Norris put aside a bit of the rent collections in order to purchase a new tool for the complex, which he always loyally ordered from his friend and bowling league teammate, Ron, the power tool salesman. And even though technically, since the tools were purchased with company money they were property of the Juniper Apartments, Norris still liked to think of them as his babies. After all, he had picked out each and every one of them from Ron's catalogue, sometimes taking days to decide between the rotary or the flat sander or between the pneumatic or compressor-driven socket set. Each tool was more than just a tool, each contained a little bit of Norris's soul.

Having finished their tour of the maintenance shed, and after walking around the grounds a little, just to see if anything on the outside could use a little sprucing up, Steve and Buck took the blue B of A money pouch and headed for the car. But as they started walking, something a little strange happened.

At first Steve hardly even noticed the anomaly but subconsciously he just had this feeling that something was a little off. As they walked, a lady and two small children exited an apartment, the children each carrying an armful of toys and the mother telling them to wait as she closed the apartment door. The kids caught Steve's attention because they were screaming and laughing like kids normally do, and they were running ahead of their mother as she screamed out to tell them to wait.

It was when the apartment door closed that Steve realized what it was. The number on the door was #23. And #23 was the unit that was vacant, and also the unit that Norris had just re-done the floors. So why were two kids and their mom coming out of there?

Well, needless to say, they lived in there. The apartment was indeed not vacant at all, and this meant, that unless Norris was wrong about which apartment number was vacant, there was exactly $575 missing from the amount that Norris should have collected.

A coincidence, you say? I think not. An entry fee to a bowling tournament, you say? I think so.

Now normally, a thing like this wouldn't have bothered Steve so much; after all, he was more of a big picture kind of guy, and in the scheme of things, what was one misappropriated rent in a sea of rents that Steve and Morty were going to collect that month. And besides, the place seemed to be running well anyway, so why stir up a bunch of trouble before Steve and Buck had to get back to Beverly Hills, better to just live and let live.

But for some reason, on this particular day, and at this particular moment, Steve just couldn't let it go. And as he stood there thinking about what to do, he thought about how long a journey it had been that had delivered him to this point, and how hard he had worked, and how so many people had tried to take advantage of him and cheat him along the way.

And in a moment that can only be described as one of temporary insanity, all the rage and disappointment and disillusionment that had been welling up inside him since the fourth grade when Paul Cotter had stolen his lunch box and defiantly ate Steve's tuna sandwich right in front of him as an unmistakable fuck you, all that pent up rage just burst forth from Steve like a giant zit that had just been popped, causing him to burst forth with pus-like words of hatred and loathing toward an unexpecting, half-asleep Norris Finch.

And so after only five days and four minutes of employment, Steve fired Norris, screaming at the top of his lungs for all the tenants to hear, "NORRIS, YOU FUCKING THIEF, STEALING THE RENTS, SITTING ON YOUR LAZY ASS NOT FIXING ANYTHING, LIVING FOR FREE IN THAT HOUSE LIKE THE WORTHLESS PIECE OF SHIT SPONGE THAT YOU ARE, GET YOUR SHIT, PACK YOUR THINGS AND GET THE FUCK OUT, NOW!"

And as if that were not quite sufficient, Steve did something extra special, just to hurt Norris where he lived. Steve went into the tool shed, ripped every power tool off the shelf and tossed them, each of Norris' "babies," one by one, out the door and onto the lawn in front of the shed, screaming like a little kindergarten child, "THEY'RE MY TOOLS NOW, NORRIS, MY TOOLS NOW, THIEF, AND I'LL DO WITH THEM WHATEVER I WANT. MY TOOLS, DO YOU HEAR ME? MINE!"

Two days later, when Steve got the Summons and Complaint, notifying him that he was being sued by Norris Finch, Steve was in his bedroom in his house in California having sex with his wife. As he thrust *his* throbbing member into *her* warm wet honey-pot, a knock came on their bedroom window. It was the process server, who upon getting Steve's attention, politely waved hello and then slipped the papers through the bottom of the window which was cracked open just about an inch or so.

Steve reached down from the bed and picked the papers off the floor. As soon as Steve's hand touched the papers, the process server said, "you've been served," kind of like when kids play tag and say "you're it." Then he wished Steve a good evening, waved goodbye and walked back to his car.

Steve, who had been unable to maintain his erection due to the interruption, sat up cross-legged in bed and began to read the complaint.

Norris's attorney and bowling teammate, Stanley Parker, had done quite a thorough job in preparing the suit. He had especially done his research when it came to establishing causes of action which had specific prescribed compensatory damages attached to them. (In lay terms, he really racked up the bucks that he said Steve owed Norris.)

Steve was pretty much unsurprised by most of the claims of the suit. It wasn't the first time he'd been sued and it wasn't going to be the last. Getting sued was just a part of doing business. And after the second or third time around you don't take it personally any more. You just realize that it's just about the money. That's all.

So as he read the list of damages, it was kind of like reading the menu at McDonalds. It was the usual stuff, wrongful termination, breach of contract, conversion of property, mental anguish, reliance, blah blah blah blah blah…until he came to the last one…..*Loss of Consortium*.

This was one he hadn't seen before! As a matter of fact, he didn't really know what it meant. *Loss of Consortium*? Now Steve remembered taking all of the tools out of the toolshed so Norris definitely *lost* the use of his tools. Was consortium just a fancy legal term for tools? No, I don't think so.

Luckily though, Steve's wife, who happened to be sitting next to him in bed reading the Summons and Complaint along with him, was a lawyer. And she knew lots of "nifty" legal terms, including, of course, *Loss of Consortium*.

As she explained to Steve, *Loss of Consortium* is a term used in the law of torts that refers to the deprivation of the benefits of a family relationship due to injuries caused by a tort-feasor, the tort-feasor, of course, being Steve.

"Loss of consortium," as his wife went on to explain, "is not a historical tort under English common law, but arrived via statute. It is often cause for compensatory damages to be awarded." His wife went on explaining that the action was originally paired in a Latin expression: *per quod servitium et consortium amisit*, translated as *in consequence of which he lost her society and services*. The relationship between husband and wife, she went on to explain, has historically been considered worthy of legal protection. The interest being protected under consortium is that which the head of the household had in the physical integrity of his wife. The undertone of this action is that the husband had an unreciprocated proprietary interest in his wife. The deprivations identified include the economic contributions of the injured spouse to the household, care and affection, and *sex*.

In lay terms, as Steve boiled it down, Norris was suing Steve because Norris couldn't fuck his wife anymore, he had lost his mojo, couldn't raise the flag, he was sailing at half mast, his noodle was over-cooked.

Having seen Norris' wife, Steve wittily commented that he had probably done Norris a big favor and with that chuckled a little, commented about how Stanley Parker's claim was clever but was still bullshit, and rested assured in the knowledge that Norris would never collect a dime from Steve – that the claims were meritless; Steve's wife pointing out that it was Norris who had stolen from Steve, that it was Norris who was in the wrong, and that Steve was certainly justified in getting rid of Norris, even if he had maybe, in the heat of the moment, overreacted just a bit, and lost his cool.

Wrong-o! Lawyer Lady. Wrong-o!

Now this is the part of the story where those of you who might be considering a career in civil litigation might want to go get one of those yellow highlighters out and take some notes because what Steve found out the very next day was that lawsuits have nothing to do with who is right and who is wrong.

They do have a lot to do, however, with how experienced the parties' attorneys are in a specific area of the law and how insurance companies make decisions on how and when to settle lawsuits.

It seems somewhere out there in the "ether," is a magic number referred to in the insurance industry as *the break-even stop loss equilibrium point*. This is the magic number where the cost of defending a lawsuit is equal to the cost of settling a lawsuit. And as such this is the point at which the insurance company decides to settle and pay the claim. Where the experience of the attorney comes in is in knowing for each lawsuit what that break-even point is and knowing to sue for exactly that amount, thereby ensuring a quick, and equitable settlement. What Stanley Parker knew, and what Steve and his lawyer lady wife didn't know was for the whole Norris incident, the magic number was $27,500 and this is exactly what Stanley Parker asked for.

And so, in the end, it was the *loss of consortium* claim, the claim that Steve had laughed about, calling it meritless, that claim that had clenched the deal for Stanley and Norris, and it was that claim which paid for the brand new uniforms and bowling balls and new shiny bowling shoes for the entire El Paso Bowling Team.

Upon reading the heart-wrenching account of how Steve had humiliated him in front of the entire Juniper complex, and how after explaining in a sorrowful, grief-stricken tone how his wife Anna Bell had "heard the whole thing from inside the house," and how upon hearing his humiliation she just couldn't see him in *that way* ever again, and how as a result Norris' manhood had simply ceased to function, the insurance adjuster called Steve on the phone and told him to just pay the poor bastard. And that was that!

Except for one little thing that always struck Steve as more than a little strange about Anna Bell hearing the whole thing from inside the house because, as you probably remember, Norris's wife Anna Bell was deaf.

Chapter 2.2

The Beverly Hills Boys Back Home

Beverly Hills, California August 1990 – Just 13 seconds after Steve had left Morty's office

Now in accordance with the elaborate and well thought out plan that Morty had just jotted down in his little blue notebook, and while Steve headed down to the Burbank Airport to get on a plane bound for El Paso, Morty began assembling his elite group of investors with an almost religious fervor thirteen seconds after Steve had left his office.

And since both Morty and Steve were big believers in Napoleon Hill's methods for deploying success, they decided to carry out their own individual parts of the plan by following Napoleon's suggestions to the letter; the first step in Napoleon Hill's recipe being the building of a *Master Mind*

Alliance, which meant assembling a team that could work together as one mind to achieve a common goal, the goal for Morty and Steve being to build a great real estate empire – Morty by raising the money, Steve by finding and buying the buildings.

Now, the book recommends that you choose for your alliance, the best and most knowledgeable people available in your field of endeavor. In practical application though, you usually have to start building a team with the people that you already know.

And so in accordance with Napoleon's recipe, as soon as he left Morty's office, Steve began building his Master Mind Alliance using the people that he already knew – cigarette smugglers, poker hustlers, recently laid off bank vice presidents, porn-shop managers and unemployed real estate agents, while Morty began assembling his team from the people *he* knew, other inept children of the rich who had inherited their accomplished parents' fortunes and who, like Morty, were looking to play real estate and somehow believed that because they had come from situations of means that they too, like their accomplished ancestors, had the talent and genius to make their own climb to the mountaintop.

Morty's first recruit was Alan Horatio Blaine, a man Steve and The Boys always referred to as "that son of a bitch."

Not that Alan was a son of a bitch; as a matter of fact he was exactly the opposite.

But Steve and The Boys just liked the way it sounded, "That son of a bitch, Alan Blaine, what was that scoundrel up to this time?"

"That son of a bitch Alan Blaine is just about the luckiest son of a bitch I ever met."

"Alan Blaine, that son of a bitch, he's got one set of brass ones on him."

"Speaking of sons of bitches, did you hear what Alan Blaine did last week?"

Sometimes the "son-of-a-bitching" would go on for several minutes before The Boys finally got down to talking business, but it was all good clean fun and saying it kind of put Alan up on a pedestal and made him a celebrity of sorts, at least among The Boys.

Besides, Steve and The Boys really looked up to and admired him.

Alan, the heir to a small Mint Julep fortune, hailed from Savannah, Georgia and was perhaps the most street smart of all. He was also the biggest risk taker of the group and was always good for a cool million or two, sight unseen, just by virtue of a phone call from Morty. He didn't need to see the property; if Steve had negotiated the deal, then that was good enough for him. Alan's motto was "always be in escrow" and Steve was more than happy to oblige.

As you know, of the group it was Steve's job to find and negotiate the killer deals that would soon be making himself and The Boys notoriously famous in the private investment community.

Even more important than that (although none of The Boys except Steve and Alan seemed to be aware of how important it really was), it was Steve's job to run at a profit the empire they would be assembling until such time as they could all cash in their chips and go home. And running an empire of rag-tag, run-down buildings filled with drug addicts, illegal immigrants, and the terminally unemployed, well that was no easy task, especially at a profit.

Alan had always liked Steve because, like him, Steve was street smart and knew how to turn a profit, even when there was no profit to be turned. And, regardless of how shitty a building was when they bought it, or how hard it was to negotiate the deal, Steve would always be able to turn it around and make it work for himself and The Boys, time after time, and without fucking it up.

As a matter of fact, there was this little running joke between Steve and Alan where every time Steve was on his way to a meeting to negotiate a deal, Alan would call Steve on his cell phone and utter the words, "And remember, don't fuck it up this time!" which became a good luck tradition for every deal Steve and The Boys ever negotiated. It was like saying *break a leg* before a performer goes on.

Morty's second recruit was Arnold G. Leventhal of the law firm of Leventhal, Vaughn, Mavis and Betz, a Beverly Hills-based firm which specialized in legal matters regarding the lobbying industry.

Arnie was the man that Steve and the Boys, except for Morty, always referred to as "that pussy." This was not like the whole Alan Blaine "son-of-a-bitch" admiration thing – but because Arnie was actually, in fact, a bit of a pussy, and if Morty had not been Arnie's friend, neither Steve nor the rest of the Beverly Hills posse would have had anything to do with him.

The Boys' general dislike for Arnie aside, Arnie was known for two things, first – he was a specialist in airline industry regulatory affairs, and second – he had completely obliterated his wrist in a freak tennis accident when, while taking his victory leap over the net, he had tripped and come crashing down on his hand, fracturing all eight carpal bones in his wrist and his radiocarpal, midcarpal and meta-carpal joints to boot (as he was always quick to point out whenever someone asked him what had happened to his wrist.)

Nevertheless, despite his injury, Arnie continued to function normally with the occasional exception that sometimes it took him an inordinate amount of time to sign and return certain legal documents, which he would blame on the fact that his wrist was bothering him.

Arnie and Morty had been college roommates at USC and had remained best friends for the last 47 years, but unlike Alan and Morty who had inherited their fortunes, Arnie had married into his.

Arnie's wife Fancy "Robbins" Leventhal, upon the impending demise of her soon-to-be late father Irv, stood to inherit half of the family's vast ice cream business fortune and as one might expect, until then, she and Arnie lived comfortably off her family's vast wealth and resided in the extremely lavish lifestyle that her father's money afforded them.

Of all the Beverly Hills Boys Back Home, Arnie was, as such, perhaps the most cautious with his investments. After all, it wasn't really his money that he was investing and it was very important for him to make a good impression on Fancy's father, a man who had never really liked Arnie that much because he said that Arnie lacked "the balls" to really "make it" in the business world.

Thus, like Morty, Arnie was a guy with something to prove, only he was apt to prove it in a more cautious manner and so began Arnie's practice of never really committing to investing in a deal until four months or so after the deal had already closed, a phenomenon he blamed on his inability to sign documents in a timely manner because of his obliterated wrist.

This way, if things went south, Arnie, "that pussy," could simply say he *wasn't* in the deal and if things went north, then Arnie could say he "*was* in the deal."

But since things so far had always gone north, Arnie's catch phrase, "I *was* in the deal," caused the other Beverly Hills Boys to poke fun at Arnie, taunting him with relentless questions of "Are you *sure* you were in the deal? Do you want to wait until we *sell* the fucking place first before you decide?"

Either way, the important thing to Arnie was to not lose face in the face of Fancy's father. And although it wasn't really fair to any of the other Beverly Hills Boys, who weren't "pussies" and who put their money up front, Morty, because he and Arnie were friends, always covered for Arnie by buying Arnie's share of the deal at the beginning and then selling it back to him at cost several months later when the merits of the investment had already been proven.

Of the biggest and most powerful members of the Beverly Hills Boys Back Home, and the one who invested the greatest share of the money in the deals that Steve and Morty were putting together was Stanton White, a man Steve and the rest of The Boys always referred to as "Stanton White" since none of the other Boys, other than Morty, had ever met him.

As a matter of fact, no one was really sure where Stanton's money came from, or for that matter what he even looked like, but one thing was known for sure – when it came to money, Stanton had shit-loads of it and the one thing he loved more than making money was giving it away, and give it away he did, to every foundation, to every charity, to every institute, to every research organization and to every cause imaginable.

Save the whales. Kill the whales. Fuck the whales. He didn't care, as long as he felt he was helping somebody by giving them money.

As a matter of fact, it was widely rumored that the only reason Stanton gave any money to Morty in the first place was that Stanton had known Morty's father, the great Saul T. Salt, and as the rumor goes, on his death bed Saul asked Stanton to please look after his *putz* son Morton, who Saul believed was likely to squander the family fortune.

The motivation behind Stanton and Morty's relationship aside, Stanton and his wife were extremely active in the business of *giving* and had founded several charitable foundations of their own including one to support the Arts in Los Angeles and another one to support the *censorship* of the Arts in Alabama. They had even had a wing of a museum named after them.

But of all the members of the Beverly Hills Boys, the one who would become the most instrumental in the goings-on of the group didn't even know she was a member at all until the shit hit the fan. She was, in fact, not a boy at all, although she *was* from Beverly Hills – Morty's wife Nicki Gamble.

No indeed, had Nicki known about the whole thing from the very start she would not have likely had any part of it. No, land-lording was not her cup of tea, and besides she had bigger fish to fry, what with running her purse business and overseeing her money managers managing her inherited fortune and all.

And besides, these days she was considering a nobler path, a run for political office perhaps, maybe for Congress, or State Senate, or something cute like City Council or something like that.

But fate had other plans for Nicki Gamble. An unmentioned gift given to her by her husband to celebrate their tenth wedding anniversary left her conscripted to a role not of her own choosing – that role being the one of landlord, and as such, a surprise member of the Beverly Hills Boys Back Home.

Nicki's involvement in the whole El Paso situation would escalate a simple story of a group of guys who bought a chunk of a small southwestern city into a nationally televised media spectacle – complete with its own theme song.

But so it was, when one day the primrose path of ambition that Steve and The Boys were leading themselves, and now Nicki down, ended up in a West Texas neighborhood called Eastwood.

Sub-Chapter 1.2

"Once Upon a Time in Little Mexico…" The Legend of Gabby the Ass-Dentist and The Mysterious Disappearance of a One Victor Tomato

El Paso, Texas – Sometime in the 1990's –The West Texas neighborhood of Eastwood

Now to say that it was pure folly for such a group of "men of wealth and taste" (to quote the prophet Jagger), to choose to build their dream in a place like Eastwood, a place of neither wealth nor taste, would be like saying that when you come to a piece of shit lying in the road and you have a choice, maybe you should step around it rather than stepping in it; it is a statement of the purely obvious.

Just as perhaps not heeding the time honored advice to "never wave your penis at a hungry dog" would be easily seen by anyone from the outside looking in, as an act of pure tomfoolery.

But how many times in history have men's penises lead them to a place they shouldn't have gone and how many roads must a man walk down before you call him a man?

I don't know, Bob, but perhaps the answer is *not* blowing in the wind, but scurrying around in the ambitions which cloud men's minds, which distract them from the obvious and which cause them to stare straight into the eyes of a growling tiger and still see a fluffy purring kitty cat.

And the neighborhood of Eastwood was certainly no purring kitty cat.

Rather, it was a beastly flurry of constant activity, a densely populated, somewhat chaotic, and loosely-held-together collection of buildings, peoples and interests. Owning and managing even a small part of this community would scare off even the most foolhardy of daredevils – except of course for Steve and Morty and the 300 or so other building owners in the area – who either out of *arrogance* believed they could tame the beast, or more than likely, out of *ignorance* hadn't realized until it was too late that they had hopped on the back of a bucking bronco and were now in for an eight-second ride of their lives.

Now Eastwood, an area of about three square miles located in the northwest section of El Paso, was comprised of about 400 or so apartment complexes, 50 or so single family homes and just a handful of retail establishments, mostly liquor stores and check cashing places.

Known as "Little Mexico," the Eastwood neighborhood had existed for some forty years now. The 400 or so apartment complexes in the area had, over the last ten years or so, become an oasis for almost 80,000 Spanish-speaking residents, mostly Mexican citizens. Unlike most groups of immigrants who come to America seeking to own a piece of the American dream, many in this community had as their goal not to join American society, but to just be left alone by it; their plan being to earn as much money as they could and to send it back to their families in a country that was *theirs*, that being for the most part, "big" Mexico.

Of the white and black people who called the neighborhood's apartment complexes their home – a definite minority – these were folks that the city of El Paso referred to as "tenants of last resort," folks who for one reason or another, criminal backgrounds, terminal unemployment, drug addiction, etc., couldn't find housing in other "more desirable" areas of the city.

And of the 300 or so middle-class white folks who resided in the fifty or so unsellable single-family homes that adorned the outskirts of the neighborhood, these folks were referred to by the City, unofficially of course, as the "angry white people" who had seen their retirement nest-eggs disappear and had bitterly tasted the flavor of *their* community change, a change they were not particularly happy about to say the least.

Now the Crestwood Apartments, the very same complex that Steve and The Boys would end up owning someday hence was typical of the neighborhood.

A 352-unit complex, it was far much more than just an assemblage of buildings which housed a population of tenants. The Crestwood Apartments was a being unto itself, a living, breathing entity which had a history, a legacy, and a personality all its own; a domain, with its own customs, its own rules, its own system of justice, and most importantly, its own economy – that economy being comprised of hundreds of home businesses being run out of hundreds of apartments by thousands of enterprising residents.

At the top of the food chain was Esperanza Villa Valla Villanova, a Columbian woman in her late thirties who not only was the manager of three other complexes in the neighborhood, but had recently become the manager of Crestwood as well. A dictatorial figure, but also seen as a benevolent woman, Esperanza's leadership provided order in an otherwise chaotic world and was the proverbial glue which held the community, especially the community's economy, together.

For it was Esperanza's brainchild, the *10 percent rule,* which provided for a hierarchy of things, a way of doing business and a code of ethics that gave the day-to-day goings-on a sense of order and purpose, the 10 percent rule being that in the 4 complexes that Esperanza managed, each and every tenant who was running a home business had to give her 10 percent of the gross receipts.

And to ensure this rule was complied with, Esperanza had established her own private collection agency/police force which were called "los Federales de Villanova," a squad of twenty armed, muscular Cuban gentlemen whose job it was to call on each and every tenant at each and every apartment at each and every complex on each and every day; to collect Esperanza's 10 percent plus their 2 percent override tax which they got to keep as compensation for their collection services.

Yes, indeed, it was very important that everyone "follow the rules," whatever those rules were, and Esperanza was the one who decided. And so in addition to the 10 percent rule there were many other rules that she implemented to keep the community running smoothly, each one of which had a monetary penalty as a punishment for non-compliance – $25 for littering, $50 for breaking a window, $75 for clogging the toilet, $100 for leaking oil or transmission fluid in the parking lot, and of course $1,000 and *death*, for not following the 10 percent rule, and that was that, no matter what!

The next most important citizen of little Mexico was "V," a small determined woman in her mid-thirties who lived in apartment 91and who was rumored to suffer from a horrific and extremely contagious skin condition which rendered her hideous-looking. That is why, it was speculated upon, no one at the complex had ever actually seen her or come in contact with her – "for fear of catching whatever it was she had."

Her supposed deformities aside, Veronica Sanchez, "V" was by far Esperanza's best "earner" and a key player when it came to the proper functioning of the community, for she provided an "immigration service" for the fine citizens of the neighborhood and kept a constant flow of new citizens and new customers coming in to the already burgeoning empire.

Yes, V was what is commonly referred to as a "coyote," a person who smuggles people, undocumented aliens specifically, into the country for a price, that price being

$1,000 each for men and woman of adult age, defined by V as those being over the age of five, and $500 each for boys and girls being of non-adult age, those as defined by V as being under the age of three, leaving room for negotiation for the adolescent pricing schedule for those customers between the ages of three and five.

Now although no one had actually ever seen V, her status as a MIP (Mas Importante Persona) was nevertheless evident in her possession of two highly regarded status symbols. First of all, she had not one apartment, but three – units 91, 92, and 93, meaning that unlike most of the other businesses at Crestwood who were only a one-unit shop, she was a three-unit enterprise and as such, *big* business. Second of all, she had her own brand new Chevy 3500 Econoline Van, brand new vehicles of any kind being a rare sight, and quite the status symbol, over at "the Crest."

And so every night at 11:00 p.m., except Tuesdays, V's brand new white Chevy 3500 Econoline Van with no windows would pull up to unit 91 North and unload a cargo of twenty or so new citizens of the Eastwood neighborhood. These new citizens would then walk to the door, enter the unit, and not be seen again till the very next day when they would exit unit 93 North at about 2:30 p.m. and start lining up in front of El Joto's apartment, the third most important person in the Crestwood complex.

Gabriel Lopez "El Joto" (the fag), as Gabriel was known as, was a slender, black-haired man in his mid-thirties who lived in unit 191. He usually wore tight jeans, an even tighter button-down orange shirt, a pair of pointy black shoes with stiletto heels, and a hairnet which was tightly pulled back as to stretch the skin on his forehead. Flamboyant appearances aside, he was someone you needed to treat with respect and the utmost of courtesy.

Now to understand his status and to appreciate just how important El Joto was to the proper functioning of the entire neighborhood's economy, it is imperative that you be aware that without the help of El Joto you couldn't work, you couldn't get an apartment, you couldn't open a bank account and you couldn't even cash a check down at La Pinchi Puta – the neighborhood liquor store, restaurant, meat market, medical clinic, funeral home, wedding chapel, check cashing place, Western Union office and menudo stand.

The key to El Joto's power lay in the fact that his nephew in San Diego (who had been born on the California side of the border just minutes after the immigration and naturalization service officers had finished searching the semi that his mother and several dozen other citizens of the city of Juarez had hidden in the back of), was a citizen of the U.S., and he had two years earlier gotten a job at the Social Security Administration Office downtown.

As the office was ramping up to go paperless, and began printing social security cards on those new plastic cards with the electronic strips, El Joto's nephew was charged with the task of destroying the old boxes of those old paper social security cards with the blanks on them to fill in people's names when they were issued a card. Somehow in the confusion of the whole ramping up thing, the boxes were misplaced and so had never been properly discarded.

Luckily, however, they turned up in the apartment kitchen of one Gabriel Villa Lopez.

Just below his kitchen cabinet, where El Joto kept the ten or so boxes of blank paper social security cards, was a counter and on that counter sat a greenish gray IBM Selectric Brand Typewriter Model 330 with the self-correcting ribbon and the automatic indentation bar.

On the counter next to the typewriter was a copy of the telephone directory for the city of Des Moines, Iowa.

And so every afternoon starting at 3:00 p.m. and going until the line went down, El Joto set up shop in the kitchen of his two-bedroom apartment. (In the mornings he worked as a busboy over at the El Paso Inn and on Wednesdays as a groundskeeper at the El Paso City Hall complex downtown.)

The line which started at El Joto's front door always stretched all the way down the parking lot and was comprised of people waiting for their brand new social security cards to be issued. As a matter of fact the line would often start forming the night before with people camping out in the parking lot so they would be sure to get a good spot on line.

And as soon as El Joto opened up at exactly 3:00 P.M, one by one they would enter El Joto's apartment, step up to the counter, hand him $100 and then be assigned a name out of the Des Moines telephone directory.

El Joto would type the name he had selected out of the directory – today he was using the "C" section – so Jim Caldwell, Sam Cooper, Barney Cox, etc. – and then with the new weekly updated circular of recently deceased card number holders his nephew had sent him the previous Friday, he would type the newly reassigned social security numbers on the paper social security cards on the blue line, just above where it said *Social Security Number*.

Most of the time, the numbers lined up pretty good with the blue line but sometimes they were a little crooked because the double-space button on his IBM Selectric sometimes stuck a little.

Having typed in their newly assigned number, El Joto would give the proud new American taxpayer their card, put $45 aside in a cigar box marked with a big red "V" drawn on the top, put $10 aside in a cigar box with a big green "E" drawn on top and place the remaining $45 into a lavender men's purse with a big diamond-looking "G" on the side.

He would then hold out his hand to receive the next $100 from his next new proud American taxpayer and so the afternoon would progress. At the end of his shift, El Joto would then count the money in the cigar box marked "V," set aside 10 percent of that for Esperanza, count the money in his purse and set aside an additional 10 percent of that for Esperanza again, and then drop the cigar box marked "E" off over at the Crestwood office, and then drop the cigar box marked "V" over at unit number 91.

It was as he was walking over to V's unit every day, except Wednesday of course, that El Joto would pass unit 52.

Gabrielle Putado, a light skinned Latin girl of El Salvadoran descent was the inhabitant of that particular domicile. She was in her early twenties, stood 5'3" tall, had long brown hair, and was very attractive.

And as it had been the custom since as long as anyone could remember, every afternoon at about 3:00 p.m., when the temperature was still hovering at about 120 degrees,

Gabby's "clients" would begin to arrive, usually in beat up sedans with faded paint, no air-conditioning, a few dents on the fender and always with a broken window that had been repaired using state of the art Mexican engineering which always included the clever use of plastic wrap, duct tape and string.

With an average four guys per carload, they would pull up in front of Gabby's door. Then, after shutting off the engine, one of the car doors would open, an empty Bud Light can, always Bud Light, would roll out of the car and fall onto the ground, and then one guy, who was always dripping with sweat and wearing a bandana on his head, would step out of the car. This guy would then walk to Gabby's door, knock 3 times, enter the apartment, spend two or three minutes inside, and then leave the same way he came in, usually with a sort of smile on his face.

For what usually took a total of about ten minutes per car load, each guy would wait their turn in the car, with the windows closed, the engine off and the Texas heat baking them to a sweaty golden brown.

And when it was their turn, each guy would repeat the same routine that his buddy had just done – walk to Gabby's door, knock 3 times, enter, exit, get back in the car, and wait.

When they were all done, the car would start, back up from the parking space, and slowly pull away.

It all seemed innocent enough, a pretty young girl making a living at the world's oldest profession, and it gave El Joto quite a thrill, seeing all those sweaty brown men coming and going from Gabby's apartment.

Besides Gabby, there were 257 additional enterprising tenants who resided at the Crestwood Apartments, each one of whom ran entrepreneurial businesses out of their two-bedroom units.

There was Antonio Gomez from unit 263 who sold roasted corn-on-the-cob-on-a-stick, slathered with a special mayonnaise and parmesan cheese mixture which he kept unrefrigerated in a one gallon container which sat just out-side the door of his apartment baking in the sun, day, after day, after day.

There was Jesus Alonzo from unit 149, who ran an auto body shop in the rear end of the parking lot.

There was Herlinda Cruz from unit 11, who sold coco-nut-covered ice cream bars out of the helado cart with the little jingly bicycle bell she had hooked up to the push-bar of her little white cart.

There was Arturo Gonzalez who sold prescription anti-biotics, which he got from the country of "big Mexico," to the poor little kids who had come down with strep-throat and to the older men and women when they had come down with a hand infection or a bad cough or a yeast infection or even the occasional venereal disease.

And there was, speaking of venereal disease, Anna la Puta from unit 311 who was one of thirty "professional la-dies" at the Crest, and who, for an extra $20, would let you do anything you wanted with the used corn cob that you had just purchased from Señor Gomez so long as it was properly lubed up and slathered with that special mayon-naise parmesan cheese mixture that he used.

Unit 257 was home to "La Salon," a hair and nail estab-lishment run by the Landito sisters, Julita and Mujita.

There was a used shoe and purse store, "La Zapateria - El Bolsoria" in units 31 and 32, respectively.

And of course there was Juan Carlos Ramirez, who ran an amateur Law and Dental practice out of the back of his truck, which was parked in front of his apartment at unit 333.

But one of the most motivated and enterprising tenants, and yet one of the most tragic figures over at Crestwood, was a maintenance man at the complex, Victor Tomatillo, a.k.a. Victor Tomato, who, until the day he mysteriously vanished, lived in unit 152. It is his story which has become the stuff of legend in "Little Mexico" and which serves as a warning to all of what can happen when blind ambition leads you to a place you shouldn't be.

The Legend of Victor Tomato

You see Victor was a man with a mission; a mission to earn $22,252 dollars, not to be sent home to his other family back in Mexico, as most of the other tenants were doing, but for a much nobler, and much local-*er* cause, to save the sight of his eldest son Gabriel.

Victor, a family man who lived with his wife Amelia and their seven children in a two-bedroom apartment at Crestwood had sworn, as his duty in life, to raise the $22,252 to pay for the operation that would save his six-year-old son.

As the story goes, Gabriel had unfortunately been born blind and was in need of an operation to restore his sight.

His blindness, not actually a birth defect but a birth injury, was the result of two detached retinas which he had suf-

fered when the obstetrician over at the El Paso Emergency
Medical Center had accidentally dropped little Gabriel
straight on his head onto the tile floor some four feet below
during the delivery.

The cause of the mishap, however, was not really completely the doctor's fault. It was, as the "incident report"
outlined, due to the doctor's new cell phone, which apparently was pre-set back at the factory on vibrate, a setting the
poor doctor was not familiar with and had never experienced before.

As the report went on to say, when Amelia, Victor's
wife, was fully dilated, and as she gave that final push
which launched little Gabriel out into the world, the doctor's cell phone coincidentally and simultaneously went off,
sending a tingly, buzzing sensation throughout his entire
mid-region, uncontrollably stimulating his prostate and
causing a sudden massive erection, which in turn caused a
sudden rise in the doctor's blood pressure which in turn,
suddenly and momentarily had caused him to "lose focus."
Ooops!

Although it could be argued that the accident was at
least partially the doctor's fault, and the problem should
have been taken care of by the emergency center, or perhaps by the cell phone manufacturer, little Gabriel was nevertheless discharged and sent home blind, without having
been given the corrective surgery which could have easily
restored his eyesight.

His parents were, however, comforted by the fact that
little Gabriel's eyesight could someday be restored with
corrective surgery as soon as Victor and Amelia Tomatillo
had saved up the $22,252 that the operation was expected to

cost. Victor, being a day laborer at the time of Gabriel's birth, and working under the table for just less than minimum wage was not likely to be able to save up such a sum real soon.

To Victor's favor however, the $22,252 price of the operation, which did not of course include the cost of anesthesia, or the two days of post-op care that little Gabriel would need after the surgery, was the amount the hospital said they could accept as a down payment because after all – there's more to medicine than just money.

Having sworn to give little Gabriel the gift of sight, Victor and Amelia had spent countless hours in their apartment lately, talking and brainstorming about how to raise the $22,252 it would take to get little Gabriel his operation. To date though, they had not come up with any good ideas.

Until one day Victor's "big break" finally came along. He was in the Crestwood office getting a case of light bulbs out of the supply closet and he overheard Esperanza ordering appliances from the Apartment Supply Warehouse, specifically microwave ovens, refrigerators and electric stove heater elements. It was at the conclusion of the phone call, that Victor received what he believed to be divine inspiration when he heard Esperanza utter the words which sent Victor's mind spinning with possibilities, those words being "put that on our account."

 You see it seems that Mr. Knapp and his business associates, the then-owners of the Crestwood complex as well as several other large complexes in town, had a $100,000 line of credit down at the Supply Warehouse, and Victor, who had just seen Esperanza order about $10,000 worth of appliances on the phone, and who was impressed with the ease at which Esperanza could get $10,000 worth of stuff by just saying "put that on our account," began formulating a plan.

Now although Victor had no idea of what an account really was or that anybody even kept track of that sort of stuff, his plan went roughly as follows:

He would call the Supply Warehouse himself when Esperanza was out of the office, identify himself as the maintenance supervisor over at Crestwood, order $22,252 worth of stuff, "putting that on the account" and then have the stuff delivered to his apartment. He would then sell the stuff to tenants over at the other apartment complexes in the neighborhood, so that Esperanza wouldn't catch wind of what he was doing. His reason for wishing to keep Esperanza in the dark about his brilliant scheme was that he didn't want to have to pay Esperanza her 10 percent override tax which she charged each and every tenant operating a business over at Crestwood for the privilege of doing business at *her* complex – the use of the word *her* implying the concepts of both ownership and control.

Well Victor wasted no time in putting his brilliant scheme to work, and as soon as Esperanza had left the office to go down to unit 53 South to get her nails done by the Landito sisters, he picked up the phone in the office, called the Apartment Supply Warehouse and ordered ten "bottom of the line" apartment-size refrigerators, charging them to Mr. Knapp's account and instructing the Supply Warehouse to deliver the refrigerators to his apartment at #152 South at the Crestwood Apartments.

But things didn't stop there. And after just a week of brisk refrigerator sales, Victor decided to expand his appliance business into dishwashers, ranges, microwaves, washing machines, dryers and his newest item juicers, which sold really well on Margarita Fridays.

And within just seven weeks of going into business, Victor and Amelia had grossed just over $17,503.17. Mr. Knapp, on the other hand, had racked up a bill at the Supply Warehouse of just over $37,503.17, the difference owing to Victor's apparent lack of understanding of the concept of cost-plus pricing, apparently seeming to favor the idea of a market-based low-cost leadership pricing schedule that he was more familiar with from having done most of his shopping down at the Wal-Mart.

Differences in marketing strategy aside, Victor, after only eight weeks of being in the appliance business, had earned just over $20,000 and was able to make a significant down payment at the Emergency Center, a down payment significant enough that the administrator in charge said the hospital could actually schedule little Gabriel's operation for the very next morning, pointing out that the balance of $2,252, not including the cost of anesthesia and post-operative care of course, could be put on Victor's account, a concept that Victor, now that he was a *businessman* understood quite well.

And so the very next day little Gabriel underwent that operation to restore his sight, and to the rejoicing of all, his surgery was an outstanding success.

As fate would have it, however, upon little Gabriel opening his eyes and upon seeing Victor's face for the very first time saying, "I can see you poppy, I can see you," Gabriel realized he was unable to move his arms and legs.

Tragically, although his eye surgery had been such a great success, he had apparently had a bad reaction to the anesthesia after receiving an accidental overdose during surgery and was unfortunately, temporarily, paralyzed from the neck down.

The doctors assured Victor and Amelia that with several months of physical therapy, and at a cost of just $18,000 more, little Gabriel would once again be able to walk.

But little Gabriel would never get that chance, because as of Wednesday, Victor would find himself both unemployed and out of business when happenstance dealt yet another cruel blow to the Tomatillo family.

You see Victor's unsanctioned appliance business was accidentally discovered by Esperanza that day while she was on her way down to get a chip in her fingernail repaired at "La Salon" in unit 53. As she passed by Victor's unit she noticed what seemed like an inordinate amount of boxes of brand new appliances stacked up in front of his front door and in the parking lot and she immediately became suspicious.

And upon checking with her assistant and confirming that she had never received her 10 percent share, she became outraged and immediately fired him as the maintenance man, confiscated his appliance inventory and then presented him with a bill for the $40,000 worth of appliances he had ordered – the ones he had sold for $22,000 (if only he had used cost-plus pricing rather than market), $4,000 for Esperanza's share of the original $40,000 that she never received, and a fine of an additional $10,000 for "Don't Follow The Rules." She then ordered him to pay her the total amount due of $54,000 within the next 48 hours, lest he had made his "final arrangements with the funeral chapel down at the Pinchi Puta and had made his peace with God." And just to drive her point home, she then had Victor and his entire family, excluding Gabriel of course, who was still in the hospital, evicted from their apartment and had their belongings tossed out into the parking lot, where she had a sign posted that read, "This is what happens for Don't Follow the Rules."

And so homeless, unemployed, out of business, and with no personal belongings, Victor with just twenty dollars in his pocket, walked off, dejected and forlorn, down the parking lot, desperately churning the occurrences of the last few weeks over in his mind and trying to think of a way to come up with the $54,000 that he owed Esperanza and the $18,000 that he needed to get little Gabriel the physical therapy that would restore motion and feeling to the young lad's lower extremities.

Now perhaps if Victor had been totally broke and without that twenty dollars in his pocket, perhaps he would have just bummed a couple of beers from some of the other guys hanging out in the parking lot working on their cars that day, and perhaps he could have just hung out, shot the shit, gotten drunk, and then just took a nap.

But fate had other plans for Victor Tomatillo that day. And as he walked down the parking lot, and as he passed unit #52 South, the apartment of a pretty, young, professional woman named Gabby Pintado, and as he saw the guys waiting their turns in their cars outside of Gabby's front door, he couldn't help think to himself that in such a moment of despair in his life that maybe a little female companionship, maybe just twenty dollars' worth, was just what he needed to clear his mind.

And so in a moment that could best be described as, "Fuck-It," Victor dragged himself up on to the sidewalk, stepped up to Gabby's door, knocked three times and waited for Gabby to answer.

"Hola, Señor Tomato," said Gabby. "Tiene algo para mi?" (Do you have something for me?)

"Si!" said Victor, "but only twenty."

"Twenty grams? Okay," said Gabby.

And Victor, not really listening, and not really hearing the word *grams*, stepped in to Gabby's apartment, for what he expected would be a quick hand-job or something, and then he would be on his way.

"Come into the kitchen," Gabby said

"Okay," said Victor as he followed Gabby

And when they were both in the kitchen, Gabby instructed Victor to lean against the kitchen counter, which he did.

Then stepping behind him, she pulled out one surgical, green, latex rubber glove from a box of 500 such gloves that was on the counter next to where Victor was leaning, stretched the glove over her right hand, and released the end of the glove around her wrist, making a slapping sound when the latex hit her upper right forearm.

With that she dipped the fingers of her glove-covered hand into a huge jar of KY Jelly that was also on the counter next to the box of rubber gloves, held her hand slightly up, rubbing her thumb and forefingers together, looked at her right hand, placed her left hand on Victor's right shoulder and said, "BEND OVER."

Well it seems for just twenty bucks, Victor was going to get more than just the run of the mill hand-job, he thought to himself. Perhaps a rim-job hand-job combination, or maybe a hand-job-prostate-massage combo, or even a tug-blow-and rim-job triple play? The anticipation was very exciting, and the further thought of getting such a good deal for only twenty bucks was very exciting as well, as Victor was now, of course, a businessman and had come to appreciate the importance of these sorts of things.

And that's when it happened. Gabby's hand passed through Victor's sphincter, and then into his lower colon, and then further up rubbing against his prostate, and then still further up going deep within his bowels and then still further up until Gabby's forearm was inserted into Victor's ass almost up to her elbow.

"Where is it," Gabby asked. "Donde esta las drogas?"

But Victor, who was distracted by the throbbing waves of pleasure he felt pulsing through his erect penis as it smashed against the side of the kitchen counter he was leaning against, and who was very much enjoying this new back door experience, didn't seem to hear her.

"Ju Pinchi Muthafucker, donde esta las drogas? Donde? Donde? Donde?" Gabby kept repeating.

But still Victor heard nothing.

And as Gabby entered still further, and further, and then still further, all the way up past her elbow, and into what must have been the beginning of Victor's small intestines, and continued to scream, "Donde, donde, donde?!"

And as Victor, began pulsing and then throbbing, and then shaking and then convulsing and then finally shooting what seemed like an endless stream of semen all over the side of Gabby's kitchen counter, and as the intense waves of pleasure began to subside, and as the blood began to return to Victor's head, it was then and only then that Victor heard the simultaneous sound of two distinct clicks, one in his right ear and one in his left.

"Las drogas, las drogas, donde esta las drogas?" Victor finally heard Gabby say.

And as he, still a little bit dizzy, opened his eyes he caught the sight of, in his peripheral vision, two men, one on each side of him, each holding a .38 chrome-plated revolver with the hammers cocked back, pointed at each one of his ears, just 2 inches from each side of his head.

And that's when it dawned on him, in a moment of sober clarity, and as small drops of semen continued to leak from his now deflating member, that Gabrielle Pintado of Crestwood unit #52 South was not, indeed, a prostitute at all. No the situation strongly suggested otherwise.
For in fact, Gabby, despite her neighborhood reputation as a receptacle for the unwanted sperm of unwashed men, was not in the business of love. No!

She was, as the evidence suggested, a member of a much nobler and more revered profession, a tradition dating back to the most ancient of civilizations, and one which is perhaps even older than what is commonly considered to be the "world's oldest profession."

Gabby was, in fact, an Ass-Dentist, a master practiced in the art of implantation and extraction, who had been keeping alive a tradition as vital and as old as the art of "keestering" itself.

For as sure as eating, fucking, shitting and dying, mankind, in his need to keep his valuables safe, (and sometimes just to see what might happen), has been ingeniously shoving things up his ass and carrying them around since the dawn of time.

And as sure as eating, fucking, shitting and dying, since the dawn of time, mankind has needed those with the dexterity and tenacity to insert and extract such ass cargo in a gentle, yet proficient manner.

And Gabby was one such person.

And so for the last "who-knows-how-many-years," for seven hours a day, beginning at 3:00 p.m. every day, seven days a week, 364 days a year (Gabby didn't work on Cinco de Mayo), Gabby had been unrolling, lubing, shoving, extracting, rinsing, weighing, re-condomizing and re-inserting grams, kilos, bricks and containers of ass cargo, and was as such, an integral and indispensable cog in the machinery of an intestinal railroad that stretched from Chihuahua, Mexico to Phoenix, Arizona, all the way to Tacoma, Philadelphia, Atlanta, LA.; although it was a route that should in no way be confused with having anything to do with the Steve Miller Band.

And neither Victor, up until this point, nor the ATF, nor the DEA, nor the El Paso police department, nor the U.S. Immigration and Naturalization Service, nor most of the people who lived in the neighborhood of "Little Mexico" had even an *inkling* of an idea that the backbone of an entire global economy was inextricably linked to the goings-on at the home of one Gabrielle Pintado, Crestwood Apartments, Unit #52 South. And so it was.

As for Victor Tomato, no one will ever know what became of him, although, as it goes without saying, he was never seen at the complex, or anywhere else in the neighborhood for that matter after that day, ever again.

Some say he was shot by Gabby's two friends after believing that he stole the drug-filled balloons that were supposed to be up his ass that day.

Others say that it was Esperanza who caused Victor's disappearance, when he was, of course, not able to come up with the $54,000 for "Don't Follow the Rules."

And still others say that it was Victor who caused his own disappearance when after realizing the futility of his economic situation simply said "Fuck It" and returned to his other family in his hometown in Mexico.

No one will ever know.

But as the sun set over the Crestwood Apartments on that warm evening, and as the sounds of bubbling mayonnaise, ice cream bells ringing, refrigerator moving, social security card typing, surgical rubber glove snapping, nail filing, pill dispensing, and the screams of "Ay Poppy, ay Poppy," filled the air, a tragic silhouette of a man, limping slowly with his legs spread far apart, a white crusty patch adorning the zipper at the front of his jeans, is said to have been seen inching down the road, with a paper sign stuck to the front of his shirt reading "Don't Follow the Rules."

(As an interesting aside, it was later estimated by the U.S. Department of commerce, that the Gross Domestic Product at the Crestwood Apartments alone, exceeded that of most small developing nations. In a study conducted by the United States Treasury Department, some years later, it was acknowledged that there was a higher than normal incidence of deceased people from Iowa working in the El Paso area, but since these people paid Social Security, federal and state income taxes, and local unemployment taxes, and not one of them had ever applied for a refund or for benefits of any kind, the statistical anomaly was found to have no significant impact on the economy as a whole and as such was simply dismissed as insignificant. The study cost an estimated $37 million dollars to complete and was never published.)

Sub-Chapter 2.1

He Who Holds Himself Out to
Be an Expert Usually Knows the Least

Van Nuys, California – Early 1990 – How Steve came to meet Morty

Harvey Mendel, an environmental consultant and part-time professional poker player from Las Vegas was an enigmatic man veiled in contradictions.

An orthodox Jewish fellow in his late fifties, he was a charming and charismatic character who stood 6'2" tall, spoke in a loud commanding voice, sported a Teddy Roosevelt mustache, and channeled a mysterious alter-ego who went by the name of Shmengey Mignone.

Shmengey, Harvey's other Harvey, was not a Jewish fellow at all, but a charming Southern Gentleman who followed the teachings of an Eastern Philosophy, dressed in all grey, wore a cream-colored Panama hat and sported a silver-tipped cane.

And unlike Harvey, who spent much of his time and energy "making a living," Shmengey was a man of leisure who spent his days courting beautiful women, studying the culinary arts, writing unsolicited book reviews for the New York Times and making rare but memorable appearances as "the man on the street in New York City" on the Channel 7 Eyewitness News.

Now as it was their custom, in the days before Morty and the Great Beverly Hills Empire, Steve and Harvey would often have lunch together to dream of "other worlds yet to be," and to discuss the mundane in the form of the environmental studies that Mr. Mandel was performing for the bank where Steve worked as a vice-president of commercial lending. It had been in this capacity as an officer of Valley Savings that Steve had gotten to know Harvey, having hired him on several occasions to perform Phase 1 Environmental Studies on properties that had been foreclosed by the bank.

They had gotten to know each other fairly well over the past two years, but as Harvey was always quick to point out, "they were *not* friends."

And it was on one such particular occasion, when the two were dining at Jerry's Famous Deli in Sherman Oaks California, that a moment of synchronicity occurred, a moment that like the perfect corned beef sandwich with just the right amount of coleslaw and Russian dressing – like Steve was eating at the time – where everything seamlessly came together and destiny was to reveal itself; that moment coming when Steve happened to mention that he was leaving the banking world and venturing forth on his own in some sort of entrepreneurial endeavor – probably in the apartment business, or the hotel business, or something like that. It was time, he told Harvey, for Steve to go out on his own and make his mark in the world. Steve was ready for a change.

It was in this very moment when Harvey Mandel, a man Steve had known only to this point to be a theorizer of big dreams and an analyzer of the mistakes of others, suddenly erupted with a passion that Steve had never seen in him before, an enthusiasm that appeared to be divine inspiration, for it was in this moment that Harvey revealed himself, his true self, to Steve.

Yes, it was as if Steve's words of entrepreneurial intent had in some way sparked something long dormant in Harvey's soul.

And so upon hearing Steve's words, Harvey, who was fastidiously taking a bite out of his tuna on rye with lettuce and tomato suddenly paused, lowered his sandwich, looked Steve almost straight in the eye and said,

"When the student is ready, the teacher will appear."

It was a Zen Buddhist saying that Steve recognized from a religion class he had taken in college. And one which Harvey obviously felt was apropos to the situation.

And then Harvey's testimony began.

An Oklahoma oil man and a self-made multi-millionaire, Harvey had, he confessed, at one time been a bold adventurer of copious achievement, his downfall ironically coming at the hands of one of his greatest successes; a windfall so overwhelmingly profitable, that it was impossible to manage and which like all things in life which are too much of a good thing, led to his utter and total demise.

"Sometimes, it is easier to manage your failures than it is your successes," Harvey told Steve, a gem of wisdom he attributed to the authorship of a famous southern gentleman philosopher known as Shmengey Mignone.

Nevertheless, as Harvey explained, regardless of his monumental successful failure, and to his credit, he had refused to let the incident crush his inner spirit and ruin the rest of his life. And so, he went on to say that although his current situation dictated that he must assume the role of a humble environmental consultant, this indeed was not the real Harvey Mendel, nor was it his destiny to spend the rest of his days living in the world of the ordinary and the mundane.

"No!" he declared. "Someday, I will be delivered back unto the mountain top, where I will see the glory again from a-high, and the trials and tribulations of the past will fall away like pebbles from a shoe that has walked the path of turmoil and found refuge in the comfort of the dream once dreamed. And on that day, I will be home and the shackles of disappointments' bondage will lie torn asunder at my feet."

And as Harvey continued to wax poetically and then biblically and then finally Martin Luther King-*ed-ly*, the conversation ultimately came down to the plain hard truth that was this:

Harvey was in a bind and these days in order to dig himself out of the financial pit that great success had put him in, he spent much of his time not only consulting, but pursuing two other endeavors which he hoped would deliver him unto salvation and at least pay the bills for a while, these endeavors being poker-hustling and law-suiting.

With regard to poker-hustling Harvey made what he called *seed money* by organizing private underground poker tournaments which he ran out of a room he rented at a weekly motel in downtown Las Vegas called the Mission Motel.

It was here, at the M.M., a flea-bag, cum-encrusted, puke-stained, run-down, shithole of a transient flophouse, in room #23, that twice a week – usually on Friday nights –

Harvey ran what he referred to as a *high stakes, winner-take-all, sudden-death contest of skill, luck and mental fortitude*, the unobvious choice of such a location for a high stakes poker event being that the cops would never think to look there. When the authorities had been called to come there in the past, most of the time they didn't show up because none of the members of the Downtown Precinct of the Las Vegas Metro Police Department wanted to go anywhere near that fucking place.

It was on Southwest Airlines' $59 round-trip flights from Burbank to Las Vegas that the Southern Gentleman of leisure and man about town, Shmengey Mignone, would promote Harvey's "high stakes contest for high rollers and V.I.P.s" to high-stakes, high-roller V.I.P-wannabes who were going to Las Vegas for a little weekend getaway or a bachelor party or whatever, and were looking for a little exclusive action, "you know, something you couldn't get on the strip."

And it was here, on these flights, usually on Friday afternoons, that Shmengey Mignone would offer, for the modest buy-in price of $100, information on how a fella might attend such an affair, and where and when such an affair might be taking place.

Will female accompaniment be available? The guy in seat 7B might ask.

"Why yes it may very well be, I do declare" would say Shmengey Mignone.

"How about booze?" would ask those USC college boys seated in row 14, off for a weekend of spending their parents' money.

"Why yes of course, libations will be provided compliments of the house, not to mention the availability of certain other stimulating concoctions of a pharmaceutical nature," Shmengey Mignone would answer.

And so it was, weekend after weekend, Harvey's alter-ego Shmengey Mignone, southern gentleman of leisure and refinement, would rally unsuspecting marks to a high stakes, winner take all, world-series-of-poker tournament which for some reason, oddly enough, was won every single time by a tall thin man of Asian descent who chain smoked, moved mechanically, seemed to display not the slightest hint of human emotion whatsoever, and wore a black t-shirt which had printed on it the words "Pai Gow."

Now the poker thing, Harvey admitted to Steve, was just a part time deal he had going which he used to fund his *real* moneymaker, which was of course *suing people*. Harvey claimed to have won over $800,000 in assorted settlements in a variety of nuisance lawsuits he had instituted over the past couple of years. His specialty, he boasted, was "product liability, stemming from a personal injury claim resulting from an initial workman's comp claim." And luckily, he continued to brag, that because his son was a lawyer "it never cost him a dime to initiate all those lawsuits."

It did cost a pretty penny, unfortunately, to hire expert witnesses, visit doctors, file motions, gather evidence and generally build a believable case that *appeared* to have merit. At least, merit enough to induce the defendant's insurance company to settle.

And thus the need, Harvey explained, to raise seed money by running the whole poker thing at the M.M.

"And what of the environmental consulting gig, why do that?" Steve asked.

"Well, it pays the day-to-day bills." Harvey replied, "And besides, it gives me an air of legitimacy and respectability in the community – you know, makes me look kosher."

Now, the perfect suit went something like this, he went on to explain:

Someone at work, let's say Harvey's girlfriend Cathy for example, is sitting and entering some data on her computer keyboard when all of a sudden the adjustable height office chair she is sitting in, inexplicable and suddenly drops two inches to a lower adjustable setting. In the drop, a disk in her lower spine is in some way dislocated, causing severe pain and suffering, rendering her unable to move, let alone work. Well, clearly she is immediately eligible for work-man's compensation benefits, and this starts the steady stream of cash flowing.

But now, what of the deeper pocket issues? Well first there is her employer, the Hughes Aircraft Corporation, who "knowingly and willingly exposed her to hazardous and dangerous conditions" when they placed her in that chair of death that they made her sit in. And what of the Herman Miller Company, that manufactured the chair, are they not also to blame? And how about the Monsanto Corporation who manufactured the rug that that chair happened to be rolling around on when it hit that snag in the defectively made carpet? And how about the Dell Computer Corporation that manufactured that keyboard that gave poor Cathy carpel-tunnel syndrome that caused her to sit funny in her office chair of death so that when the chair plummeted those two inches straight downward, she was in an odd position, exposing her lower spine to even further trauma – sounds like "contributory negligence to me."

"You see, Steve my boy, it's all about the product liability angle and going after the big fish. But not enough to really get their attention and piss them off," Harvey explained, "but just enough to be sufficiently annoying enough that you're like that fly buzzing around their head that they just want to swat, flick away, and get on with their day."

"And that's the secret my boy, keep it small while keeping it big, don't waste your time with the small fries and don't be a chaza (pig)."

"So it's all about eating French fries, then?" Steve wittily retorted.

"Yes, in a matter of speaking, it is!" said Harvey, somewhat unaware that Steve had just poked fun at what Harvey had just said.

Now the perfect lawsuit, Harvey went on to explain without missing a beat, is one that gets settled quickly, and the key to quickly settling is to know exactly how much to ask for in your complaint. "What is the magic number?" Harvey asked rhetorically.

The magic number is the amount that equals the insurance company's cost of defending the suit and the amount which is below the radar of the plaintiff's budgetary constraints – let's say $100,000.

Now down at Hughes Aircraft at the Las Vegas plant, they spend $100,000 a month on janitorial supplies. And if they get a call from their insurance company's lawyer, and she says, it's gonna cost $125,000 over the next six months to successfully defend this meritless case, so even if we win, we're still better off by $25,000 just paying the claim. Well that's a slam dunker for that division manager over at Hughes to decide.

> *"What's this extra $100,000-line item in the monthly budget Bob?" The regional manager asks him at the quarterly budget meeting.*
>
> *"Well Jim, that was that workman's comp thing with that Cathy woman and her boyfriend – that Mandel asshole – and the chair thing, if you remember."*
>
> *"Oh yeah," says Jim. "I understand that fuck-head sues like 30 companies a year. Well, what can you do?*

*Some guys have just got it all figured out." Says Jim
resignedly and philosophically.*

*"Okay, just double the janitorial supplies allotment
this quarter and we'll bury the line item in petty cash.
That way it won't hurt our performance numbers for
the division this year."*

"Sounds good Jim," says Bob

*"Sounds good Bob," says Jim, "So where do you
want to go for lunch today?"*

And just like that, Harvey Mandel and his girlfriend
Cathy get a tax-free check for $100,000.

(If only Steve had paid more attention to Harvey's advice that day at Jerry's Deli, perhaps he wouldn't have
yelled at Norris in front of his wife Anna Bell four years
hence.)

And that's when the conversation changed direction. For
it seems that Harvey's explanation of his expertise in the
ways of the world was just a warm-up, a resume if you will,
for what he was about to propose to Steve.

"You see," Harvey went on to say, "Even between consulting and poker-hustling and nuisance law-suiting," he
still suffered from a sense of unsettling boredom, a feeling
that his life lacked meaning in the grand scheme of things.

This indeed was the very feeling that was absent in Harvey's life, absent because the "incident of his unmanagea-
ble success," while not extinguishing his spirit, had extin-
guished his desire to take risks.

And so perhaps that day, in Steve's youthful exuberance,
Harvey saw a chance for his own redemption, a chance to
do it all over again – only this time secure in the knowledge
that Steve could be the one taking the risks – and that Harvey, with the expertise which comes from having been a
student at the school of hard knocks, could participate in the
adventure from the sidelines, not as a partner, but as a con-

sultant of sorts, imparting secret knowledge and wisdom which only comes to men like Harvey, who have been to the mountaintop and then fallen off.

And so on this particular afternoon as Harvey ate his tuna sandwich and listened to Steve talk about his own dreams of making it big in the real estate business, Harvey couldn't help but get caught up in the emotion of the moment. Nor could he help but realize that try as he may to be content with his current lot in life as an Orthodox Jewish Environmental Consultant Poker Hustler Plaintiff, he needed once again to be part of something more – something grand and glorious – something which would give him a feeling that there was indeed purpose in this seemingly purposeless, but controllable, existence.

And so, at lunch on that one particular afternoon, as he was washing down his sandwich with a sip of passion fruit iced tea, Harvey put forth a proposal to Steve that the two of them become "business associates," but *not* partners.

Harvey's plan was as follows: he would help find, negotiate, finance and purchase hotel and apartment deals in the Las Vegas area and Steve would run them once they were bought. And the beauty of it all was that neither Steve nor Harvey were going to have to put up one dime of their own money to finance the deals (which was a good thing because neither Harvey nor Steve had a dime of their own money to finance any deals anyway.)

And then what Harvey said next not only piqued Steve's interest, but clenched the deal in Steve's mind.

You see Harvey told Steve that he knew a guy from Beverly Hills named Salt. This guy, he said, invested in a lot of commercial real estate deals, especially in motels and apartments. Harvey said this guy would probably be interested in becoming a partner in Steve's success and that he could hook Steve up with this guy. In return for the hookup, Harvey said, Steve would agree to hire Harvey as his

Deal Consultant, stressing emphatically that Harvey and Steve's relationship was not going to be one of partners, but one of client and consultant.

And from this point in the conversation Harvey – who had in actuality never owned, managed, invested in or even had any experience with apartment buildings or hotels whatsoever, except for performing a phase 1- Environmental Study and maybe staying in one a few times – proceeded to give Steve detailed advice on how to own, manage, invest in, finance and sell apartments and hotels in the Las Vegas market.

And with his offer in place, Harvey went on to outline the details of his proposed consulting agreement, saying the two would enter into a contract that Harvey would draw up (of course), the terms of which would read as follows:

On an on-going basis, and in perpetuity, Harvey would provide consulting services to Steve and in consideration for Harvey's services Steve would pay Harvey 1 percent of the acquisition price and 1 percent of the gross rents collected on any property Steve had ever bought in the past or planned to buy in the future, forever and ever, amen.

It was a deal of biblical proportions!

Harvey then again went on to assure Steve that he was an expert in real estate acquisition and based his credentials on the fact that he had just read Donald Trump's book *The Art of the Deal*.

Steve – who was not born yesterday – upon hearing Harvey's reassurance of how valid his credentials really were, sensed that Harvey was probably a little, if not totally, full of shit!

But, nevertheless, Steve had indeed heard of Morton Salt and was intrigued with the idea of meeting him. And since he really needed the money that Harvey's hook-up – if it was real – would yield him, he decided to go along with Harvey's idea, at least for the time being, and sign the consulting agreement, a boiler-plate copy of which Harvey just happened to have right there in his briefcase at that moment right there in the deli where Steve and Harvey were having lunch.

Besides, since Steve knew a little about contract law from helping his wife study for the California bar exam a few years back, Steve knew that Harvey's contract was probably unenforceable because it was illusory and also because of a little concept in law called "the rule against perpetuities."

Harvey, on the other hand, was certain that such an agreement was indeed enforceable, as Harvey was not only a real estate expert but a legal expert as well, his confidence in the matter being based on a long standing Jewish tradition called "the transitive property of relative education." This meant that if your relative was a lawyer, as Harvey's son was, then you too were a lawyer, the reasoning behind it being that you paid for your son's education so (said in a Jewish whine) "weren't you entitled?"

Steve, in his own mind, retorted with an opinion based on another long standing Jewish tradition that he was aware of called "renegotiating the deal and then fucking your partner before he fucks you." It had been an integral part of Jewish business negotiations for as far back as anyone could remember, probably stemming from when after leaving Egypt, Moses promised the Israelites they would get to the Promised Land real soon. Forty fuckin' years later, they were still wandering in the desert, and Moses was still changing the terms of the deal adding more commandments and smashing more false idols.

In any case, the two argued silently about the enforceability of the contract in their own minds for about two minutes without saying a word, at which point Steve, with no intention of ever honoring their agreement, just simply signed the deal anyway.

And with Harvey now sporting the title of Steve's Business Consultant, Harvey set up a meeting which would take place 160 days hence, in Beverly Hills, for Steve to meet his prospective new partner, Morton Salt.

Harvey unfortunately couldn't attend the meeting because he had recently finished suing Morty on a phony workman's comp claim and as such their relationship was a bit strained.

And so for the next 160 days and 160 nights, Steve continued to listen to Harvey's ponderings, watch him analyze and re-analyze the merits and demerits of various real estate deals that Harvey knew nothing about, and long for the day when Steve could hook up with Morty, dump Harvey, and use Harvey's one-percent-in-perpetuity-for-life contract to wipe his ass with.

In the meantime, Steve could not help but think about the ultimate irony in the logic of Harvey's wisdom when Harvey had offered up to him the following pearl of consulting advice, which when Steve thought about it, was a real mind fuck.

"He who holds himself out to be an expert knows the least."— Shmengey Mignone

In offering the saying to Steve as advice, Harvey was correct, he did know the least, and thus his advice was sound, thereby making him an expert, Steve thought to himself.

"157 more days, 157 more days."

Chapter 1.3

Tryin' this mother out

Woodcrest Apartments – El Paso, Texas – August 2000 - Exactly 24 hours and two minutes before the inevitable

As 12:13 in the afternoon arrived on this otherwise average sweltering El Paso day in August, the temperature in the Woodcrest parking lot was reaching 130 degrees.

The chiller system had been down for almost thirty minutes, 28 minutes to be exact, and the situation was getting a little tenser.

Shirley Dole, of the Eastwood Community Association, had heard of the problem and was in her bedroom getting ready to go over to Woodcrest to make sure that something was going to be done.

As Shirley was drying her enormously large head of Marge Simpson-style, reddish-orange dyed hair and putting on the many pins and badges which she liked to wear over her Bea Arthur-style pant suit with the long flowing grey satin vest, Harold and Andy were out in the northwest corner of the property next to Unit 1 installing the two six-volt batteries required to power up the super-sensitive microphone spy device that they were going to use to listen for the aspirin-sized leak in the ten or so miles of piping that stretched just below the surface of the 7.8 acres of the Woodcrest property.

Andy had just gotten the two batteries out of the smoke alarms in Unit 1 and was excited about "trying this mother out" to see if it really would work as well as the package said it would.

The plan was to start at the north end of the property in front of Unit 1 and move in an east to west pattern, zigzagging their way across the complex and finally ending at the southwest corner just off of Martin Luther King Boulevard in front of Unit #352.

As Andy fired up the device he could hear a whoosh and then a crackle coming from the speaker, and as he put the pointy end of the microphone next to the ground and then as he and Harold started making their way, east to west and then west to east across the 7.8 acres, Andy was sure that in just a short while, he and Harold would be $4,500 richer.

Now in an effort not to understate the gravity of the situation it should be noted that Harold and Andy, as cool and as calm as they appeared to be, were aware that they were under a little bit of time pressure.

You see Texas State Health Code Regulations clearly state that "when a heating or cooling system ceases to function or is functioning in a diminished capacity, a landlord, apartment owner, manager and/or agent has 24 hours to repair and or remedy the situation."

The reason for this regulation is pretty simple – in Texas in mid-August it gets pretty fucking hot and without air-conditioning people could die.

The code goes on to say that if not rectified within the 24-hour time limit, the authorities have the right to take corrective action themselves, bill the apartment owner for the repairs and impose compensatory and punitive monetary fines against the owners, the manager and/or their agents. In addition, the state, at its discretion, may consider filing criminal charges against the property owners, their managers and/or agents for public endangerment, health and safety violations, and generally just to remind the other landlords out there that if the air conditioning breaks they better fix it pretty fucking fast.

And so, under the gun, Harold and Andy wasted no time getting around to "commencing to listening" and by 5:00 p.m. that afternoon, just about five hours after they had begun, they had already made their way almost 300 feet across the front lawn at Woodcrest. With only 7.7 acres and 3.9 miles of underground pipe left to cover, Harold and Andy were, however, pretty confident they would be finding the source of the leak real soon.

It was, just the same, still kind of hot out and Harold and Andy were getting hungry and a little tired. So they decided to take a short break and head down to the market to pick up a twelve-pack of Bud Light and some of those pork rinds with the chipotle seasoning that Andy liked so much.

Harold, on the other hand, couldn't eat the pork rinds because he had recently had gallbladder surgery and only had half a gall bladder left and so he didn't tolerate fatty foods too well. So Harold got a bag of Cheetos instead and one of those banana flavored Moon Pies, and a pack of one of those two-for-a-dollar Slim Jim and American Cheese Food Product Combo Packs that went really good with Bud Light. He also got a pack of Marlboro Lights (he always got the lights because he only had one lung and he was trying to be careful to live a healthier lifestyle.)

After about a half-hour and with their refreshments in hand, Harold and Andy headed back to the truck and drove the three and a half blocks back to the front lawn at Woodcrest. There they unloaded their supplies on the grass, including the tools that Andy had gathered up from the back lawn of the Juniper Apartments a few days before, and resumed working where they had left off.

Now if the truth be known, Andy wasn't exactly sure where it was they had left off. He had kind of forgotten to mark the spot with a spike or something because he was really kind of hungry before they left and was in a hurry to get some food.

But well, he was pretty sure of *about* where they had left off and he didn't want to upset Harold too much because "Harold gets a little belligerent when he's been drinking" and he was already on his third beer, and besides it was a really big place so the chance of missing the leak, even if they forget to check a few feet, wasn't that much anyway.

So, confidently, Andy picked up the super-sensitive spy micro-phone, put it down on the sort-of exact place they had left off and continued to move east to west and then west to east, carefully listening for that aspirin-sized leak that would pretty soon be making him and Harold a shit-load of dough.

They continued listening for about another hour and got about another 30 feet, and then, since it was 6:30 p.m., Harold and Andy both decided that it was "quitting time" for the evening.

Harold had already consumed an entire twelve-pack and he really had to go take a piss and Andy was getting a little hungry again and wanted to make it home for dinner before re-runs of his favorite TV show, *The Beverly Hillbillies*, came on.

The episode that was going to be on that night was the one where Jethro decides that he wants to be a big time movie producer and Granny decides to fill up the "cement pond" with those crawdads she is going to cook for Sunday supper.

As you might guess, when Jethro decides to have one of those big Hollywood parties over in the backyard next to the cement pond his new business associates and their accompanying starlets decide to take a dip in the pool, all heck breaks loose, and Jethro's budding movie career swims away with the crawdads.

Andy just loved that episode and entertained thoughts of becoming a big time movie producer himself; after all, if Jethro could do it with only having a third grade education, Andy, who had gotten all the way through the seventh grade, could do it too.

So vowing to get an early start and get the leak fixed before the 24-hour deadline was up, and before Steve found out about it and called Roto-Rooter for real, Andy walked and Harold stumbled back to Harold's apartment to get cleaned up before dinner.

Sub-Sub-Chapter 2.1

Why Build the Building When You Can Just Build the Model?

Beverly Hills, California - 1990 - Right next door to Sylvester Stallone's House – How Steve came to meet Harvey

In 1989 Eli Shalom was a Real Estate Billionaire and anyone who spent more than thirty seconds in a room with him knew exactly why. The man was absolutely electric – a ball of unbridled energy that bounced about a room giving off sparks of ideas, waves of inspiration and projections of vision.

Yes, it was Eli's contagious energy that was the attractor of his great success. Indeed, within thirty seconds of being in a room with Eli Shalom even the most beaten-down corporate dilettante could not help having entrepreneurial thoughts of his own nor could he help getting caught up in the frenzied storm of optimism that was Eli's universe.

Having moved to the U.S. from Israel in 1982 with $418 in his pocket, a Hebrew-English dictionary, and a worn pair of white slip-on loafers, he was the embodiment of the American dream. Within seven short years of arriving in the U.S. he was living in a hilltop mansion in Beverly Hills, right next door to Sylvester Stallone, with an indoor pool, a bowling alley in his basement and a disco room complete with a state of the art sound system and a diamond-encrusted disco ball. His garage housed two ivory-colored Rolls Royce convertibles with blue fabric tops and license plates that read *Oooo! LaLa I* and *Oooo! LaLa II*.

But it was not what Eli bought with his money that was important to him. It was the idea of making money as an entrepreneur – an American Capitalist – that simply fascinated him. And this was as easy to see as the look on his face when he talked about it. Yes, Eli Shalom was mesmerized by and in love with the idea of being an American businessman. Why anyone would not take full advantage of the tremendous opportunities that a country like America had to offer was inconceivable to him. And he had no time for those types of people.

To Eli, making money was his holy quest; he did it because he loved it, because it thrilled him, and because he felt there was something primal about it – like a lion stalking its prey.

It was beautiful as nature is beautiful because it was pure and simple, the only unadulterated system of human design whose beauty lie in the fact that it was completely devoid of all humanity.

And Eli had found a way of making money that was absolutely ingenious; the ingenuity of his invention being that Eli Shalom's billion-dollar real estate empire didn't contain one piece of real estate – not one parcel of land, not one shopping center, not one office building, not one apartment complex and not one industrial facility.

What it did contain was 314 sets of architectural drawings, 314 files filled with permits, surveys, title reports, legal entitlements, prescriptive easements, zoning variances and all the other documentation necessary to develop a project – and most importantly – 314 scale models of some of the most elaborate and beautiful buildings known to man. As Eli would rhetorically ask his soon-to-be apprentice Steve, "Why build the building, Stevie, when you can just build the model?" (Only in an Israeli accent of course.)

Yes indeed, Eli Shalom had made his fortune selling not real estate, but turn-key kits of everything a person would need to build all types of real estate projects imaginable; all the legal work done, all the plans approved, all the sights identified and zoned properly, all the engineering and soil testing complete, and of course, a scale mock-up of the building and parking facilities complete with tiny trees and little model people. All a developer would need to purchase such a project from Eli was money – lots and lots of money.

And Eli sold his turn-key projects to mostly foreign investors, folks who may have had trouble on their own procuring all those permits and entitlements and the like. And they were more than happy to pay Eli lots and lots of money for being the facilitator of their visions and the deliverer of their dreams.

So for the cost of a scale model and some paperwork, which he never paid for until he sold the project anyway, maybe three or four thousand dollars, Eli charged foreign developers five or six million dollars for the rights to own the concept of the project.

And the cherry on top was this: Eli was the largest depositor and stock holder of several savings and loans in the Los Angeles area, the very same savings and loans that were loaning those very same foreign investors the money to give to Eli for his projects. Talk about getting them coming and going. Yes indeed, Eli was the Master; and "When the student is ready, the master will appear."

And in 1990, Steve was ready.

Having just earned his MBA in finance and having worked in the banking industry for nearly five years, Steve had taken a job as Vice President of Commercial Lending for Valley Savings and Loan. And although Steve was impressed with his title and his vice presidential salary, there was something about his job that did bother him.

You see, as Vice President of Commercial Lending, not only was he in charge of making new loans to finance the purchase and construction of commercial property, but he was also in charge of reviewing the bank's current loan portfolio, especially those loans that may have been or were likely to become problems.

And it was while reviewing these potentially problematic loans that Steve came face to face with a phenomenon that was a little unsettling to him because it didn't jive well with his over-educated, moral, middle-class view of the universe.

It seems that many of the borrowers who were on the list of problem loans were not really interested in talking to him, and even if they had been he probably wouldn't have understood them that well anyway, as many of the folks on the list were foreigners and spoke broken English at best.

No, folks like Foo San Lu, and Avram Havnery, and Hovan Hovananian, and Ali Huchma Hieshmicha, and Hajamata Fujimoto, and Alex Jamgitchian and Eli Shalom, well they all seemed to have a general lack of concern for Steve's concerns about their loans.

And when he had been lucky enough to actually get them on the phone, they had always spoken down to Steve in a tone that suggested that he was in some way bothering them with his questions, annoying them with his clerical checklists and confusing them with his loan to value ratios.

No, they didn't have the time or the interest to talk to Steve because he was just a clerk, a loan processor, a corporate servant, there for their benefit, to loan them money and then to just shut the fuck up and let them run their businesses. Who the hell was Steve, a little corporate monkey, to tell them what to do?

And the more Steve conversed with these troubled borrowers, the more troubled Steve became, because what he found out didn't sit well with his ideas about how the world should work.

Very few of them had any sort of formal education. Many of them had little or no previous experience in purchasing or developing real estate. And most of them were not even American citizens. And here they were, all of them, earning millions of dollars a year, being landlords, and project developers, and shopping center owners.

"What gives," Steve often thought to himself. "I busted my ass to get through MBA school, I know way more about finance and real estate than any of these borrowers and here I am, earning $60,000 a year, driving a Ford Escort, while these guys who don't even speak English are driving Mercedes and Rolls-Royces and earning more in one day than I make all year."

Now for all great men and women of achievement there is a moment in life when they come to a realization that success really has nothing to do with the outside world – that everything needed to accomplish your dreams and realize your visions comes from within yourself. That genius comes from your soul, not from the validation of the world around you. It is what I like to call your *moment of courage*.

It's the very same moment that Bill Gates decided to drop out of Harvard, that Quentin Tarantino decided to drop out of high school, and that Albert Einstein decided to take an F in Physics rather than listen to his professor drone on about ideas he knew were just plain wrong.

It is the moment you accept in your heart that the current path you're on is bullshit, and the path you should be on is, and probably always has been, within your grasp.

It is in this moment, when you finally have the courage to accept what you already know in your heart, that you free yourself from the shackles of mediocrity, and become the champion of your vision. It is in this moment when your passion – what you love – puts you on a path that defines who you are.

And this moment is the birth place of your quest.

And for Steve this moment came when he accepted the fact that you don't need a degree in finance to raise money to buy property. What you need is a pen and thirty minutes to fill out the loan application form. And you don't need ten years of experience in real estate or a degree in business administration to buy a building. What you need are the "balls" to actually go find a building and then some more balls to actually follow through and buy it.

The difference between Steve and Mr. Pomgotchian, and Mr. Lee, and Mr. Havnery, and Mr. Hieshmicha was that while Steve was busy reading about buying buildings, they were out strapping on a set of "brass ones" and actually doing it. Because unlike Steve, who ten years ago was in college taking classes in religion and philosophy and worrying about concepts like good and evil, right and wrong and moral and immoral, these guys were in Bosnia and China and Iran trying to figure out how not to get shot and how to stay alive long enough to save up enough money to be able to come to America where there was real opportunity and a real chance for a better life.

And in that moment of realization Steve suddenly understood that the borrowers on that troubled loan list were indeed not men to be ridiculed but men to be admired because they were able to do something that Steve, and indeed many men, were unable to do. They were able to have the vision, the passion, and the balls to follow their dreams.

Steve had seen the truth, and the student was ready.

And that's when the master appeared.

So it was no accident that as Steve went down the list of "Possible Problem Loans" that fateful day in 1990 that Eli's name was next on the list of borrowers to call.

And as Steve called Eli that fateful day about his twenty-million-dollar problem loan, expecting to hear the same annoyed, condescending, "don't bother me" voice, imagine his surprise when he heard the great American entrepreneur Eli Shalom say, "Oh Yes! I am *interesting* to talk to you." (What he meant to say was he was interested to talk to him but he looked in the wrong part of his Hebrew-English dictionary.)

And imagine Steve's further surprise when Eli said, "Why don't you come over to my house right now and we can talk over lunch?" As Eli went on to explain, he didn't have time to be going to any bank meetings. As a matter of fact, he was so busy that he didn't even have time to leave his house. He simply worked out of an office that was connected to his bedroom and his indoor marble swimming pool and inlaid-tile hot tub, so he could always take a nap or a swim, while he worked those 23-hour work days of his.

Now what kind of a guy goes from penniless immigrant to real estate billionaire in just 5 years?

A guy with vision, a guy with passion – a guy with *balls*!

As a matter of fact, there was a refrigerator magnet on Eli's refrigerator that said, "Vision-Passion-Balls" – it was Eli's motto. And Eli's make-up was 10 percent vision, 90 percent passion and 100 percent balls. That's right! He was a 200 percent kind of guy.

When Steve pulled up in front of Eli's Beverly Hills hilltop mansion right next door to Sylvester Stallone's place, in his brand new 1989 grey Ford Escort with the "no air conditioning" and the "no radio," it was quite the mind fuck. In a single moment, the contrast of the sight of Steve's car in front of Eli's house completely shattered a belief system that had taken Steve thirty years to assemble. And everything that Steve had been taught and every idea that he had formulated on his own in those first thirty years – the self-righteousness, the middle-class morality, the Judeo-Christian values, "the study hard, earn a degree and get a good job recipe for success," all went right out the window of his 1989 Ford Escort, the window being down because he had no air-conditioning and it was hot in the Los Angeles area that day.

And if you think that just driving up to Eli's house was enough to blow Steve's mind, can you imagine what must have been going on in Steve's head when Eli's personal assistant opened the gold-encrusted black marble double doors of Eli's entranceway, invited Steve in and then led him towards Eli's office, passing the Roman statue-lined marble-floored disco with the diamond-encrusted disco ball and the hot tub in the center.

Steve's life was about to change, and Eli Shalom was about to change it.

"Come in Stevie, shalom, shalom," Eli called from the swimming pool outside his bedroom. "You want take a swim, Stevie? Come, its heated!" Steve was a little surprised that Eli called him Stevie; it was like Eli had known him for years. The only other person who ever called him "Stevie" was his mother.

So now what's going on in Steve's head? Was he confused? Was he excited? Was he in awe? Yes, yes, yes. But mostly he was curious. Why would a legend like Eli Shalom be "interesting to talk to" Steve? Surely Eli had a plan, an idea, a scheme.

And Steve himself probably had some sort of plan, some sort of idea, some sort of scheme.

And although Steve was there under the guise of talking business, and Eli had invited Steve under the same guise, they both must have known that this was just an excuse to meet one another because they could have just said what was needed to be said in a two-minute phone call.

And so it is pretty safe to say that Steve probably wanted something from Eli, to perhaps in some way have some of Eli's success rub off on him, and that Eli wanted something from Steve.

Maybe Eli would be impressed with Steve and make him his apprentice and groom him to take over the empire when Eli retired, or maybe Eli would even hire Steve to be his assistant at some fabulous salary and give him a company Rolls-Royce that had a vanity plate that said "Oooh! La La III." Or maybe Eli would just cut Steve a check for ten million dollars for no particular reason at all, just because he felt like it, because Steve was such a swell guy.

(Isn't that usually the fascination with meeting heroes and movie stars? That somewhere in the back of your mind you think that if you meet someone who is rich or famous, and shake their hand, that somehow their wealth or fame will rub off on you. That maybe if you met Bill Gates he'd be so impressed with you that he'd just give you twenty million dollars to start your own Microsoft, or if you met Quentin Tarantino that he'd be so taken aback by your storytelling abilities that he'd decide right there on the spot to make a full-length motion picture based on the story you just told him about your ride over from Pasadena to shake his hand at the opening of some film festival. Or if you met Albert Einstein, and after sharing your observations on the nature of light with him, he looked at you in amusement and said, "Why didn't I think of that?")

And so with all this speculation going on in Steve's head, there must have been some thoughts going on in Eli's as well. Why would he want to meet some "nobody," 60,000-dollar a year banker? Was it because Eli wanted to negotiate some kind of loan work-out agreement on his twenty million-dollar loan with Steve's bank? Probably not, since Eli was the bank's biggest borrower, and also its largest stockholder; if he wanted to do some kind of loan workout, he'd just call the Chairman of the Board of the bank and tell him what to do. So that wasn't it. Was it because Eli needed some professional financial banking advice? No, Eli had a team of seasoned bankers and lawyers and CPAs for that. So that wasn't it. Was it because Eli's secretary had gone home and Eli needed to have someone close by who knew how to swim just in case he started drowning in the hot tub? Again, not likely! So what was it that prompted Eli to invite Steve over to his Mansion that fateful day in 1990?

It was "balls." Steve had had the balls to call Eli on the phone. Eli was impressed with the fact that this bank vice president would have the balls to do that. So much so, that he decided it would be interesting to meet Steve before calling the Chairman of the Board of Valley Savings to have Steve fired for daring to call him in the first place.

And so as the two of them began to converse, Eli sitting in the hot tub wearing a red Speedo and Steve standing on the side wearing a grey pin-stripe banker suit that he bought at J.C. Penny, it was the unlikely beginning of their brief relationship as Master and Student, Mentor and Mentee.

Now this Master-Student sort of relationship has been around for thousands of years, dating back to Socrates and Plato, Andrew Carnegie and Napoleon Hill, and Master Po and Grasshopper.

And the reason that Students and Mentees want to be Students and Mentees is pretty easy to figure out. It is to learn and eventually become proficient enough in some sort of endeavor, to become Masters and Mentors themselves someday. But why do Masters and Mentors want to be Masters and Mentors?

Immortality and ego, of course! Because after you've made twenty gajillion dollars and bought every type of toy, house, boat, plane, train, car and collectable (including people) and political power, what's left?

The feeling that *your wisdom will live forever* and the feeling of importance and self-worth that you get spouting unquestioned pearls of wisdom to someone who hangs on your every word!

Now on the side of Eli's hot tub was a phone. And unless Steve was mistaken, the phone had 17 lines, all of which whose buttons were flashing on and off except one, indicating that Eli was talking on one of them and had 16 other people on hold, simultaneously.

And as the two got down to talking, Eli would ask Steve a rhetorical mentor-like question, like: "Stevie, why build the building when you can just build the model?" And just as Steve was about to attempt an answer, Eli would tell him to hold on for a second and then he would press one of the phone line buttons and begin speaking to the person on the other end of the phone. "What do you mean the plans aren't ready yet, damn it you son of a bitch, I need them now! Do you hear me? Now!" And as Eli screamed at the person on the phone, he picked up one of his white slip-on loafers which were next to the phone and he would violently bang the heel of the shoe on the side of the hot tub, and then he would throw the loafer across the room screaming, "Damn it, damn it!"

And then as if nothing happened, he would put the phone receiver down, look at Steve and ask him yet another rhetorical mentor-like question. "If you owned a bank, Stevie, who would you rather loan money to, a strange borrower or to yourself?" And just as Steve was about to attempt an answer, Eli again would ask Steve to hold on a minute, and then he would press another phone line button and begin to scream at another person on the other end of the phone, "I need those permits drawn up immediately and if you don't have them by 5:00 p.m., you're fired!" And then he would pick up his other shoe, and bang the heel on the side of the hot tub saying, "5:00 p.m., 5:00 p.m. damn it!" And then he would throw that shoe across the room. And then he would put down the receiver, look up at Steve, and ask him another question? "Is it better to have the money, Stevie, or to have the real estate? Money always, Stevie, money always!" And then Eli said, "Excuse me for a minute while I take this call, and could you go get my shoes for me while I'm talking to this guy?"

And as this routine of Socratic repartee continued for over 3 hours, and as Eli endlessly spouted those entrepreneurial pearls of wisdom, (while intermittently screaming at somebody on the phone and banging the chipped wooden heel of his white slip-on loafers on the side of the hot tub), and while Steve carefully hung on every word that Eli told him as he fetched his shoes over two dozen times as Eli held court in his hot tub, the two of them exchanged, although Steve never got a chance to utter a word of his own, bits and pieces of dreams and visions, hopes and ideas, and ways and means, until it was time for Eli's massage, Steve opting not to have a massage because it appeared to include a "happy ending" and Steve was a family man.

(As an interesting aside, it should be noted that during that three-hour time period while Eli and Steve were talking, Eli sold three deals over the telephone and earned just over eighteen million dollars, while Steve sustained irreversible water damage to his J.C. Penny suit from the chlo-

STEVE O.

rinated bubbles that were coming off the hot tub and earned $47.18, mostly from his mileage reimbursement for driving out to Eli's house.)

When they were through talking, Eli wished Steve well and told him he was totally confident that Steve had everything it took to become a total American success in his own right. "Just remember Stevie, why build the building when you can build the model?" And with that said, Eli had his assistant get Steve a refrigerator magnet, which said "Vision, Passion, Balls" to take with him and a chicken salad sandwich on rye bread and a Diet Coke to eat in his car on his way back to the office.

When Steve got back to the office at Valley Savings, upon walking in the door everyone stood up and applauded. Apparently word had gotten out that Steve had had a meeting with the great Eli Shalom. And even more spectacular than that, word had gotten out that while Steve had been driving back to the office Eli had called Scott Brawny, the President of the Bank, and wired the full twenty million dollars due on his "troubled" loan. (What Scott didn't know was that Eli had, just before calling Scott, called the Chairman of the Board of Valley Savings and arranged to borrow forty million.) Boy, what had Steve said to Eli to get him to work out the problem so fast? Even Scott hadn't been able to even get Eli on the phone, let alone negotiate a twenty million-dollar settlement. That Steve was a genius!

On the following Friday night a special awards dinner was held in Steve's honor at a fancy restaurant in the Valley, where Steve was presented with a certificate of achievement for the largest loan workout in the bank's 75-year history. Steve was also presented with an award for "Employee of the Year" and Scott Brawny made a speech telling every one of the banks 225 employees in attendance about Steve's courage and determination in facing Eli Shalom. "Bravo Steve," said Scott, "bravo."

On the following Monday morning at 9:01 a.m., when Steve arrived at the office, there was a note on his desk from Scott Brawny asking him to come up to Scott's office for a meeting later that afternoon at 3:00 p.m.

And as 2:55 rolled around, and as Steve was riding up in the elevator to the 11th floor of the Valley Savings Building where Scott's office was located, he wondered to himself about the subject of the meeting that Scott had called. Was it to give Steve a promotion or even a raise for the outstanding work he had done on the Eli situation? Was it to assign him another project that needed to be handled that Scott knew *only* Steve could take care of, or was it simply to commend him one more time for the courage and initiative he had shown in contacting Eli in the first place?

It surely was, Steve acknowledged to himself as he entered Scott's office and Scott began to speak. "Steve, you are to be commended for your courage and determination. What you did took the spirit of a maverick, some real 'out of the box' thinking."

"The trouble is," Scott continued, "that although that type of thing is great, and it saved the bank twenty million dollars, we can't have that type of thing going on around here. You're too much of a wild card and even though what you did saved us a great deal of money, the Board and I can't help but wonder, maybe if there was a next time the whole thing might backfire and we might lose a lot of money. So rather than risk it, we're just going to have to let you go."

Un-fucking-believable!

But then again, to Steve, it didn't really matter. As a matter of fact, they had done him a favor. He was going to quit anyway because he was no longer a corporate guy, he was an entrepreneur and he was ready to head out into the business world on his own, confident of his ability to succeed. After all, he had been mentored by the master.

"Scott?" Steve said as they both returned together to Steve's desk and as Steve packed up the *Vision-Passion-Balls* refrigerator magnet and his Employee-of-the-Year trophy, and headed to the door, "Why build the building when you can build the model?"

Scott looked puzzled, but Steve knew what it meant. And with that, Steve walked out the door, got into his 1989 Ford Escort with the no-air conditioning and the no-radio, and drove off down Van Nuys Boulevard fading into the mid-morning smog.

Chapter 1.4

What Is That Little Blue Flame?

Woodcrest Apartments – July 2000 – 6:00 a.m. the next morning, just about six hours and 14 minutes before, well, you know!

At 6:00 a.m. the next morning Harold and Andy left their apartment and returned to the front lawn. This time Andy had been smart. Before he and Harold had called it a day the night before, Andy had marked the spot with a half-full (apparently Andy was an optimist) Bud Light can left over from the twelve-pack that Harold and Andy had been drinking on the front lawn the night before. To Andy's dismay, however, when they arrived on the scene that morning, Andy discovered that the front lawn was littered with hundreds of identical Bud Light cans strewn about and lying in pretty much the same area that he was pretty sure he had left his "marking" can just eleven and one-half hours before.

Seems the one thing Andy hadn't figured on, was that all forty tenants who lived in the apartments next to the front lawn were all big Bud Light fans too, and not really good garbage picker-uppers. The only difference between the cans the tenants left and the can that Andy had left was that many of the tenants' cans were not half-full, but half-empty, indicating that the tenants, unlike Andy, were mostly pessimists.

Nevertheless, Harold and Andy weren't going to let a small set-back like that stop them from watching the upcoming *Retro Sports Bonanza Highlighting the Year 1955* and featuring the famous Rocky Marciano/Archie Moore fight and the 1955 All-Star Game on ESPN that coming weekend, and Harold needed to get that ninety-day delinquent portion of his cable bill paid real soon.

So, Harold and Andy picked the spot where they were pretty sure they had left off and began combing the property east to west and then west to east with their super-sensitive spy micro-phone.

It had been eighteen hours since the chiller system went down but Harold and Andy were pretty confident they'd find the leak and get things up and running by 11:30 a.m. – thirty full minutes before the 24-hour deadline. "But heck," Harold figured to himself, "the Health Department probably didn't know exactly when the chiller went down so if worst came to worst nothing really bad would happen until the following day anyway." With this thought in mind, Harold lit up a Marlboro Light, took a deep half-breath and went back to listening to the ground.

Unfortunately, Harold's figuring was wrong.

In fact, just 14 minutes after the chiller system had quit working, the tenants in unit #13, who coincidentally were two months behind on their rent and were scheduled to be evicted, were on the phone to the Department of Human Services to let them know that the chiller system at Wood-crest wasn't working.

They also just wanted to make sure that they didn't have to pay their rent and that they couldn't be evicted until such time as the chiller was fixed. While on the phone they also figured they might as well mention that their living room window had been broken by someone who threw a frying pan through it from the outside and that it had been broken for two days and no one had come to fix it. Oddly enough, the broken glass and the alleged frying pan were on the out-side of the apartment, scattered about the grass patch in front of the apartment, the disarray clearly indicating an exit wound rather than an entrance wound had occurred. Nevertheless, the Department of Human Services took note and said they would continue to monitor the situation and take corrective action if necessary.

Coincidentally, and at about just the same time, the ten-ants in unit #21 made a similar phone call alerting the local news desk down at Channel 5 Eyewitness News that the chiller was down. Also, coincidentally, the folks in unit #21 were also behind in their rent but took comfort in the fact that since the chiller was down, they too didn't have to pay.

And as 27 additional and similar phone calls poured out that fateful July afternoon to various city agencies, health authorities, community associations, action committees and finally to the District 13 Office of then-City Councilman Jim Jameson, it was sure as shit, that everyone in the City of El Paso knew, to Harold's dismay, that the chiller system at the Woodcrest Apartments was down and had been down since exactly 11:46 a.m. the previous morning.

As 9:30 a.m. approached, Harold and Andy had made their way through the second row of apartments, about 200 feet south of where they had begun listening to the ground just 21 and one-half hours before.

At exactly 9:32, and at the exact moment that Harold had fired up his lighter to light the last cigarette left in his pack of Marlboro Lights, Andy screamed out to Harold and waved him over.

There was no doubt about it, Andy could hear a definite hissing sound coming from the ground and when Harold bent over to put his ear to the ground, lit lighter still in hand, he could hear it too. And then the most amazing thing happened. As Harold's lighter touched the ground, a small wave of blue flame seemed to bubble up and dance around for just about three or four seconds and then go out.

"That's weird," Harold said.

"Light it again," Andy said.

And as Harold touched the ground with his lit lighter the wave of blue flame started up again, bubbled around and then, about three seconds later, just blew out. "That's so weird," said Andy.

"Never seen anything like that before," said Harold. So Harold lit it again, and just like the first two times, the wave of blue flame came up, bubbled around and then blew out. "Go get Joey," said Harold. "Maybe he knows what this is, after all, it's right here in front of his apartment." (Joey was the groundskeeper at "the Crest" and like Harold and Andy, also lived there. As a matter of fact, he lived in Unit #1 north, his front door being not more than 15 feet from where Harold and Andy were now standing.)

And so while Andy went to get Joey, Harold continued to light, watch and re-light the ground where that strange hissing noise was coming up from. After Harold's lighter ran out of butane, Joey (who Andy had found in the maintenance shed taking a mid-morning nap because he was exhausted due to the fact that his girlfriend Clarissa, who suffered from Tourette's syndrome and often kept Joey up all night screaming profanities at him and banging him in the head with spastic arm movements, wouldn't let him sleep) gave Harold his lighter, and when that ran out, Bill from unit #14 South, who lived in the unit right in back of where the discovery was occurring, gave Joey his lighter who then gave it to Harold, and when that one ran out, the guy from the ice cream truck who came over to see what was going on gave his lighter to Bill who in turn gave it to Joey who in turn gave it to Harold. And this went on for about another 45 minutes until the crowd of maintenance guys, tenants and passersby got bored with the whole thing and just kinda moved on.

Figuring it was some natural freak of nature or something, Harold and Andy dismissed the whole thing and got back to focusing on the situation at hand. The fact of the matter was they had found the leak. And with only two and one-half hours left before the 24-hour deadline was up, they figured they should probably go to the plumbing supply warehouse, get the pipe and supplies they needed and come back and fix the chiller.

It was getting close to break time, however, and Harold was out of cigarettes so on the way they decided to stop at the 7-Eleven to pick up some snacks, another twelve-pack, and a jumbo pack of Bic disposable lighters for later.

Chapter 2.4

John "Bing Shu" Hu –
The Parable of the Yuan and the Shekel

Arcadia, California 1990 – Three days after Steve had lunch with Harvey Mendel and 157 days till Steve was to Meet Morty

John "Bing Shu" Hu was a man who some say was utterly devoid of a soul. A cold and calculating man who seemed incapable of experiencing emotion, his only passions in life being those of chain-smoking, gambling, and the obsessive pursuit of the one "big deal" that would deliver him from the status of normal businessman to billionaire mogul/real estate genius, literally overnight.

His passions and his dreams notwithstanding, these days John was eking out a living as the head of a cigarette smuggling ring that imported tax stamp-free cartons of cigarettes from a warehouse located somewhere in Hong Kong to an unused bedroom in his luxury home located in the expensive section of Arcadia, California.

Arcadia, or Arc-Asia as the locals call it, is a city of about 100,000 residents, 50,000 of whom are Chinese. It is located just east of Pasadena, California.

John, or Bing Shu as his sidekick Wilbur called him, was rumored to be a part-time member of the Chinese Mafia, a degenerate gambler and an investor in "low end" real estate deals in the greater Los Angeles area.

But the most interesting habit that John will always be remembered for was that for some reason when he spoke English he began every phrase with the sound HHHHHHHHHHHHHHHA, and ended every phrase with the sound HHHHHHHHHHHHHHHHHHO! Aside from this linguistic idiosyncrasy, about 33 million dollars in unpaid debts, and his total lack of compunction, John was pretty much just a regular guy.

You see, due to the Savings and Loan Crisis of the late 80s and a series of unfortunate real estate investments in the downtown Los Angeles area, John had fallen on hard times and had found himself turning to the cigarette smuggling trade in order to fund the enormous negative cash-flow situation that his once great real estate empire was now suffering.

Like all men of entrepreneurial achievement who had "been to the mountain top," John found it hard to come to terms with the fact that he was no longer there. But with a monthly overhead of almost $50,000 and a monthly income of only $20,000, it was just a matter of time until John's world was going to come crashing down around him and he knew he had to do something soon.

Regardless of the fact that he was nearly broke, John did manage to maintain several vestiges of his former success.

The first being his brand new 1989 Mercedes 450 SEL AMG – a black, souped-up top-of-the-line Benz that he bought eight months earlier for $120,000 (still owing the full $120,000 on it because he hadn't made a payment on the car since the day he bought it.) This car, which he kept in his next door neighbor's garage fearing it would be re-possessed if he parked it in his own driveway, was equipped with a .44 caliber Luger which he kept in the backseat compartment that separated the two rear custom bucket deer-hide seats, and to John it was more than just a car. It was the vehicle John used to maintain the second vestige of his former success, his weekly gambling trips to Las Vegas.

You see, aside from being addicted to the thrill of ciga-rette smuggling and real estate investing, John was also ad-dicted to the rush of giving most of the money he stole from the tax authorities right back to the casinos at the Pai Gow poker tables and the sports books that were popping up on the "new" strip just being built in Las Vegas in the late 80s.

His favorite place to stay and play was the Luxor Hotel, partly because as he drove up to the entranceway in his sleek Mercedes he could imagine himself to be like one of those ancient Egyptian Pharaohs pulling up in his ornate chariot to oversee some magnificent battle, but also because if you stayed two nights at full price you would receive a third night for absolutely free; and times being what they were, John appreciated a bargain when he saw one.

Now at around the very same time that John was living in Arcadia and coming to terms with his new found finan-cial reality, Steve coincidentally was also residing there and also coming to terms with a new financial reality of his own. You see, Steve, like John, had also found himself a casualty of the Savings and Loan Crisis of the late 80s, his casualty stemming from his "great success" (curse you,

Harvey Mendel!) in being laid off from his job as a Vice President of Commercial lending at Valley Savings.

Now although Steve and John lived in the same city, and for that matter, only several blocks from one another, they had never met or even crossed paths. You see, the Chinese population and the non-Chinese population of Arcadia usually kept pretty much to themselves, leading what you might call "separate, but equal" lives; sort of like the deep south in the early sixties. Besides, even if they had crossed paths before, neither one of them would have remembered, since to John most of the white people looked pretty much alike and the same could be said for Steve's view of the Chinese.

Steve, armed with an MBA and a middle class work ethic, had set out several years earlier to conquer the banking world and as you know, had risen to the ranks of Executive Vice President in charge of Commercial Lending at one of the San Fernando Valley's largest financial institutions, Valley Savings and Loan.

With his modest corporate salary and his expense reimbursement account, Steve, his wife and their two small children had set up house in Arcadia and purchased a modest three-bedroom home just south of Foothill Boulevard in the less expensive, but still nice section of town.

Unfortunately, thanks to his recent lay off from the bank, Steve, who had suddenly found himself awakened with new courage and an entrepreneurial sense of adventure had also found himself without a job. And like all men of corporate achievement who have "been to the mountaintop," Steve found it hard to come to terms with the fact that he was no longer an "executive."

Ironically, just two weeks after being laid off, Valley Savings, like so many other Savings and Loan Associations of its time, fell victim to a change in federal banking regulations and as a result was declared insolvent and was subsequently shut down by the FDIC.

When this happened Steve took great solace in the fact that his former boss, Scott Brawny, and the rest of the fifty or so vice presidents at Valley Savings also had found themselves without jobs, the only difference being, at least in Steve's mind anyway, that unlike Steve, who had discovered the secret of financial success from reading Napoleon Hill's book *Think and Grow Rich,* these poor bastards didn't have a clue and as such were destined to just get another corporate job and live out the rest of their lives stuck in middle-class existences of boredom, ass-kissing, and meaningless repetition.

Aside from this perception in Steve's head, however, at least these guys would have jobs, but Steve didn't care because, thanks to his meeting just two days before with Harvey, he knew, or at least he had a glimmer of hope, that he was destined for something greater.

Also, luckily for Steve, when he was fired, Scott – in the midst of all the confusion going on with the insolvency thing – forgot to fill out the proper termination documents and when the FDIC took over the bank just two weeks later, Steve was still listed on the bank payroll as a bank officer. As such, like Scott and all the other let-go vice presidents, he received a severance check for 6 months' salary which came to a little over $30,000.

And so armed with his impressive resume, his $30,000 severance check, a water-damaged suit from J.C. Penny's and a copy of Napoleon Hill's timeless business classic, *Think and Grow Rich,* Steve set out to conquer the business world – exactly what business, Steve had no idea, and how he was going to build an empire, yet alone make a living, with almost no investment capital, was beyond him.

But surely, Steve thought to himself, if he just closed his eyes, stepped on the gas, and hoped for the best, something would indeed come along.

And of course, as he had hoped, it did. Steve's first real break, as he waited to see if Harvey's opportunity was going to pan out, came along in the form of Milton Lamshon, a man in his early eighties who for some strange reason was afflicted with a condition in which he had no function in his salivary glands. As such, in order for him to eat he had to carry around with him a bottle of artificial saliva which he would squirt into his mouth between bites of food when he went to lunch every day at his favorite restaurant in Sherman Oaks, California, *Jerry's Famous Deli*. His unusual condition aside, for the past fifty years Milton was a 50 percent owner in one of the most successful real estate auction firms in the Los Angeles Area, Lamshon & Flanx.

After a life-long partnership with his business partner Charlie Flanx, and for reasons that only Milton and Charlie will ever know, their relationship suddenly came to an abrupt and bitter end one day in May of '89, and as a result of their surreptitious dispute, Milton moved his office directly across the street to a three-room luxury suite in the Bank of America Building on Ventura Boulevard in Sherman Oaks. Charlie stayed in the run-down office that he and Milton had shared across the street for the past fifty years, and both swore a blood oath of hatred for one another and began a feud which resembled that of two pirate ships, firing insults and accusations at one another like cannonballs across the busy sea of cars that was Ventura Boulevard in Sherman Oaks California.

It reminded John Hu, who was a long-time client of both Charlie and Milton, a lot of the Pirate Battle Show at the Treasure Island Hotel & Casino which he would go to watch outside in front of the hotel while chain smoking an entire pack of Marlboro Lights in between his five-hour sessions of Pai Gow and the occasional throw at the craps table.

Milton, just like Steve (except he was 86 years old) had gone out on his own for the first time in his life, and was looking for a new partner for his brand new real estate auction firm, Lamshon & Associates, a firm for which Milton coined the catch-phrase *The Best Real Estate Auctioneer in the Business.*

Charlie, who was now also left to go out on his own, and who was also looking for a new partner for his brand new real estate auction firm, Flanx & Associates, coined what he said was a much better and much more original catch-phrase than Milton's, his phrase being Flanx & Associates – *The Finest Real Estate Auctioneer in the Business.*

And so both of them, armed with new catch-phrases and both looking for a new partner, and both of them knowing Steve from his banking days at Valley Savings when Steve had hired them both to auction off some bank-owned properties, offered Steve an ownership share of their new firms, respectively.

Milton wrote his offer on the back of a white matchbook cover, simply scribbling the words 50/50 and signing his name underneath as Steve and Milt were having lunch together at Jerry's Famous Deli.

Charlie, on the other hand, wrote his offer on the outside of a manila windowed envelope containing a $500 savings bond made out to Steve's newborn son, sort of a little signing bonus, while they were having lunch at La Trattoria, "a real restaurant – not like that piece of crap cheap-ass deli that that cheap bastard Milton took Steve to," as Charlie put it.

And as to why both of them were so eager to partner up with Steve in the first place was a bit of a mystery to Steve who had no experience whatsoever in the auction business. But Milton and Charlie both believed that Steve was "connected" in the banking business and as such could line them up with plenty of auction business from all those banks that were foreclosing on commercial properties as a result of the whole Savings and Loan Crisis thing.

Also, they both probably liked the idea of screwing each other out of something the other one of them wanted and "winning" Steve was a way of proving, once and for all, who the better businessman was.

And so the competition raged for several weeks and like any couple who has been together for fifty years, there are bound to be some issues and things are bound to get personal.

And as Charlie was quick to point out, "Milton was a shifty, talentless, free-loader who had sponged off" Charlie's "talent and kindness for the last fifty years" and who if not for Charley, "would be lying broke and penniless in the streets of downtown L.A. sucking dicks for spare change so he could buy a can of condensed chicken soup, not Campbell's, but the generic brand, to feed his degenerate family and his lazy, worthless self."

Milt, quipped back at Charlie's tirade saying that Charlie could "suck his eighty-six-year-old shriveled dick after he fucked Charlie's wife up the ass, and then when he came, Charlie could lick up the cum with his tongue, spit it in a jar and carry it over to the sperm bank located on the corner of Ventura Boulevard and Go Fuck Yourself Charlie, so that future generations could witness the magnificence of Milton's talent as it paled in comparison to Charlie's worthless whore-like essence and fuck you Charlie, fuck you, fuck you!" Milton even got so enraged that he went to spit on Charlie's new business flyers but unfortunately realized that he had left his bottle of artificial saliva in the car, rendering him spit-less.

(As an interesting side-note to this story, Charlie Flanx was the guest of honor at Milton's funeral where upon delivering the eulogy, he tearfully acknowledged that he had loved Milton like a brother and that Milton Lamshon was the best friend he had ever had. Forty-seven days later, Charlie, sadly, passed away.)

In the end, and the $500 savings bond notwithstanding, because Charlie had only offered Steve a 30 percent interest in the company, Steve went with Milton's offer and set up shop in one of the three luxury offices that Milton has just rented on the 11th floor of the Bank of America Building.

And it was here, just 23 days after meeting Harvey Mandel for lunch, and just after two minutes of becoming Milton's new partner, on the 11th floor of the Bank of America Building in Sherman Oaks California, in January of 1989, that Steve and John "Bing Shu" Hu met for the very first time, their meeting being the instant beginning of a business partnership that would meld two great and ancient cultural traditions into a real estate investment machine that Steve and John were both sure was destined for fantastic success.

John had come to Milton's office to discuss auctioning off some of those buildings in downtown L.A. that he had gotten stuck with and that were currently bleeding him dry. Several of them were already in foreclosure and he was desperate to get them sold and to get the banks off his ass.

Steve, upon hearing John's predicament, and having been a banker for the past several years and thinking he knew what he was talking about, explained to John how he could renegotiate some of the terms of his delinquent loans and buy some time to either get the buildings sold at a better price or maybe even get them rented and cash flowing again.

John, who had no idea what Steve was talking about but who never thought much of anything through and who just liked to close his eyes and throw the dice, responded to Steve's idea by uttering his favorite catch phrase, "Good idea," only John, who began every sentence with the word HHHHHHHHHHHA and ended every sentence with the word HHHHHHHHHHHHHO said, "HHHHHHHHHHHA – Good Idea – HHHHHHHHHHHHHHO."

And as the two began to talk, it became immediately clear that these two entrepreneurial men of ambition were destined to be partners; for not only did they have a lot in common, not only did they live in the same city, and not only did they share similar business goals, but they also shared a similar philosophy of life and success, both philosophies rooted in thousands of years of ancient yet parallel traditions.

Now as you may well know, two of the oldest cultures in the world are that of the Chinese and that of the Jews. Both date back almost 6,000 years and both carry on ancient customs of wisdom, diet, food preparation, religious beliefs, family values and business practices. It is this final category, business practices, that concerns this parable called:

The Parable of the Yuan and the Shekel

Now in pursuit of the Yuan (a Chinese monetary unit), and influenced by the writings of Sun Tzu in his timeless classic *The Art of War*, a tradition of "winning by deception" had evolved and become an integral part of Chinese business culture.

And as it had come to pass one day, three Chinese businessmen, partners in a real estate investment venture, set out to buy an apartment building.

And as it was their custom in these sorts of transactions, the Chinese investor group was more than happy to offer full price for the apartment building they sought.

And their offer, as you would expect, was immediately accepted by the Seller who was happy to get the full asking price of five million dollars, believing that the deal would close within thirty days and he could take his money, buy a yacht and sail around the world.

But as sixty days passed however, and then ninety days and then 120 days, and then 150 and then 180 the Seller grew weary, always hoping the Chinese businessmen would finally close the deal, but always being disappointed at the last moment by one sort of unexpected delay or another.

And finally on day 191 the Chinese group of investors wired over the money to consummate the transaction. Only mysteriously, the amount wired was only three million dollars.

"Surely, this must be a mistake," thought the Seller. And so he called the Chinese businessmen on the phone.

"No, it is no mistake," replied the Chinese investor group. "You see, the transaction has taken so long that the value of the property you are selling us has declined in this declining market and is now only worth three million dollars," explained the Chinese investor group.

"But it was you who stalled for so long that caused me to lose two million dollars," whined the Seller.

"Yes, we were quite clever to deceive you with our original offer," the Chinese group replied humbly.

And so realizing that he should have probably sold his building to someone else for maybe 4.5 million dollars and taken his money right away, but accepting the fact that market values had declined, the seller accepted the three million dollars, paid off his existing mortgage of $2,999,000 and bought himself not a yacht but a canoe so that he might paddle about the pond that was located in the local community park.

And once the Chinese investor group had successfully purchased their building for three million dollars, all of the partners went to celebrate their two million-dollar victory by going out together to a nice restaurant, having a great dinner and buying whores for one another as a gesture of appreciation for a job well done.

Now in pursuit of the Shekel (a monetary unit of the ancient Hebrews), and influenced by the writings of Sholem Aleichem, the Jews had a similar and parallel tradition of employing deception in order to win a business negotiation.

And as it had also come to pass one day, three Jewish businessmen, also partners in a real estate investment venture, set out to buy an identical apartment building right next door to the one that the three Chinese businessmen had set out to buy.

And so, as it was their custom, the three Jewish businessmen substantially made an identical "full price" offer to the Seller of the apartment building that they desired to buy. Although their offer for the building that was listed on the market for five million dollars was $4,999,999 – one dollar less than the original Chinese offer; an inconsequential difference of less than one hundredth of one percent of course, but an amount significant just the same because it illustrated the Jewish investor group's unwillingness to pay full price for anything........ever!

And the Seller, upon receiving the Jewish businessmen's offer, and having done business before with the Chinese, decided cheerfully to accept the Jewish group's offer, and looked forward to closing the transaction in the next thirty days so that he too could buy a yacht and sail around the world.

But this Seller too, annoyingly watched as sixty days came, (at which point the buyers renegotiated the deal and lowered their offering price to $4.5 million) and as ninety days came (at which point the buyers *re*-renegotiated the deal and lowered their offering price to four million dollars), and 120 days came (at which point the buyers *re-re*-renegotiated the deal and lowered their offering price to $3.5 million) and finally as 180 days came (at which point the buyers lowered their offering price to $2,995,000 knowing full well that the Seller's outstanding mortgage on the building was $2,999,000 and even though they could have given him at least $3 million so that he could have gotten out of the deal whole, decided to really "fuck him" so that not only would he have to sell his building for $2 million less than they had originally agreed, but that he would have to actually pay an extra $4,000 out of his own pocket in order to close the deal.

And so sadly and reluctantly, and knowing full well that the market had declined over the last several months, and also having come to realize that the Jewish investor group would probably tie the property up in litigation for the next five years while the market continued to decline, the Seller finally relented to the merciless "Jewing Down" he had just received, and took the

$2,995,000, selling his boat for $4,000 to finally close the deal.

"Take the building and choke on it," said the poor Seller.

"If you have any more buildings we can buy, just let us know. We will be happy to pay you almost full asking price for them," replied the Jewish investor group.

And then, just as the Chinese group had done, the Jewish group ceremoniously honored their victory. But rather than just going out to celebrate their victory and buying each other whores, as the Chinese investor group had done, upon the closing of escrow, the Jewish investor group returned to their office, re-printed a copy of their partnership agreement, reviewed the agreement and then proceeded to reinterpret and argue over the terms of that agreement, bickering about the percentage of ownership each partner had in the deal and whose idea it was in the first place to buy the building.

And as time passed, this "re-negotiation" continued on tirelessly for about three years until the building they had purchased had in turn been sold.

And in the end, the losers of the partnership dispute, took the winners of the dispute out to lunch at the Deli; promising to pay but sticking them with the check anyway, and then paid the legal bills of the winners of the dispute as a gesture of appreciation for a job well done, a custom very similar to the Chinese practice of buying each other whores.

The End

Thus is the story of the *Parable of the Yuan and the Shekel*; the moral of which is that when selling your apartment building, it's best not to do business with either the Chinese or the Jews.

And so, sharing a common background and many thousands of years of rich cultural tradition and history, it was no surprise that only one hour from the moment they had first met, John and Steve, the Yuan and the Shekel, found themselves as business partners.

And just a short two days later, and as an army of name-less, faceless Chinese immigrant workers were stacking cartons of stamp-less cigarettes in the back bedroom of John's Arc-Asia Mansion, John and Steve were off riding together in John's Mercedes SEL, on their way to Las Vegas to begin their legendary real estate buying spree by purchasing the very same hotel that for some reason John Hu was very familiar with, especially room #23, and the very same hotel where Shmengey Mignone had been holding his notoriously non-famous underground poker games – The M.M.

As they drove, John was talking to Steve, who he had recently nick-named K.J., a biblically referenced handle which Steve would later find out stood for the questionably honorable title of King of the Jews. Although the nick-name originally was meant to be pejorative, as it referred to the fact that every time Steve and John went out to dinner, Steve would stick John with the tab, it eventually became a term of endearment and respect as John came to revere the fact that Steve had consistently, and on numerous occasions "out-deceived" him in a business negotiation, a skill that John "Bing Shu" Hu truly, truly admired.

Steve had likewise nick-named John, K.C., a zenistically-referenced handle which stood for King of the Chinese, which referred to the fact that John was so cold and calculating that it seemed he lacked both any sense of humor or conscience and for that matter, any emotions whatsoever.

And from that moment on, John and Steve were a team, the Yuan and the Shekel, K.C. and K.J.; and as it was destined to be, 6,000 years of beautiful tradition were joined together to form an Apartment Buying Machine the likes of which they both were sure the world had never seen before.

They called their new company the "American Capitol Group." (The word *Capitol*, like the building in Washington D.C., was supposed to be spelled *Capital*, like money, but John, who had sent in the incorporation forms, was not a really good English speller.)

Chapter 1.5

Shirley's Kids

Woodcrest Apartments – El Paso, Texas- August 2000 as Harold and Andy were down at 7-Eleven picking up some more Bic Lighters.

When Shirley Dole first got the call about the chiller being down at Woodcrest she was not surprised. She had seen this kind of thing before. And she knew that the broken chiller system was just the tip of the iceberg, a symptom of a much deeper and more serious problem. It was the tell-tale sign of the evil sin of greed which had caused out-of-town landlords like Steve and his partners to purposely neglect and run the Eastwood apartment buildings into the ground.

Dole lived only a few blocks away, and had driven by it many times on her way to the hairdressers for her weekly rinse and color; she was familiar with the property.

She had seen the abandoned couches, and the broken windows, and the sea of Bud Light cans and bottles glistening in mid-day sun.

She had smelled the bags of hominy with the drippy gravy sitting outside of tenants' doors, and the discarded diapers, and the rotting pile of palm leaves that the guys trimming the trees at some fancy building downtown had brought over to Eastwood and had dumped in the vacant lot next to the Woodcrest driveway.

And she had seen the bullet-riddled corpse of the dead drug dealer who, after being shot down the street in a drug deal gone bad, fled through the Woodcrest parking lot to escape but ended up bleeding out right there in parking space #23.

And she had heard the cries of the poor little children who were traumatized by the site of the dead drug dealer just lying there, as the kids went through his pockets looking for valuables.

It disgusted Dole as she patrolled the neighborhood every morning taking pictures of the blighting conditions that were ruining her beloved Eastwood.

And as if the trash situation wasn't bad enough, these God-damn illegals were dumping motor oil and transmission fluid and anti-freeze all over the parking lot when they worked on their cars after work every day, and what's worse, the God-damn slumlords were letting them do it.

It's no wonder, Dole would say to herself, that people were getting cancer, it was all those poisons that the Jews were having the Mexicans spread around that was causing the whole thing, it was a conspiracy for certain, as if it weren't bad enough that the Jews controlled the media, now they were trying to control her neighborhood as well.

And it was for this very reason that she had just founded her new private law enforcement organization to make sure that the conditions that were ruining her community would be rectified, a group she called S.T.O.P.E.M (Stop Terrorizing Our People Empowerment Movement). You see, as the current, self-appointed head of the Eastwood Community Association, a non-profit group which Shirley had founded with her husband Barry about six years before, Shirley understood the real cause of the problems of the neighborhood.

"Those greedy out-of-town slumlords were letting *her* community go to hell. Their greedy money-grubbing immoral business practices were turning *her* community into a slum." (Or as the El Paso Neighborhood Services Department preferred to refer to it as "an area manifesting blighting conditions.")

And Dole simply was not going to just sit back and let it happen, not in *her* neighborhood, and furthermore, as she had said on many occasions, regardless of how much criticism she received from the local landlords, or the neighborhood tenants for that matter, she was simply not going to go away. After all, Dole was the head of the Eastwood Community Association and as such she was there to help *her* people.

Yes indeed it was *her* job, as the self-appointed leader of all twelve of the groups she had created to date, to protect the Eastwood community from the blighting conditions caused by the evil doings of the out-of-town landlords like "that towel-head son-of-a-bitch Ranbir Sanni who was one of those Iranian Jews or something," and who she had personally seen to it was thrown in jail. Her new Public Enemy Number One was "Beverly Hills Steve," a Jew of a different color whom she angrily referred to as Beelzebub – the Devil. If she didn't protect *her* fellow tenants of the Eastwood Community against the evil out-of-town forces, who would? As she stated on many occasions, this was *her* community, *her* people and *her* mission and by God she simply was not going to go away.

Funny thing was Shirley didn't live in an apartment building at all. As a matter of fact she didn't even technically live in Eastwood, and as such was not even a member of what the City of El Paso unofficially called "the angry white people," who actually owned homes in the Eastwood area. She lived about three blocks away from the official border of the neighborhood and about seventeen blocks away from Woodcrest, on a street which only had single family homes. Shirley's house was one of the nicest on the block. It had four bedrooms, a porch, a large kitchen and a big back yard. But she did technically live *close to* Eastwood.

Perhaps what was really strange was that, as you know, more than 90 percent of the people who resided in apartments in *her* Community of Eastwood were Hispanic, most of them undocumented aliens who didn't speak English.

And what was even stranger than that was that Shirley not only didn't speak Spanish, but she wasn't particularly fond of the Hispanics and their "backwards" culture either, especially Mexicans, who she said, "had no respect for cleanliness, drank too much, ate animal guts like menudo and tongue and who smelled like pork fat and ass." And yet, these were *her* people, and she was *their* leader. Or so Shirley Dole would have liked the world to believe. The truth, as we will soon see, was far more interesting and far more sinister.

Inconsistencies in her logic aside, and despite her comical "Bozo the Clown" appearance, Shirley Dole was, in fact, a force to be reckoned with.

She had built alliances with the City Zoning Department, the Neighborhood Services Department, the City

Prosecutors office and the office of the local councilman Jim Jameson.

She also had an extensive collection of Elvis Memorabilia which she displayed in one of the four bedrooms in her house that she had set aside as a shrine to the late King.

But Dole's true talent laid in her ability to draw financial support for her non-profit 5013c Eastwood Community Association, which incidentally had neglected to file a tax return since its inception nearly six years before. Shirley assured everyone that this was merely an oversight and that her husband would be getting around to doing the books real soon.

In an ingeniously crafted "racquet" which drew on the legal resources of the City of El Paso, the financial support of the local car dealership Stylus Chevrolet located in Eastwood, and the endless supply of slum-victim horror stories supplied by the few English speaking tenants living in the Eastwood area, Dole had single handedly constructed an extortion machine that would have drawn the envy of Meyer Lansky, Al Capone and even Tony Soprano (if he had been a real person.) It truly was a work of art.

Veiled in the guise of helping "Shirley's kids," which was sort of like Jerry's Kids – only Shirley's kids could walk – Shirley Dole, with the help of the City, raised hundreds of thousands of tax-free, non-profit dollars. And this is how she did it:

Each time a new apartment building was sold and then bought by a new owner in the Eastwood area Dole would pay the property a visit. She would explain her mission of building a wonderful, new park in Eastwood. This park would be a beacon of light, a safe haven, a sanctuary against the drugs and violence which ran rampant in their blight-filled, drug-ridden neighborhood.

It could be a place where kids could be given the opportunity to grow and flourish in a nurturing and healthy environment. Where they could get healthy and nutritious meals on the weekends and where they could build lasting positive memories of their childhood spent growing up in the Eastwood area of El Paso, Texas.

And now, the icing on the cake! The park was to be named for a fallen El Paso Police officer, Parker "Park" Parkinson, who had given his life in the line of duty protecting the citizens of El Paso against crime and injustice. (In actuality, Officer Parkinson had been killed in an unfortunate freeway accident when upon being rear-ended, his Ford Crown Victoria exploded – it was the model that didn't have an automatic fuel cut-off switch and was later recalled – but that didn't make as good a story and since he was the only officer to die recently, Dole was forced to make the best of the story that she had.)

Now, usually this is what would happen.

The new building owner, in the spirit of community support and mostly just to get rid of her, would offer Dole a modest donation of maybe a few hundred dollars. And when they did this, it really pissed her off. She wasn't born yesterday. She knew that apartment buildings cost millions of dollars and so anyone who could afford an apartment building could certainly afford to give her more than a few hundred dollars. After all, they were rich, and probably Jews.

And parks cost money too, lots of money, maybe even as much as $5,000,000. (Actually, Dole wasn't really sure what it was going to cost to build a park, they hadn't gotten to that part of the plan yet, but she figured first things first. Raise the money and then we'll see.) So Dole would ask for a real donation, one that would make a difference, say $100,000 or so. And 99.999 percent of the time, and except for the time that the owner of the local Chevy dealership gave her a real donation, "probably because he wasn't a

Jew," the new owners would chuckle, explain they couldn't afford a donation like that, and send her on her way.

But little did they know that was not where the story was going to end. Not by a long shot. Shirley Dole was simply not going to go away.

About a week later, just as sure as the sun rises and sets over the greater El Paso area, Jake Jacobs, City Building Inspector with the Neighborhood Services Department would show up at the apartment office door, armed with a shiny new badge, a list of anonymous complaints and a 100-page ticket book for issuing citations for zoning and health code violations rumored to exist at the property.

And just like Dole, he was simply not going to go away. He was a man with a mission. He was a man with a purpose. He was a man driven to make a difference, and as he would explain as he peeled off the pages and pages of citations he'd written from his 100-page ticket book, he was a man who was "just doing his job." But job or not, for Jake, it was personal.

You see when Jake was just a boy, his father, a meter reader for the electric company in Chicago, had been accidentally killed by a faulty wiring box which had not been properly grounded when it was installed by the new "out-of-town owner" of an apartment building.

When Jake's father touched the handle on the box to open the door and read the meter, he was instantly incinerated – to the point where even Jake's mother was unable to identify the body. The incineration was so severe that even Jake's father's gold fillings had melted making his identification, even from dental records, nearly impossible. The only thing not incinerated in the electrocution was a small ceramic ash tray Jake had made at school the previous week and given his father that very morning for Father's Day. The inscription on the bottom of the ashtray read, "Be Careful Out There, I Love You Daddy - Jake."

At the funeral service, what was left of Jake's father's ashes were spread over a scale model of the Chicago electric generation plant, and as those ashes were sucked in to the $1/100^{th}$ scale-size induction fan, the choir sang an old Marty Robbins' song called "Burn Me Up" while Jake silently swore to himself, that nowhere, anytime, anywhere, would anyone have to die the senseless death his father had just succumbed to at the hands of careless and non-caring out-of-town apartment landlords.

Needless to say, when Jake arrived at a property, there were going to be citations written.

Now back to the workings of Shirley Dole's ingenious financial plan.

After Jake would issue a hundred or so citations for violations varying from broken windows, to peeling paint, to too many cats in one apartment, to faulty wiring and even sometimes one just for his dad, the case would be turned over to a special court downtown at El Paso City Hall.

This court, the "Environmental Services Court" had been established especially to deal with zoning and health situations of this very kind and had complete authority to enforce and implement any and all directives, orders, and recommendations that the Neighborhood Services Department deemed necessary. There was no appeal process, no change of venue requests and no chance of hearing the words "not-guilty" anytime in this courtroom.

The judge who presided over the court had been appointed by none other than Jim Jameson, the then-City Councilman of the, you guessed it, Eastwood District, and good friend of Shirley Dole.

And so day in and day out, the environmental services court would hear horrific stories of blighting conditions caused by the greed and intentional neglect of out-of-town landlords and would impose fines for each violation in the amount of $2,500 and send the out-of-town landlord and their Mormon Attorneys (for some reason every attorney who practiced law in the County was a member of the Church of Latter Day Saints) down to the cashiers office to pay their $250,000 fine.

And this is where the plan got really interesting.

Enter Sue-Ann McDonald, a recent graduate of the Brigham Young University School of Law, a young eager attorney who had just gotten her first job with the El Paso City Prosecutors office.

Upon her hiring, she replaced the long-standing veteran prosecutor Enrico Corleon, who had stepped down from the position he had held for thirteen years when his torrid love affair with Eastwood Chief Building Inspector Maria Rodriguez Flanders came to light after the tragic suicide of her husband Tim.

Tim Flanders, who decided that life was no longer worth living without Maria, had hung himself in an act of desperation, after coming home early one day and discovering Maria and Enrico in the shower together (they were supposedly inspecting the fixtures.)

At the sight of seeing Maria and Enrico naked together, inspecting what Maria claimed was a clogged pipe, Tim became so distraught that he tragically, yet innovatively, hung himself by unraveling the wire binding in Maria's citation booklet that was lying on the kitchen counter of their apartment, tying it around his neck, nailing one end to the kitchen window sill of their second-story apartment, and hurling himself out the window singing La Vida Loca, scattering on the sidewalk below the unused carbon copies of the citation forms that were in his hands as a result of his dismantling Maria's citation book.

Maria, after she was finished writing a citation to the building owner for excessive litter on the ground around Tim's body, was devastated.

News of Tim's tragic demise rocked the Neighborhood Services Department, and especially hit the City Prosecutors Office hard. It looked bad, real bad, that the Chief Prosecutor and the Chief Inspector's illicit affair had been the cause of an apparent suicide, not to mention the fact that they were sleeping together. There was supposed to be an arms-length distance between the two positions so as to preserve the fairness and integrity of the whole zoning enforcement process.

And so with deep regret, and with a heart-felt thank you for their thirteen years of outstanding service, Maria, who was replaced by Jake Jacobs, and Enrico, who was replaced by Sue-Ann McDonald, were demoted to assistant inspector, and assistant city prosecutor, respectively. And so it was.

Now with the changing of the guard at the Neighborhood Services Department and the City Prosecutors Office, a new day and a new way of doing business had dawned. You see Sue-Ann McDonald was a different breed of City Prosecutor. She represented a kinder, gentler nation and a kinder gentler City. She wasn't there to blame, or punish, or exact her pound of flesh, *she was there to help*. In fact, that was Sue-Ann McDonald's very motto, "We're here to help." And help she did.

You see, within minutes of successfully prosecuting her out-of-town *friends* and exacting her $250,000 pounds of flesh on their exploitative, unknowing asses, Ms. McDonald would approach her new allies in the hallway just outside the courtroom and propose a *win-win* plan that would benefit all of the parties concerned.

Her plan would usually go something like this: First, "We can help you, the landlord." Then, "Granted," she would say, "the $250,000 fine was a bit excessive." What if she could get that down to about, say, $75,000? Would that work?

"Oh, yes I thought it would!"

"Now," she would say, "the City of El Paso doesn't really need the $75,000. That would just go into the coffers of the City Treasury where it wouldn't do anybody any good, but what if we could get that money back to the community, meaning the community of Eastwood? Then the money could go to make necessary improvements in the neighborhood – to make life better for all the hard-working people struggling to make a better life for themselves, especially the kids." And when she said kids, she was specifically referring to "Shirley's Kids," you remember them, the kids who didn't have a park to play in, the kids who needed a park.

Now given the choice of paying a $250,000 fine, or donating $75,000 to build a park that would make kids happy, what shrewd business-person wouldn't go for the park?

And so, what seemed like an unreasonable request for a donation when Shirley Dole had asked for it a month earlier, in light of current circumstances seemed a very reasonable request indeed. And just to put the icing on the cake and to make sure that these well-meaning out-of-town owners would continue to stay on board, Sue-Ann McDonald would insist on the signing of what she called "A Settlement Agreement."

Once signing this document and making certain promises to perform certain work at certain times for certain sums of money, the City would agree to basically leave the out-of-town owners alone. That was unless the out-of-town owner failed to at some future date in time, to perform said certain work at certain times and for certain sums of money.

And since those out-of-town owners had signed that certain document called the Settlement Agreement, if they did fail to perform on something like, let's say, giving an additional $75,000 to the park to pay for some playground equipment, or in case another police officer was tragically killed in the line of duty and we had to build another park in his name as well, well then, Ms. McDonald wouldn't have to waste all that time getting Jake to write up all those citations, and going to court, and filing pleadings, and answering interrogatories and all that other legal stuff; she could just call Lieutenant Blumberg down at the 4th precinct and have that silly out-of-town landlord thrown in jail for contempt of court until such time as he complied with the terms of the agreement, it was just like debtors prison. Seems fair enough, where do I sign?

Now it was just about 10:30 a.m. as Shirley Dole was getting ready to go over to Woodcrest to see what was up with the chiller, and as you might expect, knowing what you now know, when Dole called Eileen, over at the Woodcrest Office to let her know she was on her way, Eileen was, as you might expect, a little rattled.

"Eileen," Dole asked "did Beverly Hills Steve not pay the electric bill this month? Is that why the chiller is down?"

Eileen assured her that the bill had been paid and told her she had paid it personally one month in advance from rents that she had skimmed from the June receipts just in case Steve decided not to pay on time. (It was Eileen's habit to skim from the receipts a little each month because this way, if Steve didn't follow through on paying for things that she ordered against Steve's wishes, then at least she could pay for it herself.)

"Stealing a little from Steve each month was for his own good." Besides, it was good to have a little extra money lying around just in case she found some real good stuff for sale on television and needed some cash to buy it. It was precisely in such an instance that Eileen had discovered that Super-Sensitive Micro-Phone Spy device that she later sold to Andy. Speaking of which, she thought to herself, "I

135

wonder if Andy and Harold have gotten back from the plumbing supply warehouse yet."

She also wondered to herself, whether, since Dole had called, that maybe this might be a good time to call Steve and let him know what was going on with the chiller and such, as it was probably her moral duty to at least inform him of the situation.

Then after pondering the idea in her head for a few moments decided, Naahh!

Thus, with Eileen's philosophical dilemma squared away, she put down the phone, and awaited Dole's arrival at the office of the Woodcrest Apartments.

It was almost 10:30 a.m. and with only one-and-a-half hours to go, Eileen decided to say a little prayer and ask for help in returning Harold and Andy from the plumbing supply store as soon as possible.

She also asked her son Frank to run next door and get one of the envelopes full of money that she was keeping under her mattress just in case there was a wrong which needed to be righted when Shirley Dole arrived.

Chapter 2.5

My Sister Agnes Could Literally Go at Any Moment, (Snap your Fingers) Just Like That

Las Vegas, Nevada 1990 – The M.M.

The first property that the American Capitol Group pur-chased, the Mission Motel, was located in Downtown Las Vegas just two blocks from Las Vegas High School and right next door to Binion's Famous Horse-Shoe Hotel and Casino. The M.M. had 152 rooms and was the crown jewel of the downtown Las Vegas "strip."

Filled with transients, hookers, drug addicts, degenerate gamblers, sexual deviants, and people who for whatever

reason just didn't want to be found, the M.M. was a dilapidated assemblage of buildings with a hundred-year-old mission (hence the initial M. for *m*ission) structure in the front,
and 140 cheaply built motel rooms in the back. (Hence the
initial M. for *m*otel)

It had roof leaks, damp hallways, moldy ceilings, crack-
ing plaster and one of the most eclectic collection of human
body fluid stains ever assembled, all of which were en-
crusted on the many damp and dank surfaces of the motel
floors, sheets, headboards, ceilings and walls.

The stains included blood, puke, urine, feces, and the
most common stain of all, the ever enduring, and hard to
get out "jizz" stain, which would always be artfully scattered about the room, like one of those modern art surreal
paintings so popular in the late sixties, in places that bog-
gled the mind as to *how they got all the way up there in the
first place*, and which kinda crackled and flaked when you
touched them.

Amenities aside, the M.M. was a gold mine, a real cash
cow, as each of the 140 "guests" in the back all paid in
cash, never asked for a receipt, and would usually just slip
the $100 weekly rent for their room under the door when
the manager, Mary, knocked on it every Friday morning
between 10:00 and 11:00 a.m.

The tenants in the front "mission" rooms of the motel,
however, did not pay rent. They were all relatives of
Mary's who, over the span of Mary's 34-year tenure as
manager at the motel, had one by one become permanent
tenants, drifting and trickling in as they sought to escape
desperate situations in other states that fortunately did not
have reciprocity with the State of Nevada.

Having finally found refuge from the cold unjust world
that had made them victims (through no fault of their own,
they would always insist), and which had left them unable
to work, take care of themselves, and/or to have non-

dysfunctional relationships with other human beings, this rag-tag collection of hopeless, angry, refugees (all of whom had that sense of white trash entitlement, sharing the belief that the world owed them something because they were the *real Americans*) all found sanctuary in the bosom of Mary, in the manger of the mission section of the M.M. in downtown Las Vegas.

Mary's son Ron lived in unit #4, and worked (in actuality he didn't really work, he just stayed in his room and smoked pot all day – it would probably be more accurate to say they he *got paid*) as the handyman over at the M.M.

Ron had landed at the M.M. after being paroled from the Utah State Penitentiary where he had been doing "two to five" for involuntary manslaughter. As the story went, one day while he and his dad, Mary's fourth husband, were having a few beers on the front porch of their trailer back in Provo, Utah, they had gotten into a heated discussion over whether Miller Lite was actually less filling than Bud Light, even though, they both agreed, that it still did have great taste.

As the debate went on, one thing led to another, and as tempers flared things got way out of control. In the heat of the moment Ron became so enraged that he broke the neck off a long neck bottle of Miller Lite, stabbed his father in the neck, and as the blood spurted from his father's jugular vein, Ron, who was temporarily blinded by the spurting river of blood, proceeded to actually, and mistakenly (as his Public Defender maintained) saw his father's head clean off with the jagged edge of the bottle.

As the Defense contended, Ron, who had just done two hits of LSD, was temporarily disoriented and hallucinating, and thought he was just cutting branches that overhung a red Amazonian jungle river as he floated helplessly with the current in his Bud Light glass bottle canoe. Luckily, for Ron, the Provo Utah District Attorney's office didn't give a fuck about Ron's father's death and cared even less about Ron. As they saw it, it was just a case of one piece of shit red-neck recidivist taking another one out of the system, a kind of favor of sorts, and as such, they offered Ron a plea bargain in exchange for community service. And so, a crime that would have normally been ruled as a homicide was instead determined to be involuntary manslaughter.

Mary's Sister Gertrude lived in unit #2. She helped Mary at the Motel and liked to think of herself as the assistant manager because she took care of things when Mary wasn't around.

Mary's nephew Lenny lived in unit #5 with his two cousins Linda and Ted who were both married, to each other.

Johnny lived in unit #7. Mary wasn't exactly sure how she was related to him but more than likely it was by marriage to one of Mary's seven daughters who were the product of six different marriages over the years. She couldn't really remember all of her daughters' names but it didn't really matter because none of them had spoken to her in quite some time.

Johnny was well known at the M.M. for being a bit of a perv. It was rumored that he liked to engage in auto-erotic asphyxiation, the act of depriving oneself of oxygen for the purpose of achieving or enhancing orgasm.

Just in case you're new to the subject, there are few things you should know about it. First of all, various methods are used to achieve the level of oxygen depletion needed; such as a plastic bag over the head or self-strangulation, typically by the use of a ligature (In medicine, a ligature is a device, similar to a tourniquet, usually of thread or string, tied around a limb or blood vessel to restrict blood flow. Also, in auto-erotic asphyxiation the preferred ligature used is usually a scarf, and thus the practice is commonly known as "scarfing.")

The practice of auto-erotic asphyxiation, sometimes referred to as breath-play or edge-play, can be dangerous even if done with care, and has resulted in some accidental deaths – often this is due to loss of consciousness caused by partial asphyxia, leading to loss of control over the means of strangulation, resulting in continued asphyxia and death.

Now, in addition to tales of auto-erotic adventure, it had also been rumored that Johnny had an extensive collection of porn and one of the largest collection of dildos ever assembled; what he did with those dildos, the world will never know. But we do know this; he kept them in a suitcase in the entranceway closet of his apartment and liked to check on them several times a day to make sure they were all still there and would line them up in order of size, color and shape. He had named each one of them, his four favorites being a green dildo adorned with various leaves and berries that was his special holiday dildo called the "Mistle-do"; a muscular, Caucasian, Germanic-looking dildo called the "Cock-a-Nator"; a stubby white dildo with an unusually large mushroom helmet head called "Penisius The Roman Centurion"; and a remarkably large black dildo he excitedly referred to in as the "Nigga-Please."

As the story goes, one tragic July morning while Johnny was "scarfing," the Velcro release rescue mechanism he had rigged to the back of the Harley Davidson scarf he was using to strangle himself failed to work in the manner that he had anticipated, and as he slipped into unconsciousness and was eventually drawn toward a white light that was coming from the hole in the glory-hole booth in the great adult-bookstore beyond, his last thought was that he had forgotten to turn on the air conditioner in his apartment.

As it was pretty normal for Johnny not to leave his apartment for several weeks at a time while he went on drinking and asphyxiation binges, no one noticed him missing, and as such his body was not discovered for over two months – where it sat basting in the damp, 110-degree heat of his furnished two-bedroom apartment at the M.M. Oddly enough, no one really was alarmed by the smell of simmering flesh coming from his apartment, and for two months those who passed by the front door of Johnny's unit took a sniff, assumed somebody was cooking barbeque, and then simply moved on.

One day a hooker who had lent the key to Johnny's room for twenty bucks accidentally stumbled on Johnny's body while she was washing up in the bathroom. After going through his pockets, stealing what drugs he had left in his bedroom drawer, and after taking his suitcase filled with the largest assortment of dildos she had ever seen, she promptly reported the incident to Gertrude, who was filling in for Mary while Mary was next door at Binion's Horseshoe Hotel and Casino. It was Thursday and they were having the all-you-can-eat barbeque buffet and for some reason, Mary had been craving barbeque for just about the last two months.

Perhaps the most tragic yet comical figure at the M.M., and the most famous tenant living in the Mission section of the Motel, was Mary's older sister Agnes. Agnes, like Job of the Old Testament, was suffering from an array of physical afflictions which rendered her day-to-day existence a living hell. Her only pleasure left was the one she derived from chain-smoking pack after pack of Camel unfiltered cigarettes – which she did from the moment she awoke at 7:00 a.m. every day till the moment she went to bed at 3:00 a.m. the next morning. She was, as you might guess, suffering from the late stages of emphysema and lung cancer, not to mention diabetes, insomnia, colitis, perpetual diarrhea, Parkinson's disease, epilepsy and one of the most severe cases of psoriasis that the doctors had ever seen. She literally, as Mary often commented as she would snap her fingers saying the words, "could go at any moment......just like that."

There was really nothing the doctors could do for her emphysema or her lung cancer other than give her an oxygen tank which she wheeled around with her on a little cart everywhere she went, inhaling a whoosh or two when she began to feel faint or tired or out of breath. And as far as her other ailments were concerned, they were pretty much untreatable as well. But as for her skin condition, there was hope.

Agnes's dermatologist had given her a new experimental psoriasis cream which had actually proved quite effective. It was .01 percent zinc oxide, a 2 percent 50:50 mixture of sulfuric acid and nitric acid (which for you chemistry buffs out there makes $C_3H_5(NO_3)_3$, more commonly known as nitroglycerin), and 1 percent inert absorbents, particularly kieselgur, which when combined with the nitroglycerin makes, as Alfred Nobel discovered in 1867, a substance which he patented and later called dynamite.

These active ingredients were combined and delivered in a 50:50 base of pure methyl alcohol, to ensure quick evaporation of the lotion, and a jellied refined petroleum mixture which used as a thickener a combination of co-precipitated aluminum salts of naphthenic and palmitic acids. (Again for you chemistry buffs out there, this combination of gasoline and acids was developed by a team of Harvard chemists led by Louis Fieser during World War II and is commonly referred to as NAPALM). The jellied substance was used to ensure smooth and even application of the active ingredients in the psoriasis cream.

Every day Mary would help Agnes apply the cream liberally all over her body using nearly an entire tube each day to cover the 100 or so itchy scaly patches which nearly covered Agnes's entire body. The cream would dry and disappear quickly, thanks to the methyl alcohol base, and as it evaporated, you could see a translucent, wavy wall of fumes drifting outwards and then upwards all around Agnes's body. It was really kind of cool. It looked sort of like air coming out of the back of a jet engine or how the hot air rising off a desert road forms a sort of wave-like mirage as it starts to cool at the end of a hot summer's day.

Now, needless to say, as was hinted to by her emphysema and lung cancer, Agnes was not new to chain-smoking. She had smoked eight or so packs a day of Camels (the unfiltered ones) for the last sixty years and today was no exception.

She was sick nowadays, however, and had to modify her smoking habits a little, so she devised a method of smoking which could deliver both the nicotine she craved and the oxygen she needed to stay alive.

With a cigarette in her shaking, palsied right hand, and a soft plastic oxygen mask – hooked to her little portable green oxygen tank – in her shaking, palsied left hand, Agnes would bring the unfiltered Camel up to her lips, take a long, slow, steady deep drag, hold it in for five or six seconds, remove the cigarette just about an inch away from her mouth, and then exhale slowly making a kissing shape with her lips.

As the smoke exited her mouth and hovered in the air an inch or so from her face, she would then bring the soft plastic oxygen mask up to her face with her shaking, palsied left hand, press the mask against her mouth and nose, and squeeze the mask until it made a very distinctive "Chhshsh" sound as the oxygen from the tank rushed through the tube up into the mask and into her waiting lungs.

When Agnes was through inhaling her shot of oxygen, she would stop pressing the mask which in turn would shut off the air flow from the tank, making a distinctive "tup" sound.

She would then hold the oxygen in her lungs for about only 1 second (she didn't want to waste any time getting to the next drag of her cigarette) before exhaling, and then, drawing the cigarette up to her mouth with her shaking, palsied right hand, begin the whole rhythmic process over again, finishing usually half a pack at a time before taking a break to pee and then take a nap. As you passed Agnes's front door, you could often hear the sounds of her ritual, repeated over and over again and over again:

Chshshshsh....Tup. Exhale. Drag. Exhale.

Chshshshsh....Tup. Exhale. Drag. Exhale.

Chshshshsh....Tup. Exhale. Drag. Exhale.

It sounded just like one of those life support machines you see in the intensive care ward.

One fateful evening, just as Mary had finished rubbing Agnes down with an entire tube of that experimental psoriasis cream the doctors had given Agnes, and as Agnes was sitting in the courtyard watching the wavy fumes dance off the surface of her skin as she dried off, and as she took a drag of her cigarette and then took a drag of her oxygen, and then a drag of her cigarette again, a small ember from the tip of her unfiltered Camel flaked off and lodged in the soft clear plastic oxygen mask.

As she brought the mask to her lips, and as the oxygen from the portable green tank hit the nitroglycerin-dynamite-alcohol fumes and mixed with the smoldering ember, Agnes, completely and utterly exploded, and as Mary had so prophetically predicted, was literally gone, (snap your fingers), just like that.

For one brief fiery moment, the lights of Vegas were completely overshadowed by a bright white flash and then a giant fireball that mushroomed a thousand feet in the air and seemed to dance and swirl around, like a blender filled with Trix Cereal, all raspberry red and lemon yellow and orange-orange.

As the tenants stood in the courtyard in awe, lighting joints and roasting hot dogs on sticks in the outskirts of the flame that had engulfed Mary's beloved older sister, they began to sing the words to *Amazing Grace* only sung to the melody of *House of The Rising Sun*. When the flames subsided eleven minutes later the only thing left was the mangled wreckage of an ownerless little portable green oxygen tank, the charred sticker still affixed to the top surface of the tank.

It read *Extremely Flammable – No Smoking.*

Chapter 1.6

Joey Poney Had Lost the Sense of Smell

Woodcrest Apartments – June 2000 - 9:45 a.m. the very same morning while Harold and Andy were at 7-Eleven buying some more Bic Lighters for later to light the ground with

It was about 9:45 a.m. and as Harold and Andy were making their way through the beer aisle at the 7-Eleven, Joey Poney, the grounds picker-upper guy at Woodcrest was beginning his daily rounds back at the complex.

Joey, who was eighteen and lived with his mother and his Tourette's-afflicted girlfriend in unit #1, was a man of special talents, two of which, when combined, gave him the exact qualifications to be the best picker-upper guy "the Crest," and for that matter the entire City of El Paso, had ever seen.

First, it was rumored that Joey had been perpetually stoned for each and every second of his life for the past five years, although this rumor was unverifiable since Joey had absolutely no sense of time, five minutes being easily mistaken by Joey as five days or five months or five years for that matter.

Second, and probably most important, it was rumored that Joey had completely lost his sense of smell, the cause of which was a rare "reefer" lighting accident.

When the flame from a blowtorch he was using to stoke up one of the "biggest most humongatorius doobies he had ever rolled" suddenly surged out of control it singed the inside of Joey's nose clear up through his sinus cavities, burning all his mucous membranes and sending a giant stream of smoke exiting through his eye sockets.

Had he not been sitting less than three feet away from his two-gallon mega-stonacious super-bong, as the story goes, and had he not sucked up through his nose the nearly two gallons of leftover ganja water sitting in the holding tank of his bong, who knows what might have happened.

But this little accidental incident turned out to be a blessing in disguise and gave Joey, using the benefit of his olfactory handicap, the power to become the best, most awesome picker-upper guy ever.

You see, the truly great thing about Joey, since he had almost no sense of smell and never got nauseous because of all the marijuana he smoked, was that Joey could pick up anything, no matter how gross, no matter how disgusting, no matter how toxic, no matter how foul-smelling and no matter how long it had been baking in the hot Texas sun.

And that's not where his talents stopped. You see Joey was somewhat of an expert when it came to the subject of trash; his favorite subject that he liked to talk about was the difference between "White Trash" and "Mexi-trash."

As Joey would explain, white people's trash contained four major elements – cigarette butts, Little Debbie snack cake wrappers, empty Bud Light bottles and broken glass. Mexican people's trash also contained four major elements, however Mexi-trash is far more organic in its contents than white trash, Joey would go on to explain. The four major components of Mexican trash were pork fat, hominy, chicken bones and used toilet paper, the last requiring further explanation.

Now as far as Joey could ascertain, the reason for this cultural anomaly was probably that the plumbing in Mexico was not really that good and so since toilet paper may have tended to clog up the works back home, people simply got in the habit of throwing it in the garbage.

It was due to its highly organic content, especially the used toilet paper, that made Mexican trash so much more aromatic, and which made Joey's olfactory skills in not being able to savor its aroma, all the more valuable in his position as picker-upper guy at Woodcrest.

As you know about 90 percent of the tenants at the complex, and for that matter, the entire community of Eastwood, were indeed Hispanic, and as such, 90 percent of the neighborhood's trash was Hispanic in nature, as well.

One other difference that Joey had noticed between white-trash and Mexi-trash was the manner in which it was packaged and disposed of.

White-trash was packaged in store-bought garbage bags like the Hefty CinchSak or the Glad Tuff Bag and was disposed of by throwing it out the window with the bag usually breaking open upon impact with the ground and the trash usually scattering within a three-foot radius around the point of impact.

Mexi-trash, on the other hand, was packaged in used grocery store bags, both paper and plastic, and was usually discarded by placing it just outside the front door. Although under this method there was no collateral damage caused by impact, the Mexi-trash was equally as untidy and just as difficult to pick up because the used grocery bags, both paper and plastic, usually broke or split open when Joey would pick them up, sending streams of organic liquids and putrid solids oozing down Joey's arms, onto his shirt and then to his pants and this, after a while, attracted flies, and Joey didn't like flies.

Joey's average day went something like this:

After smoking his "wake and bake" doobie at about 9:00 a.m., Joey would leave his apartment to start picking up trash. Within three steps of his front door he would begin to encounter a forest of reused ripped plastic grocery bags baking in the early morning sun filled with wet slimy piles of leftover hominy, chili beans, chicken bones, pork blood, cow intestines, corn cobs, dirty diapers, used condoms, vomit, used tampons, used panty liners, blood soaked rags, the occasional severed finger, some left-over KFC original recipe drumsticks and wings, and of course, used toilet paper.

If the wings looked good and there was enough meat left on them, Joey would usually put a few of the leftovers in his pocket to nibble on for later, but for the most part Joey didn't usually eat from the garbage.

Joey would then pick up each of these bags by hand and then walk them over to a portable trash bin that he would wheel around with him throughout the day, up and down the hundred or so grass rows that went from east to west throughout the 7.8 acres of the Woodcrest property.

Tumbling over the occasional abandoned couch, chair or TV set and always navigating through a sea of empty Bud Light cans and bottles that numbered in the thousands, and yes, always Bud Light, Joey would be mesmerized by the shininess of the silvery cans and the brown-ness of the bottles as they glistened in the sun. Sometimes he would just stand there and stare at them for minutes at a time, thinking about what it would be like to be in a real sea, traveling on a boat made of hemp and smoking an endless doobie that stretched to the moon and beyond.

When his portable bin was full with bottles and bags, he would wheel it to one of the six big metal dumpsters sitting in the parking lot near each of the driveway entrances, and empty it before returning to where he left off.

At 10:00 a.m. Joey would head to the maintenance shed to take his ganja break, which usually only lasted about 15 minutes but which to Joey seemed like they lasted for "like three hours or something."

After his break Joey would continue his routine till lunch, at which time he would go back to his mother's apartment, light up his bong, and smoke a good half-ounce of that "really good Columbian shit" he had gotten over at Promontory Pointe, another complex owned by Steve and The Boys, which was just down the street. That Columbian lady manager Carmen had given it to him as a tip for doing some chores for her over at her house a few days before.

After lunch Joey would return to work and continue "picking-up" until it was about 4:00 p.m. each day, and just as he was finishing his late afternoon doobie (a tradition for Joey kind of like English Tea), the auto repair industry would start ramping up in the parking lot.

By 5:00 p.m. things were in full swing – oil changes, radiator flushes, transmission overhauls, and the occasional tire change. And what always impressed Joey, especially after he had smoked his 6:00 p.m. just-before-dinner doobie, was the array of beautiful colors that all those automotive fluids would make as they mixed together on the ground of the complex parking lot and then flowed like a magic green, black and red river out to the storm drain and into the sewer system of the City of El Paso.

And this was Joey's existence, day in and day out, day after day, week after week, month after month, and year after year. (Actually it only seemed like that long to Joey, because he was always stoned. In actuality, he had only worked at Woodcrest for about a week now, and he was planning to quit because he heard they were hiring test subjects down at the Medical Center to undergo a new form of heroin substitution therapy, and Joey figured if you could get paid to get high, well that was "like totally kick-ass sweet."

Chapter 2.6

The Shooting Cans in the Desert Incident

Las Vegas, Nevada-Still 1990 – Still at the M.M.! Two days after Steve met Morty, and 32 minutes after Morty had instructed Steve to get rid of John Hu by whatever means necessary

Now whether or not John Hu intended to kill Steve or to just intimidate him into letting John back into the M.M. deal will never be known for sure. But what is known for sure is this:

It had been two weeks since Steve had met Morty and it had also been two weeks since Mary's sister Agnes had exploded in the courtyard of the M.M. and things were beginning to get back to normal.

For Steve and John, however, things were not going exactly according to plans. You see even though the damage to the motel from the explosion had been minimal, the place didn't seem to be doing as well as Steve and John had expected it to when they first bought the place.

John was sure he had done well when he first negotiated the purchase of the M.M. for a cool one million dollars.

The terms of the deal which he went over again in his mind were as follows:

All Apartment Capitol Group would put $100,000 cash down and the Seller, Mr. B, would carry a note for the remaining $900,000 payable at nine percent interest, due in ten years and amortized over a period of 35 years.

Mr. B, the seller of the motel, had owned the property "on and off" since 1957, having sold the property under similar terms 33 times in the last 34 years – John and Steve becoming the 33rd owners of the motel, a number that John said was lucky because it showed up numerous times in Chinese numerology charts and was the name of his favorite brand of cigarettes that he imported, tax-stamp-free of course, from Hong Kong – *Lucky 33's*.

On all previous 32 occasions and with the 33rd being no exception, Mr. B had always retained, after the sale of the building, a copy of the key that opened the drop-safe located in the M.M. front office, where the weekly cash receipts were deposited by Mary shortly after she collected the weekly rents on Friday morning.

He also kept the key to the coin-operated washing machine and dryer, which was located just above the office, on the second floor of the mission section of the motel.

Mr. B kept the drop-safe key and used it to "skim," on a regular basis, his illicit share of the weekly rents.

The laundry key he kept just for the fun of messing with the new owners, which he did by randomly taking out, and then sometimes adding back the quarters that were accumulating in the coin box of the washing and drying machines, creating an erratic pattern of profit and loss which when discovered by the new owners was just funny as hell, at least to Mr. B.

Now just as John was sure that he had negotiated a great deal on the M.M., Steve was also sure he had brilliantly arranged the financing on the deal.

Scraping together what was left of his severance check that he had gotten when the FDIC closed Valley Savings and Loan, Steve came up with $33,000.

This sum of money, and a fond memory of a loan committee meeting that was held just weeks before the bank was closed in which the Bank's President, Scott Brawny, paced back and forth at the head of the table, his hair slicked back, his pants fastened tightly to his Gordon Gecko brand suspenders, a lit cigarette in one hand and a cup of black coffee in the other, repeating the phrase over and over, "We're fucked, we're going to take it in the shorts," was all Steve had left of the experience.

Steve raised the remaining $67,000 he needed to close the M.M. deal by obtaining cash advances on the nearly twenty credit cards that he had been pre-approved for just shortly after the news of his severance windfall had hit the data banks of the three major credit reporting agencies. With interest rates that ranged from 2 percent for the first two months on his Capital One Hassle-Free Small Business Master Card to interest rates that reached the then-legal limit of 22.5 percent on his MBNA Platinum Deluxe Visa, Steve assembled a financial package that would cost the All Apartment Capitol Group a "weighted average cost of capital" (a term Steve had learned in MBA school) just over

16.5 percent, the combined monthly minimum payment, being just under $4,000 a month.

That sum, when combined with the $5,162 they would be paying Mr. B, made their total monthly mortgage obligation on the motel just under $9,200 per month. This left plenty of money, or so Steve thought, to pay the electric bill, the water bill, the gas bill, the sewer bill, the trash bill, the payroll bill, the motel supplies bill and the voluntary donation to the Las Vegas Firemen's Development Fund, which the local Fire Marshall would collect personally on the second Tuesday of every month.

Now Mary, the manager of the M.M., was a feisty older lady of about seventy or so who resembled, both in personality and in appearance, the character of Granny from the TV show *The Beverly Hillbillies*.

She was shifty, wiry, argumentative, stubborn and used to doing things her own way. She had run that place for Mr. B for 34 years and she "wasn't gonna let some snot-nose Jew fuck kid from California" or his "slant-eyed yellow bastard friend" tell her how to do things.

This was especially true when it came to collecting the rents, which in Mary's head were *her* rents. As such, it was her custom to collect the rents using the "one-for-you/two for me" method which came out roughly to a 30/70 split with 30 percent going to Steve and John and 70 percent going to Mary and Mr. B, their split being determined on a first-come first-serve basis which meant that if Mr. B got to the drop-safe first with his secret key before Mary went over to Binion's Horseshoe Hotel and Casino, then he got half. If he didn't, then he was just "shit out of luck."

After several weeks, and with only 30 percent of the rents actually making it to the deposit window over at Nevada State Bank, All Apartment Capitol Group's bank account was beginning to feel the pinch. Although they were collecting some laundry income from the quarters in the coin box of the washing and drying machine, this cash flow was erratic, (thanks to Mr. B) and was simply not sufficient to bridge the gap between the motel's enormous cash outlay and its meager cash inflow.

As any first year business school student could tell, and as Scott Brawny had so succinctly put it, "Steve and John were fucked – they were going to take it in the shorts."

After owning the place for just 153 days, they had lost over $21,000 and with the mortgage payment to Mr. B due in seven days, and with only $257 left in All Apartment Capitol Group's account, and with Mr. B already chomping at the bit to take the place back and sell it to the next poor bastard, Steve knew that if they were to stay afloat, he would have to arrange some "bridge financing" to get them over this tough transitional period.

So as Mr. B was home, busy looking for those foreclosure forms that he had stashed away in his desk drawer, and as he and his real estate broker began to discuss the purchase terms for the next and 34th sale of the M.M., Steve was on his way down to Morty's office in Beverly Hills to pitch him on the M.M. deal and ask him if he would consider becoming a partner.

Morty, as we already know, had bigger plans than just the M.M. but was still willing to include the Las Vegas property in the empire-to-be with one stipulation – that John Hu be removed from the deal immediately. Morty eloquently told Steve that as far as he was concerned, the Chinese were not to be trusted, that they were deceitful in their business dealings, "were apt to offer full price" and that they were predisposed to gambling, a pursuit which Morty was intolerant of because it involved the inability to control the outcome of all events, a concept that Morton Salt was not really familiar with nor one that he had any interest in.

As such, declared Morty, "John Hu could just go pound sand."

As his reasoning for the stipulation that John Hu be "disposed of" sooner rather than later, Morty stated that there was no room for "outsiders" in the "Master Mind inner circle" and that John was not a member of what Morty liked to refer to as "the Tribe." As such, and with complete disregard for the fact that John was half owner of the M.M. and partners with Steve, John was, as Morty put it, "burnt rice" and had to be "disposed of" immediately before he stunk up the kitchen, by any means appropriate."

But, just the same, in a half-hearted effort to appear righteous, as Morty fancied himself a just man, he told Steve to tell John that Morty was going to buy John's interest in the motel for a fair price, which to Morty meant for as close to nothing as possible.

Now as one might have expected, upon hearing Morty's offer John did not take the news well; the repercussions of Steve's having to tell John that John was out of the M.M. deal culminating in a little incident which came to be known as the "shooting cans in the desert" incident and it went down something like this:

While John and his sidekick Wilbur and Steve were whizzing their way back to Las Vegas from Arcadia in John's black Mercedes SEL-AMG as they had done so many times before, and as they were somewhere between Barstow and Baker on the I-15 freeway about forty or so miles from the California/Nevada border, John suddenly got the idea that it would be fun to stop on the side of the road and walk a few hundred yards into the desert and shoot cans with the .44 Luger that he kept in the rear seat console of his car.

Coincidentally, this idea of "shooting cans in the desert" came to John "out of the blue" just seconds after Steve had finished explaining to John how his meeting with Morty was going to affect John's stake in the M.M. deal.

Now at first, everything seemed to be "okie dokie" as Steve proceeded to explain to John that in order to save the deal it was going to be necessary to take on another partner who could infuse some money into the project, to which John initially replied, "HHHHHHHHHHHHHHHA Good idea HHHHHHHHHHHHHHHHHO."

It was when Steve explained that Morton Salt was going to buy John's interest in the project for the same amount that John had invested in the project in the first place, which was $500, that John seemed to get upset, although it was hard to tell with John because he was a person who seemed to be completely devoid of any emotions whatsoever, but upon hearing Steve's presentation of Morty's $500 proposal, John ever so slightly raised his voice while muttering, "HHHHHHHHHHHHHHHA Maybe not a good idea HHHHHHHHHHHHHHHHHO."

Well I'll tell you what wasn't a good idea, and that was telling a known smuggler and rumored member of the Chinese Mafia who had a loaded .44 next to him in the console of his car as you drove through the middle of the fucking desert with no one else around for miles, that you and your new Jewish partner were planning to fuck him up the ass with a giant $500 eggroll, and then when you were done you were going to pull it out and ask him if he wanted to eat it.

And what was even more of a "not good idea" was that after telling John the "bad news," agreeing with John, as Steve did, that "yes, it would indeed be fun to go shoot some cans in the desert."

And with that, they pulled over to the side of the road, got the .44 Luger out of the rear seat console and walked up a hill of sand about 400 yards until when they looked back, they couldn't see the road anymore.

What was Steve thinking? Who the fuck knows! Although as they were walking it did occur to him that maybe it was not really cans that John was planning to shoot out there in the desert.

As a matter of fact, when he looked at John, and then at Wilbur, and then down at his own hands, he realized that all three of them had forgotten to bring any cans. All they had brought was the Luger and a clip loaded with 15 rounds of ammunition.

But upon pointing this fact out to John that they indeed had no cans to shoot, John replied, "HHHHHHHHHHHHA There's always a few cans laying out here K.J, we will just go and pick them up HHHHHHHHHHHHHHHHHO." To which K.J. replied, "Good Idea."

Now as Steve began to consider the possibility that John was "pissed," a thought which hadn't really occurred to Steve until this moment because it was hard to conceive of John having any emotional reaction to anything in the first place, Steve began to play through in his mind how this whole little "shooting cans" thing was going to play out.

First he imagined John just turning around and shooting him three or four times in the torso.

Then he imagined John walking up behind him and shooting him in the back of the head.

Then he imagined Wilbur pretending to accidentally shoot Steve while Steve was out setting up the cans that he was going to find out there in the desert.

And then he imagined John turning around and shooting Wilbur, just to show Steve what a truly cold and calculating psychopath he really was, that he really was pissed and that he wasn't fucking around and that if Steve didn't let John back in the deal, Steve was going to be next.

Surprisingly enough, for Steve it was just like watching a little movie in his head and for some reason, feeling removed from the situation, he wasn't scared at all by the possibility that in all likelihood, he was about to get shot.

It is perhaps this cool, calm reaction to the whole situation which may have very well saved Steve that windy desert morning somewhere between Barstow and Baker just 400 yards off the I-15 Freeway.

As the three of them arrived at the top of the sandy hill and looked out at the flat rocky desert that stretched out for miles before them, John turned to Steve and said, "HHHHHHHHHHHHHHA this is a good place to shoot from HHHHHHHHHHHHHHHHHO."

Steve looked around and then agreeing with John said, "Yes, this is a good place. And since we don't have any cans, let's fire off a few rounds at those cactuses out there."

And then John turned to Steve and uttered the very words which Steve will always remember as providing him with his moment of salvation, if indeed it was John's intention to shoot Steve in the first place and if Steve did indeed need some salvation, when John said, "HHHHHHHHHHHA Do you want to shoot first? HHHHHHHHHHHHHHHHO."

Was John just "fucking" with Steve – was he playing some kind of game of "chicken," or some kind of game of Russian-Roulette to prove who the better man was?

Was John just lulling Steve into some sort of sense of security before he shot him?

Or was he just trying to intimidate Steve by letting him know that he, John, was in control and putting the thought into Steve's mind that even though he wasn't going to kill him that day, tomorrow, depending on how Steve and John worked out the whole M.M. situation, he could change his mind and kill him anyway?

Well, the truth is we will never know. You see, if this had been a movie or a TV show, Steve would have agreed to shoot first and would then have taken the gun from John's hands, turned around, shot Wilbur in the chest and then turned the gun on John and emptied the rest of the clip into John's body and head until he ran out of bullets.

That's the way situations like this usually play out in the world of entertainment. And yes, thoughts of shooting John and Wilbur did occur to Steve, but in his heart of hearts, he was not a killer, and in moments of truth like this, your real nature tends to come out and take over.

So in real life, this is what happened.

Steve agreed with John and said he would shoot first. He then took the gun from John, took the safety off, raised the gun to eye level and aimed at a cactus about one hundred feet away.

And as John and Wilbur stepped back a little behind Steve, Steve then proceeded to fire, one shot, two shots, three shots, four shots, pop, pop, pop, pop, pop, pop, pop, pop, pop, pop, pop, click, until the entire 15 shot clip was spent.

When Steve was done firing, he lowered the gun, looked off towards the cactus and said to John, "how did I do?" To which John replied "HHHHHHHHHHHHHHHA pretty good K.J, pretty good, HHHHHHHHHHHHHHHHO."

But seeing as that they had brought only that one clip of bullets with them and had no other ammunition in the car, it became clear, at that moment, that John and Wilbur's turn to "shoot cans," or cactuses for that matter, would have to wait for another day.

As it also became clear to all those present that day, Steve had either proved himself to be an amazingly clever individual, or the luckiest son-of-a-bitch on the planet.

Chapter 2.6

Frank Gerber – Heart Attack Justice

El Paso, Texas 1992 – Two Years Later - The Boys buy Pinewood Villas Apartments

In 1989 Franklyn Delano Gerber was 34 years old. He had a regular nine-to-five job and worked selling and repairing computers at a local computer retailer in El Paso, Texas. He had worked there for several years, getting paid under the table and making, by the way, a pretty good living.

On September 11, 1991, the Internal Revenue Service conducted an audit of El Paso Computer Solutions, Inc. and determined that the store had not only employed Frank under the table but all of their other nine employees as well. As a result of the audit, it was determined that El Paso Computer Solutions, Inc. owed the IRS back payroll taxes in the sum of $87,013.75, and that each of the employees who worked there owed their own portion of FICA taxes which at the time was 2.9 percent of their wages. When the dust had settled, and when the owners had closed the store, Frank Gerber owed the IRS $1,041.36.

Now most guys would have just paid the taxes, gotten another job, and got on with their life, but not Frank. You see, Frank was a man of principles. And so rather than pay the IRS their share of his wages, Frank decided to beat the bastards at their own game and "go underground." His decision was based on his intimate knowledge of the IRS code, especially one particular section which stated in no uncertain terms that after ten years any liabilities either unrecognized or unrealized would become null and void and as such, uncollectible by the IRS.

Thus, Frank's plan was simple. He would move in with his mother, become untraceable by having no bills in his own name, not officially work and not show up on the books of any employer until September 11, 2001, a date which Frank referred to as "independence day" and which, in anticipation of the fact that he had beat the IRS at their own game, had booked a five-day vacation to New York City, to begin with a visit to the famous World Trade Center which would include a tour of the observation deck on the top floor of the South Tower sometime on the morning of September 11, 2001.

Now, although it seemed, at first, like it might be tough going, going underground seemed to come naturally to Frank. As a matter of fact, he really liked it. When he moved in with his mom Eileen, in the summer of 1992, she was managing the Pinewood Villas Apartments and living rent-free in a nice, but modest three-bedroom house that was located directly in front of the apartments and was part of the property.

At the time Frank moved in, the complex wasn't really doing all that well financially. The vacancy rate was way up and there were a lot of tenants who just didn't pay their rents on time. The place was owned by some guy from Utah and was managed by a local property management company called Eastwood Property Management; Eileen worked for them.

Now Eileen had been managing Pinewood Villas for about two years now and all the while Eastwood Management was unaware that she was living rent-free in the 3-bedroom place in front of the complex. This meant she was costing the complex about $1,000 a month which Pinewood could have been earning by renting out the house to a paying customer. And although upon arriving at Pinewood Villas she was supposed to move in to the manager's unit in the back of the complex – a one bedroom place with a small kitchen – Eileen had decided to give herself a promotion and move into the three-bedroom house, as she needed the extra rooms and the backyard would be the perfect place to have those Saturday morning garage sales it was her habit to throw.

You see Eileen's daughter Jenny, a part time legal secretary who worked for a small law firm downtown, was married to this guy, Gary, who used to beat her up every week or so, although he was always sorry afterward and would promise Jenny he would never do it again, until he did it again.

So every week or so, when Jenny decided to leave Gary for good, and until she decided to go back and give him another "one last chance," Jenny would stay with Eileen over at Pinewood Villas for a couple of days while she was preparing to file those divorce papers she never quite got around to filing.

And now with Frank's predicament, Eileen needed at least a three-bedroom place so Frank could have his own room.

And have his own room he did. Not only that, but he had his own private entrance through the back door, and his own private bathroom which was connected directly to his bedroom.

His mom had given him the master bedroom in the house as she had no "man in her life" at the time and didn't really need the privacy. Anyway, she didn't need a man, she had Jesus.

And also, she was pretty sure she had this stomach tumor that had been growing inside her for about a year now, which she was saving up from the money she earned at her garage sales every Saturday morning to have removed. The tumor, she said, made it difficult for her to sleep through the whole night so even if she had a man, which she didn't, she'd "just keep him up all night anyway – besides men were lying-cheating-drunken-scum and who needs that?"

To make the situation even sweeter, Frank's room was located only two blocks away from the local Domino's Pizza Store and only one and a half blocks from the local 7-Eleven.

And as it was his habit while on his way home each day from picking up his mid-afternoon pizza, Frank would stop by the 7-Eleven and pick up the ingredients he needed to make his favorite meal, "Pizza with Links."

So after picking up the jumbo pack of Oscar Meyer Hot Dogs, a large can of Cheez Whiz and a 42-ounce Super Big Gulp of Classic Coke (Frank was a traditionalist as well as a man of principle), Frank would return home to his room and begin to assemble his own all-you-can-eat pizza buffet.

After pouring the entire package of hot dogs, uncut, directly on top of his pepperoni, sausage and double-cheese pizza, and after squirting an entire can of cheddar & bacon flavored Cheez Whiz all over the top in swirling, curly-q patterns that Frank liked to imagine were the hills and valleys of pre-World War II Italy, Frank would sit down, cross-legged on the floor, his pizza feast in front of him, his World War II reenactment board game in front of that and his mom's 27-inch color TV in front of that, and then, slice after slice, gulp after gulp, would proceed to devour his entire "buffet" while moving the little toy soldiers and tanks on his war board and watching Morey Povitch re-runs, turning up the sound on the TV only at the end of each half-hour segment to find out who indeed the "baby-daddy" was.

"Ah, this was the life!"

On the day Steve and Morty bought Pinewood Villas, the first complex that they had purchased together in El Paso, Steve met Frank's mom Eileen for the very first time.

And they failed to hit it off almost immediately.

For it was there in the kitchen of Eileen's rent-free three-bedroom house that was located in the front of the Pine-wood Villas complex, that for the very first time in his life Steve came face to face with what it really meant to be "the owner" of a business.

And what it meant was this, "that it is more important to do the right thing for you and yours than to be liked by them and theirs."

And there were plenty of things that Eileen didn't like.

Now for starters she didn't like that Steve told her it was not alright to use part of the Villas' rent receipts to buy food for her refrigerator or to buy any more bird feeders. (She had a thing for bird feeders and had almost twenty of them out in the front yard of the house.)

Eileen didn't like that Steve suggested that maybe she should stop having garage sales every Saturday morning. It wasn't that Steve didn't like garage sales, it was just that the stuff that she was selling at her weekly sales all had Home Depot price stickers on them and so Steve deduced that it was more than likely that the previous owners of Pinewood had in fact been paying for the purchase of these items on their Home Depot charge account. And from there things just escalated.

And when Eileen asked Steve if he had a Home Depot charge account and Steve said that he did, Eileen asked Steve if he could get her a card as well, you know, so she could buy "supplies" for the building.

And when Steve said no, and suggested that she open up her own account at Home Depot, Eileen became enraged. She couldn't believe that Steve was going to make her pay for her own supplies, which Steve knew weren't supplies at all, but inventory for her garage sales.

And when Steve suggested that perhaps she should move into the one-bedroom manager's unit at the back of the complex so he could rent the house out and make the place another thousand dollars a month, well that was just the final straw.

"Who the devil does this Beverly Hills brat think he is?" thought Eileen to herself. "Who is he to come in here to my complex, to my home, and to tell me what to do?"

And as she continued to rant and rave about how unfair Steve was and how she had never been so outraged or treated so badly, and how the old owners of the Villas let her run things the way she wanted and how Steve was not a very nice person and how she didn't see how she could work for a guy like Steve, Steve simply suggested that maybe she shouldn't.

And that was that!

And at this, Eileen warned Steve that he was under the influence of Satan, that he would definitely burn in hell, and that he could take his manager job and go straight to the devil with it.

She then went off to tell Frank that they were moving.

Now what always impressed Steve about this, and indeed about subsequent situations of this type, was that for some reason every time Steve tried to stop people from doing what they shouldn't have been doing in the first place, they would get all enraged and accuse him of being a bad guy.

But Steve wasn't a bad guy, was he? "No!" he thought to himself. He was just a businessman, trying to run a business.

"But, the old owners had never said anything about me having garage sales," Steve imagined Eileen saying, "and after all, the old owners had never actually counted the rents, or put limits on my charge account. The old owners never checked to see if I used the money they gave me to really fix the air conditioner. And besides, I don't really get paid all that much considering all the hard work I do around here and I've come to rely on the 'little extra' that I get taking an extra dime here and there."

Well the old owners had never had to answer to Morton Simon Salt, and the old owners had perhaps, never heard the iconic words of Saul T. Salt, who had told Morton Salt, who had in turn told Steve, that "you may feel bad firing someone for not doing a good job, but imagine how bad you'd feel if the business went under and your children starved!"

"Good riddance!" Steve thought to himself. And for almost half a second there Steve felt pretty good.

And then the reality kicked in, there was no one to manage their new property, and with Steve having to get back to Las Vegas by the next day to collect the receipts at the M.M., he realized he needed to find a new manager real fast.

What to do? What to do?

Well as it happened, as Steve was helping Eileen load boxes of bird feeders into her Ford station wagon with the wood paneling on the outside of the doors, and as she was warning Steve about the foibles of being a minion of Satan and how hot it was in hell – even hotter than El Paso – Steve happened to walk by Frank's room and saw Frank sitting there, cross-legged on the floor enjoying his pizza and link buffet.

And as Frank sat there with pepperoni grease dripping from his chin, stuffing links into his mouth with his left hand and combing his long black hair with a rounded styling brush with his right, Steve stared at Frank, thinking to himself, "Should I ask?"

And knowing full well, intuitively, that he shouldn't, Steve went ahead anyway and asked Frank if he had any experience in management, Steve referring to apartment management of course.

And Frank, referring to his WW II board game experience of course, said "Yes."

And then not wanting to ask too many more questions, the answers to which might disturb Steve's convenient fantasy that Frank was qualified to manage the complex and that Frank wasn't the lazy fat bastard who sat on his mother's floor all day eating pizza and playing board games that he was, Steve asked Frank if he wanted to be the new manager of Pinewood; a decision that was motivated by Steve's desperation to fill the position immediately and also reinforced by Steve's romantic view of the universe in which he believed that anyone, given the chance, could succeed.

"Can I keep my room?" Frank asked, going on to explain that he had his war board all set up for the Allied liberation of France and didn't really want to disassemble the pieces now that they were all set up.

"Sure, why not?" answered Steve reluctantly, not really wanting to continue using the house as a manager's unit but fearing that without doing so Frank might not take the job, and that would've left Steve in an awful bind.

And so, there it was. Franklyn Delano Gerber was now the new manager of Pinewood Villas Apartments, which was lucky for him because not only didn't he have to move out of his room, but he was going to actually start getting paid to stay home and eat pizza.

And being as Frank confided in Steve that he "never really cared that much about his mother to begin with," he told Steve he had no problem making sure she was gone by sundown and he would make sure she didn't come back to the property ever again.

And all was well!

Oh wait; there was one "small" hitch to the arrangement, however.

Frank, as you remember, was underground. He couldn't get a paycheck. Actually, he could get a paycheck, but it couldn't be more than $365 dollars a month. Anything in excess of this amount would have to be remitted by his employer to the IRS. Steve saw this garnishment as a way for Frank to pay off his small debt to the IRS while living rent-free at Pinewood. Frank was a little bit more emotional about the issue, saying "those fucker's weren't going to get a dime" out of him.

And so they solved their little dilemma with the following arrangement that Frank suggested and that Steve readily agreed to. Steve would pay Frank exactly $365 a month and Frank would agree to take the rest of his salary, another $500 a month, on "independence day," when the ten-year

IRS statute of limitations ran out. The money would come in handy for his celebratory trip to New York.

Now whether or not Steve intended to ever honor his "arrangement" with Frank is not really the point of this story. For it is unquestionably a part of human nature, to agree, for the sake of expediency, to something that you might not otherwise agree to; and to tell someone something that they might want to hear, in exchange for something you might want to hear, at least for the moment anyway.

Such are the words of the prophet Meatloaf, "I swore that I would love you till the end of time."

It is pretty clear however, that the likelihood of Steve ever having to honor such an arrangement with Frank was nil at best, for how many apartment managers last in such a position for a period as long as ten years anyway? Not many.

And even if he did, wasn't Frank's arrangement with Steve an illegal one? After all, conspiring to defraud the IRS? If Steve didn't honor the arrangement, could Frank sue him for the money? Not likely; illegal contracts are not enforceable in a court of law.

So then what is the point of this little sordid tale?

It is a moral one, a tale of what Steve, being the philosopher poet that he was, would call "heart attack justice;" the idea that in the end, you don't have to worry about the other guy and his crazy scheme because when a person sets out to do evil, they inevitably become the architects of their own destruction.

And that wasn't your problem, especially if what they wanted to do was a benefit for you!

And if that kind of thinking was good enough for the R.J. Reynolds Tobacco Company, then it was good enough for Steve.

Yes indeed, it wasn't really moral to purposely set out to screw someone, but if they wanted to screw themselves, well that's a whole other story.

And so it was with Frank.

And with Steve's moral dilemma squared away, and with Frank sporting the title of Manager of the Pinewood Villa Apartments, Steve got in his car and headed for Las Vegas to collect the rents over at the M.M.

Chapter 2.7

Make It a Loss

Beverly Hills, California – April 14, 1993 – The art of Stealth Investing by Saul T. Salt

Now for those of you out there considering a career in real estate investment, this is the time where it might be a good idea to go get a yellow highlighter and take some notes because this is where I explain about the deal structure of the Pinewood Villas Apartments' purchase, a structure invented by the late great Saul T. Salt, and a structure which was to become the archetype for every other deal that Steve and The Boys Back Home would ever do.

It is a deal structure which answers the questions: *Why don't rich people pay taxes?* And *Who owns that place, anyway?*

Now Morty and his band of merry-very-rich men, although they were not entrepreneurs at heart, were however – because of their breeding – practiced in the art of "Stealth Investing," the main tenet of this art being that no one looking in from the outside should ever be able to tell who really owns a property.

This way, if anything ever goes wrong, say someone tries to sue the property, or if there is some kind of unlikely disaster like a gas explosion or something, or just any other kind of unpleasant trouble, the owners can distance themselves from the problem and the aggrieved party could, as Morty liked to say, "Pound sand."

This is how "Stealth Investing" works:

First of all, every property purchased was always a separate limited partnership or LLC.

This way, if one property ran into trouble, it wouldn't affect any other property because of common ownership issues.

The second step was to name the Partnership with the most generic, forgettable, hard-to-pronounce and hard-to-spell name possible, the best one always being the property's address, like the 201 South First Street Limited Partnership, for example. This not only confused lookers-on, but made it very cumbersome to fill out any legal documents, such as law suits for instance, since it was usually unclear, for instance, how the number 201 was written, in other words, was it the *numeral* 201 or the words *Two-Zero-One* or the words *Two-O-One* or a combination thereof such as *2-Zero-1*, and so on – the combinations were endless.

The purpose of using these types of names became clear when Steve would receive a citation or a law suit, which when not made out exactly correct, to the right party, he could simply dismiss, saying, "that's not us." This especially pissed off process servers and legal clerks because it meant they couldn't carry out their jobs in a timely fashion, and would often have to fill out and re-serve the papers, three or four times, before finally serving the right party.

Step three in the art of "Stealth Investing" was to appoint a General Partner or Manager for each generic Limited Partnership or LLC that owned a property.

This General Partner or Manager would never be a person. Rather, it would be another generically named Corporation or LLC, the difference being that this Corporation or LLC was merely a shell corporation which had no assets, and therefore, had nothing to lose.
The fact that these entities had nothing to lose gave them the freedom to conduct business affairs, such as entering into contracts or hiring employees, without the burden of much civil or criminal liability. This business theory "of having nothing to lose" was known to Steve and The Boys as the *Janis Joplin Doctrine*.

In accordance with the doctrine, Steve named his shell corporation *Anthroncointelligistics*. It was a particularly good name for his little shell company because it had a lot of vowels strung together, was hard to pronounce correctly, and even in pronouncing it correctly, it gave a person an uncomfortable feeling of uncertainty about what they were referring to. Was it a management company? Was it some kind of religious cult? Was it a computer company? Was it some kind of medical device manufacturer? Ehhhh!

Having designated a partnership to own the property, a corporate General Partner to run the property, and a manager of the General Partner Corporation to run the corporation, this is where the spider web of actual ownership really got complex.

You see, it was the Limited Partners who were the actual owners of the Partnership. And these Limited Partners, like all the other partners, were never people. They were always yet another assortment of legal entities, however, usually of a more personal nature, like a family trust, or a foundation, or a development corporation, or a Real Estate Investment Trust, or a Pension Fund and although there was only one partnership, and one manager, there were always numerous Limited Partners, even if all the Limited Partner entities had the same owners. Got that?!

Well just in case you don't, let's go through the Pinewood Villas' "spider web of stealth" to see how it worked.

Pinewood Villas was owned by the 40Four31 N. 22nd Street Limited Partnership. The General Partner was the Anthroncointelligistics Corporation, which was managed by Retro Capital Management LLC which was in turn managed by Steve but since Retro Capital Management was organized and registered as a Delaware LLC, it was not required to list its corporate officers. Thus, no one other than Steve knew that he was the manager of Retro Capital Management. Are you with me so far?

Now there were four Limited Partners in the Pinewood Villas' deal.

First, there was the Salt Family Trust, which was comprised of the four children and eleven grandchildren of Saul T. Salt.

Then there was the Leventhal Family Trust, comprised of the four members of the Leventhal Family including Arnie and Fancy, and their two children, and the Robbins Family Trust comprised of Fancy, and her two brothers, Sid and Marty.

Then there was the Stanton White Foundation, which was founded by Stanton and his wife to support the arts in the Greater Los Angeles area.

And finally there was the Gamble foundation, founded by Nicky's grandfather, an organization that gave money to support cleaning products research.

So there you have it, a small El Paso apartment building complex with a corporate structure more complex than Exxon.

Now, it's funny that I should mention Exxon, because despite Frank's obvious inexperience in running a property and despite Steve's inexperience of operating in the El Paso real estate market, at the end of nine months Pinewood Villas Apartments had generated windfall profits.

It was so successful that it even made the cover of Apartment Management Magazine, a fact which Morty made sure to tell everyone he knew, including Harvey Mendel!

It was important that everyone know how successful Pinewood Villas had been because not only did spreading the word boost Morty's credibility in the investment community, it also attracted other "wanna-be" entrepreneur investors to the ranks of Morty's band of merry-very-rich men, which Steve had begun to refer to as the Beverly Hills Lunch Club.

The notoriety that the 97 percent cash-on-cash return that the Villas was generating (this meant if you invested $100,000 in the property, at the end of the first year you would have $197,000) had already made news down at *The Greenes*, a restaurant which was located on Wilshire Boulevard, just four blocks west of Santa Monica Boulevard, in Beverly Hills.

It was here at lunchtime, at The Greenes, where all the "real" investment deals in Beverly Hills went down and it was here, in March of 1993, that the room was "abuzz" with the news of Morty's windfall success.

Anybody who was anybody all knew that "El Paso was hot right now." And anybody who was anybody knew that if you were going to do some investing in Texas, Morty was the guy to see.

In fact, Steve and Morty's Beverly Hills crew had made so much money, that when Steve sat down to fill out the 1992 Partnership Tax Return, he was afraid they were going to have to pay a windfall profit tax, (a tax that had been on the books since the early 80s when Congress passed federal legislation that levied such a tax on oil companies because of the profits they earned as a result of the sharp increase in oil prices brought about by the Arab oil embargo. The tax was ended in 1988 by President Ronald Reagan but Steve didn't know that.)

Now part of Steve's job as Manager of the Manager of the Manager of The General Partnership was to prepare the yearly tax returns and this meant not only figuring out the taxable profit or loss of the Partnership, but also allocating, according to their ownership percentage, to each partner, (which was sometimes difficult to figure out for Arnie) their share of the partnership profits, or losses, and their share of various deductions and tax credits.

The IRS form used to do this allocation is called a K-1, and guys like Morty and the other members of the Beverly Hills Boys were used to receiving lots and lots and lots of K-1's at the end of the year.

Now anyone who has ever filled out a tax return knows the drill. The whole idea of the exercise is to minimize your tax liability by finding as many expense deductions and tax credits that you can. With that being said, Steve set out to, at least on the books, minimize the gain that the Partnership had had that first banner year.

As he poured through the many pages of his GAAP (Generally Accepted Accounting Principles) and GAAS (Generally Accepted Auditing Standards) Tax Guides, he began to assemble what was really a pretty decent attempt to minimize the IRS's share in the whole thing. As a matter of fact, when he factored in all the start-up costs of all those legal entities they had created to own and operate Pinewood Villas; he was surprised how well he had really done.

With the tax return almost completed, and the K-1's ready to go out to the Partners, Steve sent a preliminary copy over to Morty's office for his perusal and approval. When all was said and done, Steve had gotten the initial, actual profit, down from just over three million dollars to a respectable, taxable profit of just over $800,000. He was proud of the job he had done and was sure that Morty would be happy.

On April 14th, at quarter to five that evening, just as Steve was sitting down to a late afternoon snack, the phone rang. It was Dolores, Morty's private secretary.

"Oh, hi Dolores," Steve said. "Did Morty get a copy of the K-1"? Steve asked.

"Make it a lawss," Dolores said.

"Excuse me"? Steve queried.

"Morty says make it a lawss," Dolores replied.

And as Steve sat there in his kitchen, staring incredulously at the phone, shaking his head in disbelief and wondering how he was going to turn the biggest percentage profit since Exxon's Arab Oil Embargo windfall into a loss, Dolores simply hung up the phone, "click."

In the end, after rewriting the terms of the partnership agreement, and after allocating and re-allocating all of the income to the other investors and allocating all of the expenses to Morty, Steve, coming to grips with the fact that Morty's reality was, indeed, the *only* reality that really mattered, found a way to legally "make it a loss," at least for Morty anyway.

As for the other partners, they all made huge profits. And as it turned out, luckily for Arnie, Arnie had indeed "been in the deal."

Chapter 2.7

"The Morningwood Canteen" and "The Blumberg Doctrine"

El Paso, Texas 1994 – Eleven buildings later – The Boys buy Morningwood Apartments

Thomas Tuttle was used to handling rough crowds. An ex-army man, Tom had been a corporal in the Quartermasters Corps at Fort Bragg in North Carolina until the disappearance of some inventory items from the Fort Canteen ended in his court-martial and eventual dishonorable discharge from the army. After a short period of wandering and self-reflection, and short stints as a bounty hunter, a bartender in a strip club, and an unplanned appearance on

STEVE O.

the pilot episode of truTV's newest reality show *Stupid Idiot*, Tom finally landed a full-time position as assistant manager of the Come & Go Adult Emporium in downtown El Paso. It wasn't his first choice as a career but it was a steady paycheck and it kept him busy during the evening hours from 6:00 p.m. to 3:00 a.m. Tuesdays thru Sundays.

It was the very fact that Steve employed "these types of people" in positions of authority and responsibility that so confused and irritated Lieutenant Blumberg of the Neighborhood Enforcement Division of the El Paso Police Department.

No, in Blumberg's eyes there was no room in the property management arena for people with checkered pasts, questionable morals or criminal backgrounds, and it was people like Steve – the out of town landlords – who were hiring these miscreants to run and manage the over 400 apartment complexes that comprised the neighborhood of Eastwood.

You see, it was Blumberg's job to "build alliances between law enforcement and local business owners – especially apartment complex owners – and foster a spirit of mutual cooperation that would benefit the community as a whole."

As such, Blumberg had two major responsibilities; the giving out of bullshit community service awards at local community meetings, and helping to establish community standards to guide in the running of the community's apartment complexes.

Now in actuality, Blumberg had no authority to do either of these two things, and as such, his position was, for the most part, a public relations job.

But it was important that it be perceived by the public that the City had a hand in the running of the Eastwood neighborhood; an area that in reality no one could really run or control but that, just the same, would make everyone feel better if there was at least some illusion of control.

And it was for this reason that at a meeting of Shirley Dole's Eastwood Community Association, after giving Steve's wife an award for "Most Improved Complex" for her outstanding work at the Pinewood Apartments over the last two years, that Lieutenant Blumberg issued the Blumberg Doctrine – a set of guidelines for hiring apartment managers and screening potential tenants in the neighborhood with the voluntary proviso that all such selections would be given to the Lieutenant for his review and approval, or disapproval as would most likely be the case.

Now despite the fact that he had no experience whatsoever in either property management or actual law enforcement for that matter, Blumberg was no fool. He believed, and he was absolutely right, that most of the crime problems in the Eastwood area were in some way attributable to both the incompetent actions of the individuals who managed the more than 400 apartment buildings that made up the majority of the community, and the questionable make-up of the tenant populations of the community's complexes.

And Blumberg simply couldn't understand how smart guys like Steve and all of the other out of town owners (Blumberg assumed they were smart because he assumed they were wealthy) could entrust the running of such large and valuable pieces of property to alcoholics, welfare cheats, the disenfranchised and ex-cons, or fill their proper-

ties up with criminals, drug addicts, the chronically unemployed and illegal immigrants.

It was infuriating!

And what especially pissed Blumberg off was the fact
that nine times out of ten, when the "shit hit the fan" with
these loser managers, as it almost always inevitably did,
and they ended up stealing money, or worse, from their naïve employers (the out-of-town complex owners), or when
some tenant would commit some heinous criminal act
against property or personage, it was always these very
same landlords, like Steve, who would come crying to
Blumberg like a bunch of little babies who had just had
their toys taken away from them by some bully down at the
local playground.

What did they think was going to happen when they
gave the combination of the safe to the bank robber, or the
keys to the asylum to the inmates?

Why didn't they "get it"?

But what Blumberg didn't get was that these owners *did*
get it. And for the most part these out-of-town owners
weren't naïve at all. They were, however, folks caught between a rock and a hard place – folks who had for the most
part unknowingly stepped into a bad situation, or at least a
situation that they thought was controllable. They were also
folks who were heavily invested – financially at least – in
the community but who had no local resources other than
money to run their operations. And when I say resources,
I'm referring to human resources. So to address Lieutenant
Blumberg's question, why didn't Steve and those other out-
of-town owners hire qualified, competent people to manage
their complexes?

Because the only people willing to manage run-down apartments in shitty neighborhoods like Eastwood, risking their lives dealing with the chronically unemployed, sometimes-violent alcoholics and drug addicts, criminals, and illegal immigrants who made up the tenant populations of these buildings, were the chronically unemployed, sometimes-violent alcoholics and drug addicts, criminals and illegal immigrants themselves!

And you could go one step further to ask, as Lieutenant Blumberg had, why weren't Steve and other owners like him more selective about who they rented to? Why did they fill their buildings with undesirables? Why didn't they just screen their potential tenants more carefully? Maybe, if they cleaned up the tenant population a little, they could attract more "quality" people to work at and manage these complexes!

Because, as anyone who has ever run an apartment complex in a shitty neighborhood would know, and as Lieutenant Blumberg hadn't and didn't know, was that you don't choose your customers, they choose you.

After all, in real estate it's location, location, location!

And Eastwood was not the location that someone who had a good credit history, or a steady job, or no criminal record, or even someone who had something as basic as an actual driver's license or an actual social security number, would choose to live.

Especially when for only a few dollars more a month, they could live in a safer neighborhood which actually had an actual grocery store other than 7-Eleven and an actual branch of Bank of America instead of just the 10 percent check cashing store down at the Pinchi Puta.

No, Eastwood was a neighborhood of last resorts.

And as such, the reality was that Steve and the other owners like him had no choice but to take the desperate rejects that buildings in nicer neighborhoods wouldn't take – because they were their only potential customers.

It was a vicious cycle – bad conditions attract bad tenants who create more bad conditions. It was also a problem way beyond the power of any local business owner or even any city agency to really make a dent in.

If only Lieutenant Blumberg had been there that day the lady in unit 43 set the bushes in front of her apartment on fire when she decided to have a barbeque but didn't own a grill, perhaps he could have advised her not to dump an entire 10-pound bag of charcoal and an entire container of starter fluid into a plastic garbage can and then cover it with an air-conditioning register vent which she unscrewed from the wall in her living room so she could use it as a grilling surface; perhaps then he'd understand.

And perhaps had Lieutenant Blumberg been in the rental office that morning when the nice single mother and her two children came to rent an apartment, he could have used his keen apartment manager skills to properly screen her. She had proper ID, and a good credit history and a good job. Why he would have certainly rented to her. And how disappointed he probably would have been to later learn that the two-bedroom unit she just rented came to be occupied not by her or her cute-as-a-button two little children, but by a group of 33 of her cousins, nephews, nieces and uncles, who upon her getting the keys, promptly moved in to the unit and set up camp.

Perhaps he might realize that knowing what to do in theory and actually doing it were two very different animals.

And that brings us back to Thomas Tuttle, Steve's choice, in direct disregard of the Blumberg Doctrine, as the new part-time manager of the Morningwood Apartments, a smaller 20-unit building located on the outskirts of Eastwood near downtown El Paso. It was a building that Steve and Morty had just purchased for quite the bargain in this up and coming section of the city and it was in generally good condition. The tenants of the building were, although, as they say, a pretty rough crowd.

So who better than Thomas Tuttle, a man used to handling rough crowds, as the choice to be the manager of such a complex, a complex located, coincidentally, directly next door to the Come & Go Adult Emporium, a pornographic mecca which attracted a mostly deviant crowd of fisters, felchers and fellators who were drawn to the establishment because of its state of the art, surround-sound glory-hole booths, equipped with both air-conditioning and padded vinyl floors – it was the place to be if you were into that sort of thing.

And since Thomas worked at the Emporium during nighttime hours only, he was luckily available during daylight hours, to fill the part-time position of apartment manager at Morningwood, a situation he agreed to accept with one proviso – that he be allowed to operate a convenience store out of his manager's unit at the building.

Now everyone has a dream and Thomas was no exception; Thomas' dream was to own his own convenience store, an idea he had fantasized about almost constantly as he, for almost the last three years now, had languished away behind the counter of the Come & Go. And as he sold John Holmes brand signature dildos, and ball-in-the-mouth leather masks, and desensitizing creams, and velvet handcuffs, he dreamed of the day when he could do something that would really make a difference in the world – when lotions and potions and whips and chains would be replaced by Slim Jims, and Moon Pies, and cigarettes and beer.

Yes, Thomas' store would be the best convenience store ever known to civilization and it would be called The Canteen, an obvious throwback from Thomas' military days, the days before the court martial and the dishonorable discharge which had left him feeling isolated and purposeless. Yes, like all men who had been to the mountaintop and subsequently fallen off, Thomas was in need of redemption. And this was his chance.

In exchange for the duties of collecting the rents, calling Steve if something broke, and alerting the proper authorities should a murder take place on the premises, Thomas would receive a free apartment at Morningwood, $100 a week in cash, and the promise of entrepreneurial opportunity. Thomas set up shop in unit A of the complex and commenced to canteen*ing*.

Seeing as that he had a felony record and all, and would likely meet up with some bureaucratic obstacles, he decided to forego the usual permitting and licensing procedures normally associated with opening such an establishment and instead just simply went down to Costco, bought what he thought he would need for the first couple of weeks, and decided to sit back and see how things went, before rushing off to fill out a bunch of forms and paying all those permit fees that the folks down at the City usually require.

And within two weeks, business was a-booming. Why when word got out at the local high school that you could pick up an entire case of Bud Light and a carton of Marlboros for only twenty bucks, and still have change left to buy a Suzie-Q or a Moon-Pie, kids were lined up in front of Thomas' door from the second they got out of school at 3:00 p.m. until 6:00 p.m. when Thomas had to leave to go to work at the Come & Go.

Why Thomas had been so busy that he had forgotten to call Steve and tell him that he had used the 19 rents he had collected so far that month to buy more merchandise for his canteen, an amount Thomas was confident he could replenish quickly considering the brisk sales his new establishment was experiencing. He also forgot to tell Steve that some guys from some place called the ATF, whatever the fuck those initials stood for, had come by with some kind of "warrants" or something like that and had asked to speak to the owner of the building, who Thomas let them know was not him, but Steve. The guys seemed polite enough and left Thomas a card and a really big stack of papers, asking that Steve contact them immediately.

Steve checked the Morningwood bank account that afternoon in anticipation of sending the monthly mortgage payment off, had found it to be hovering at pretty close to zero, and became immediately concerned when he was unable to get in touch with Thomas by telephone. He decided to go over to the complex and confront Thomas about the missing funds, after taking the precaution of calling Lieutenant Blumberg to alert him of the possible *misappropriation of funds* situation.

The Lieutenant, upon hearing the news, immediately feigned concern, advised Steve to proceed with caution in confronting Thomas, and then hung up the phone, turning to his partner Louise, shaking his head in an "I told you so" sort of motion and saying in a disgusted tone, "these rich assholes never learn, they never learn".

And as Steve drove away from Morningwood in his truck that day, with the thought of possible charges looming for Thomas' having sold alcohol to minors, but without the missing 19 rents, or yet another manager for one of his many El Paso apartment complexes, he couldn't help but think of the words of Lieutenant Blumberg about hiring the incompetent and empowering the unqualified.

And he couldn't help but think to himself, "Blumberg, you son-of-a-bitch, you were right after all, I'll be God-damned!"

Touché Blumberg, touché.

Chapter 22

The Little Old Lady
From Unit Number B

**Anthony, Texas (about 20 miles north of El Paso)
1997 – Fifteen buildings later – Spanish Hills
Apartments**

Now, it's pretty clear to all of us that the letter *B* is a
letter, and not a number, and so it would probably have
been better if the little old lady in unit B referred to herself
as the little old lady in unit *letter* B, but she didn't. What is
probably also confusing, and what is not clear at all, is
whether or not the little old lady from unit *number* B ever
actually existed, but everyone who knew Steve seems to
remember her and that's what's important. Now when I say

remember, I don't mean like you remember something that definitely happened to you last Tuesday. It was more like when you remember something that happened a few years back or maybe even something you remember from a dream that you once had. And whether it really happened, or whether it only happened in a dream, the memory is still a memory of an experience you had, something that sticks in your mind and made you feel a certain way.

The little old lady had been living in Unit Number B at the Spanish Hills Apartments in Anthony, Texas for as long as anyone could remember. She was at least ninety years old but rumor had it that she had come from the old country sometime around the turn of the century, which would have made her closer to one hundred. Judging by her accent, the old country she had come from must have either been Armenia or Mexico; it was really hard to tell because her accent sounded like a little bit of both. Maybe she had stopped in Mexico for a while on her way over to Armenia, or maybe she had stopped in Armenia for a while on her way over to Mexico. Anyway, somehow she wound up in Anthony and that is where she had been since the building had first been converted into apartments. You see about 35 years ago or so the place was a chicken farm and the ten buildings that were spread over the acre or so of land that the property was comprised of were at one time chicken coups. Each of the ten buildings was a duplex, meaning they had two separate apartments in each building. So there were twenty units total at Spanish Hills.

What was unique about Spanish Hills, in terms of our story, was that it was the first property Steve had bought on his own without any help from, or involvement by, his usual partners, the Beverly Hills Boys Back Home. In truth, Steve had asked Morty if he wanted in on the deal, but Morty declined, saying the place was too small to bother with. Also, Morty didn't really care for chicken.

Although it was a little scary at first, Steve liked the idea of being an "owner." He could basically run things the way he wanted without having to check with his partners; he was the boss, or as the tenants called him – El Jeffe. And when he went to pick up the rents each month the tenants would all call out to each other "El Dueno esta aqui," which in Spanish means *the owner is here.*" Steve liked the way that sounded – *the owner*. It reminded him of why he wanted to get into the apartment business in the first place.

When Steve was a boy, probably no more than four years old, he lived in an apartment building in Brooklyn, New York. As he remembered it, it was a two-bedroom one-bath apartment with a dining room and a kitchen. It was on the second floor of a six-story brick building in an Italian neighborhood. It was nothing fancy, but it was clean, and it was comfortable, and it was home.

Every Friday morning Steve's dad would let him go with him when he went down to the building office to pay the rent. The landlord's name was Mr. Moskowitz and his office had bookshelves, filing cabinets, a supply closet and a large cherry-colored desk with a red leather swivel chair. Steve could tell by the size of his desk that Mr. Moskowitz was a very powerful and important man, maybe even more powerful and important than Steve's dad. Steve would always stand next to his dad's feet and gaze upwards as his dad would take his checkbook out of his jacket pocket, write a check out for Mr. Moskowitz and then ask Mr.

Moskowitz for something – like a light bulb, or a new sink, or even new carpet.

It was the way Steve's dad asked that let Steve know that Mr. Moskowitz was in charge; it was the same way that Steve would ask for things from his dad, who he knew was the boss of him.

When Steve and his dad would get back to the apartment, Steve would always rush through the front door like he was in a hurry to do something, walk intently over to the living room and sit down at his dad's desk, pulling out as many office supplies as he could find from the drawers and spreading them out on the desk top. For the next several hours Steve would sit at that desk and pretend that he was Mr. Moskowitz. He made notes on index cards, stapled papers together, and pretended to make important phone calls, yelling at imaginary vendors and handymen over the telephone about something they had forgotten to do or something they had done wrong.

When Steve's Mom would call him from the other room and say "Stevie, come in the kitchen and get some lunch," he would always reply in a hurried and slightly annoyed tone, "Not now Ma, I'm busy doing work business." From the moment Steve stepped into Mr. Moskowitz's office for the very first time, and the moment he saw that big red desk, he knew what he wanted to be when he grew. He wanted to be a landlord.

Now on the second day after Steve bought Spanish Hills he got his first call ever from little old lady in Unit Number B. What really struck him as strange about the call was that the little old lady in Unit Number B identified herself as

The Little Old Lady From Unit Number B. Didn't she have a name?

In a high pitched, crackly voice and speaking in a foreign accent in sentences that would go up in volume and pitch at the end of each, she began to speak, "Ello, ello? This the liddle ol laydeee from unit noomber bay. I luv evrybudeee, and yu are nice man. I just col to ask the questuns, becuz I live here for thirty-sevon years and I hear you buy the plez new again. So I joost wander, for my aparta-ment I could have the waater."

 "Water?" Steve asked.

"Jes" said the little old lady. I live here thirty-sevon yirs and I wait for the water but I still not hav the waater. I open the sink but it don't go with waater, no drip, drip. I flusha da bathrum bol, but the poop, she jus sis there, no swim around. So I don't ask much, but it is really hot for summer and I jus want the drink of wooter. So you turn on water, okay? Okay. Guudbye."

"Oh wait, just one more thing, fur de window, maybe I could get the gless?"

"Glass?" Steve asked.

"Jes, the gless," replied the little old lady. "Becuzz the window don't have the glass and it is hot for summer you know and with the no glass, the air-cundishunneng flies away like the little bird to the outside, and so it's too hot here. So yu ken send the glass for the windows. Thank you, you are niz man. Okay? Okay. Goodbye."

"Oh wait, one more thing. If it wouldn't be too much for you trouble, you cuud send the light bulb because at night it so dark and I kent see the roum to go for the walk with my walker and take the doggie for the walk. So you could send the light bulb, okay? Okay. Goodbye."

"Oh jess, one more thing. The lectric for the TV, because I like to watch the show on the TV but the plug, she has no lectric and so there is no light for the TV so the screen is too dark to see the show. So you bring lectric for the plug. Okay? Okay."

"So, to recap," Steve said, "You've lived here 37 years, you have never had water, glass in your windows, light bulbs in your apartment, or even electricity; how does your refrigerator work? To which the little old lady replied, "Refrigerator?"

Oh my God! Steve couldn't believe it. But now, Steve was the owner, and as the new owner of Spanish Hills, he promised the little old lady that he would come over to the apartment the very next day and inspect her apartment and make a list of everything that was broken and then he would fix it right away.

"Right away?" The little old lady asked.

"Right away," replied Steve. And with that being said, the little old lady thanked Steve, told him she loved everybody and told him that he was a nice man. Then she said "goodbye" and hung up the phone, saying the word "click" right before she hung it up.

At 10:00 a.m. the next day, as Steve had promised, he pulled into the dirt and gravel driveway at Spanish Hills. Toolbox and clipboard in hand, he got out of his car and walked up to the first duplex, building #1. The two doors in the front were marked with silver-colored letters, *A* and *C*. "Oh" Steve said to himself, "I get it," referring to the numbering system of the apartments, "it's an odd-even sort of thing, so the next building should contain units **B** and **D**." So Steve walked over to the next building, building # 2. The two doors in front of building #2 were marked with similar silver letters which said **D** and **E**. So where was unit **B**? Steve walked over to building #3 and those two doors were marked **F** and **G**. Still no unit **B**. And as Steve walked over to building #4, and saw the silver colored letters **H** and **I**, he really began to wonder where unit **B** was.

After checking all ten buildings, and all twenty units, **A** through **U**, he frustratingly counted out the letters of the alphabet on his fingers, realized **U** was the 21st letter in the alphabet, and then, in a moment of quiet acceptance, he made peace with the fact, that if you skipped the letter **B**, and counted **A** through **U**, that was 20 units. And since he was sure there were only twenty units because that's what it said in the escrow documents, he came to the conclusion that there was no unit **B**, letter, number or otherwise.

When the phone rang in Steve's office the next morning, he glanced at the caller ID display on his brand new phone – it read "Spanish Hills Apartments."

When he picked up the phone, a shrill high-pitched voice on the other end said, "Ello, Ello, this the little old lady from unit noomber bay, I luv everybody and you are a niz man. Why you no come? I wait fur yu all day but you no come to visit me, you don't like me no more? Pleaze come to see me becuz I really need the waater because it is so hot today."

"Also I bake you cookies."

And then Steve asked, "Are you sure you live in Unit Number B because I came yesterday but I couldn't find your unit. I checked all the units and there was no Unit Number B."

"Well," said the little old lady, "I live here for 37 years and I am pretty sure I know where I live."

Steve, figuring maybe he misheard her because of her accent, thought maybe she lived in *D* or *G* or *P* or *T*, since they all kind of rhymed. He probably just misunderstood her.

So Steve drove back down to Spanish Hills, this time knocking at first on doors *D, G, P* and *T*, and when no little old lady was to be found in these first four attempts, Steve proceeded to knock on every door at Spanish Hills. And after asking every tenant if they knew where the little old lady from Unit Number B actually lived, they all remembered seeing her, though they weren't sure when, but none of them could remember for 100 percent sure which unit she lived in, although they were all pretty confident it was Unit Number B. And when Steve asked where Unit Number B was, all of the tenants would point to a different part of the property and say "it's over there somewhere."

Starting with that second day Steve bought Spanish Hills he never stopped looking for the little old lady from Unit Number B, and starting with that second day after Steve bought Spanish Hills and until the day Steve sold the place, the little old lady from Unit Number B would call Steve every morning at exactly 10:03 a.m.

The conversation was always the same, with the little old lady introducing herself, making the statement, "I love everybody," and then proceeding with a list of things she needed. It was the fourth time she called, however, that Steve would always remember, because it was on this fourth call, when Steve asked for her phone number so he could call her back, she replied in those haunting words that became the stuff of urban legend in Highland Park, Texas.

Upon asking her for her number, the little old lady from Unit Number B paused, thought about it for a moment and then said to Steve in a questioning tone, "phone numer? I'm nut sure the phun numer because "I don't have a phone."

Chapter 2.8

Carmen Villanova and
"The Pride of the Pretty Bull"

**El Paso, Texas 1998 –Twenty-Two buildings later -
The Boys buy Promontory Pointe**

In May of 1998, Carmen Villa Valla Villanova was released from a Maximum Security Penitentiary in Utah,
where after serving two months of her 111-year prison term
on drug related murder charges, she was paroled. The story
was that her sentence had been reduced for good behavior,
but the truth made far more sense. The truth was that Ms.
Villa Valla Villanova was politically connected and when
her brother Victor, a wealthy Columbian "coffee" producer,
had donated a large sum of "coffee" money to a certain gu-

bernatorial campaign, Carmen had suddenly found herself with a full pardon and sitting on a Greyhound bus bound for El Paso Texas.

She had been assigned by her brother Victor to travel to El Paso and replace her cousin Esperanza Villa Valla Villanova as manager of four apartment complexes in the Eastwood area, Promontory Pointe being one of them. Not that Victor owned any of these complexes, but nonetheless he and the entire Villanova family, what was left of them anyway, had a proprietary interest in the management of these properties. And with the recent accidental beheading of Esperanza Villa Valla Villanova, Carmen's cousin, Carmen was needed to ensure that the tradition of the10% rule would continue on, as this provided a reliable and necessary supply of investment capital for the Villanova family to continue to expand their already burgeoning "coffee" business back in Columbia.

On the day that Steve met Carmen, The Boys had owned Promontory Pointe for almost a full eighteen minutes. She had been there for almost three months and by this time she was not only managing "the Pointe" but 10 other complexes in the neighborhood as well; not bad for a person who had just gotten out of prison just 90 days before.

Steve's first thought upon seeing her was that Carmen didn't really look like she belonged in Eastwood. She was well dressed in what appeared to be an expensive woman's business suit, her hair was meticulously styled, her nails were manicured, and the diamond ring on her right ring finger was at least a carat or more.

Nevertheless, there she was, the incumbent manager at The Promontory Pointe Apartments, the latest addition to "The Empire," and the Boys' 22nd such purchase in the area.

And as it was Steve's custom to keep on the old employees of any new complex that The Boys took over, Steve of course made Carmen the "new" manager.

And it soon became clear that this was a very good decision, as Promontory Pointe was, to date, the biggest complex Steve and his Beverly Hills posse had purchased so far, having 452 units, two swimming pools, and two large fully landscaped courtyards; and Carmen seemed to have things very much under control.

At a cool $6.5 million, it was quite the deal, as Morty bragged to his friends, because on Promontory Pointe they had financed the entire purchase price by having Steve personally guarantee the loan, which was kind of funny, because Steve didn't have anything close to $6.5 million dollars in his bank account to guarantee anything.

And so Morty went on and on, saying to his friends that he had just bought this giant cash machine for absolutely nothing down, with no risk, and even if the place "went south," it was Steve who would be "on the hook," not him. And so if something went wrong, the bank could just "pound sand." Morty just loved saying that – "Pound sand. Pound sand!" Anyway, it was the perfect deal, at least for Morty.

Now Carmen, it seemed, was a natural born leader who commanded respect and obedience, and the maintenance crew at The Pointe seemed to immediately sense this about her.

Yes, her unique experience in collection and money management techniques combined with her extensive knowledge of automatic weapons made her the ideal candidate to keep track of the massive amounts of people and cash rents coming in and out of the office on a daily basis. It also made it clear that she was definitely someone you needed to take seriously and not someone you wanted to piss off.

The tenants at The Pointe could sense this too, as on her very first day in command she had sent out a notice to all the tenants informing them of the new and improved, "$ For Don't-Follow-The-Rules" policy.

This meant that if a tenant littered outside their apartment they had to pay Carmen a $35 fine. This meant that if a window happened to get broken in your apartment, not only did you have to pay for a new window, but you had to pay Carmen a $100 fine. This meant that for any reason at all, if Carmen decided you had to pay her a fine, then you had to pay her a fine.

And to enforce this new and improved policy, Generalissima Carmen Villa Valla Villanova organized herself an on-campus police force to make sure that all the "Don't-Follow-the-Rules" procedures were enforced; but unlike her cousin Esperanza, who had tragically entrusted this task to a group of Cubans, Carmen, who didn't like the Cubans because she felt they were too "revolutionary", empowered a completely Mexican unit to get the job done.

It was just like being back in Columbia, and Carmen loved it – she felt right at home! And when Morty heard about the take-charge management policies that Carmen had implemented, Morty loved it too. It was like running that small South American Country that he and Nicki had always dreamed of owning.

Now having imposed martial law over at The Pointe and the ten other complexes in the neighborhood, Carmen had gone on to organize her new "Villa Nova Nation" by establishing a hierarchy which made the Promontory Pointe and her other ten properties a microcosm of the Spanish speaking world.

With Columbians on top, followed by other South Americans, followed by Central Americans, followed by Cubans, then Puerto Ricans and finally, at the bottom rung of the ladder, Mexicans, Carmen gave order to a formerly unruly group of complexes, and had benevolently dictated her way to financial security for herself, for Steve and The Boys, and for all of the other owners involved in the ten other complexes that she was in charge of in the neighborhood. She, like Fidel Castro and Francisco Franco – her two idols, was a hero.

As a matter of fact, within twenty-one days of Carmen taking over any complex in the neighborhood, the occupancy rate was usually up to 95% percent, collections were at 100 percent and the usual petty crime rate of domestic disturbances and minor drug infractions were down to zero. As a matter of fact, the properties were often so quiet that the El Paso Police Department would often think there was something wrong with the dedicated 911 phone line they had set up to service the Eastwood area.

And that wasn't all, the properties that only 90 days before had looked a lot like the Crestwood Apartments – a beer can and hominy-littered wasteland of entrepreneurial home-based illegal enterprises that was typical of most of the complexes in the neighborhood – didn't have one beer can, no trash of any kind on the ground outside, no cars being worked on in the parking lot, not one broken window, and all the garbage in the trash bins in the parking lot were packaged in spotless green plastic bags and neatly stacked in the center of the bin, with not so much as a piece of paper spilling out of the bin and onto the parking lot surface below. It was a miracle.

Yes, indeed Carmen had proven herself to be a much better manager than her cousin Esperanza, God rest her soul.

Now for all great leaders there is a defining moment – one which either solidifies their power or one which tears them asunder and sends them off into exile. For Fidel Castro it was the Bay of Pigs, for Napoleon it was Waterloo and for Carmen Villa Valla Villanova it was:

The Incident of the Pretty Bull

Carmen's first act as manager of any complex that she took over was always, of course, the implementation of the 10% rule. This was the rule which said that for every dollar that someone earned at a property, ten percent went to Carmen and an additional two percent went to Los Federales de Villa Valla Villanova, as Carmen's Mexican Police force came to be known.

Each morning Los Federales would collect the 10% plus 2% sales tax from all of the home-based businesses that were operating at the properties, keeping their 2 percent for themselves and kicking the remaining money upstairs to Carmen. It was a win-win situation for everyone, the tenants made money and received protection, Carmen funded her Los Federales, and Carmen served her beloved tenants and earned her benevolent dictator fee to which she was "humbly" entitled.

Just as an amusing aside about Carmen, Carmen had two phrases that she just loved to say, "En my hoomble upinyone" (In my humble opinion) and "Nu metta whut" (No matter what.) They were her "catch phrases" and not only did she love to say them, but people loved to hear her say them.

Sometimes, they would even just start up conversations with her about nothing at all just hoping to hear those seven words which captured the humble authoritarian determination that was the very essence of who she was. It was like tuning in to watch *Different Strokes*, just to hear Gary Coleman say, "What you talkin' 'bout Willis?"

As a matter of fact, people liked Carmen's catch phrases so much that they often repeated them to one another, as they did their own impression of Carmen saying them. "*En my hoomble upinyone*, I think I'll have the burrito and no matta how big it is I'm gonna finish it, *nu metta whut!*"

Yes, there was no arguing that Carmen's benevolent dictatorship had turned Promontory into a Latin utopia and all the citizens of The Pointe seemed to be happy and content; it was the perfect situation and everybody cooperated. That is except for one, and only one, time.

This one time came to be known as the "Orgullo de Bellatoro" incident and it was to become Carmen's defining moment.

Now for those of you who don't speak Spanish, the word *orgullo* means **pride** and the word *de* means **of** and the word *Bellatoro* is somebody's name which literally translates as **pretty bull**. So roughly translated, the incident of which I speak was called the *Pride of the Pretty Bull* and it went down something like this:

Now for some reason or other, Arturo Bellatoro, a Cuban refugee who lived in unit #123 at the Promontory Pointe Apartments, had not only refused to pay a $25 fine for "Don't-Follow-The-Rules" when he was caught throwing his cigar butt on the ground, but he had also refused to pay his share of the ten percent sales tax levied on his home-based cigar and cigarette manufacturing operation that he ran out of his apartment.

As Bellatoro had proudly and publicly stated in no uncertain terms to all his neighbors, he hadn't swam the 63 miles of shark infested waters from the coast of Cuba to the shores of Miami to be enslaved again, especially by the damn Columbians, which according to Arturo's Latin hierarchy that he carried around with him in *his* head, put the damn South Americans at the bottom of the rung.

No señor, no kidnapping, coca leaf-growing, plantain-eating pinchi muthafucker was going to tell him what to do. "And that was that, no matta wat!" he said, making fun of Carmen's favorite catch phrase.

Now when Carmen heard that Bellatoro was Cuban, she wasn't surprised. She knew how stubborn and arrogant those people could be, with their false pride and their sense of entitlement. And it wasn't the first time she had run up against something like this!

But, in a way, she could sympathize with Bellatoro because she knew about pride and she knew that he had lost his entire family on that treacherous swim over from Cuba,

Bellatoro being the only one to make it across without being torn apart and eaten by sharks.

She could sympathize because Carmen too, had lost most of her original family in Columbia when a rival "coffee" producer and former friend of her father's had launched a "coup de gras" against her father and the entire family, kidnapping and subsequently executing everyone but Carmen and her "brother" Victor.

Carmen had always carried around a little bit of guilt about the whole incident, since it was she who was entrusted with paying the ransom money to secure her family's release.

And although Victor had given her the money to deliver to her father's former business partner, she just couldn't let herself give in to the demands of her father's former friend.

And although kidnapping is very commonplace in Columbia, and seen as just a part of doing business, and although she knew that if she paid the ransom, most likely her family would be returned unharmed, Carmen decided to roll the dice and call the bluff, just because she didn't like giving in and because she believed that giving in showed weakness, and in a competitive business like the "coffee" business, she knew that "once you showed weakness, you lost your edge, and once you lost your edge – that was that, no metta whut!"

But alas, hindsight is 20/20 and when Carmen failed to deliver the ransom money, her father's former business partner had no choice but to execute his captives in a manner befitting the situation, a manner which he had learned from watching his favorite scene in his favorite movie,

Scarface – the famous "chain the guy up to the shower rod and carve him up with a chainsaw" scene.

And so as Carmen stubbornly looked on, and as her entire family was carved into pieces and placed into greenish-black Hefty brand jumbo CinchSak bags, her father's former business partner, a proud man himself, both reminded and warned Carmen that it was her pride that had forced his hand and that "someday, like the mighty palm, she too would break apart and tumble to the ground under the weight of her own pride and self-importance." It was quite the poetic warning indeed.

Now had Bellatoro just kept his proud Cuban mouth shut, and had he just simply refused to pay the "Don't Follow the Rules" fine, Carmen might have, for sentimental reasons, considered letting the whole thing go.

But Bellatoro had spouted off in front of the neighbors, and he had made a scene when Los Federales came to collect the ten percent excise tax, crying out for all the neighbors to hear, "Viva La Revalucion, down with Villa Valla Villanova!"

And this simply could not stand! No matta whut! His actions threatened to undermine Carmen's authority and make a mockery of her regime and he needed to be made an example of.

So when Carmen had Bellatoro brought to the office in a greenish-black Hefty brand jumbo CinchSak lawn and leaf bag that day, and when upon his arrival she had him dumped in the deep freezer in the office kitchen so he could cool off for a while, no one was surprised.

After about ten minutes in the freezer Carmen had the Los Federales let Bellatoro out of the bag and had him seated in the chair in front of Carmen's desk. As he picked ice crystals off his eyebrows, and as Carmen tapped her finely manicured nails on the large cherry desk, the two stared intensely at each other, playing a game of Latin "Pollo" to see who would speak first, for they both knew that the one who spoke first showed weakness, and as such, would not prevail.

And as visions of sharks ripping Bellatoro's beloved Anna's tattered flesh flashed through his head; and as visions of bullets being pumped into her father's smoking chest, and the sight of limbs and heads falling onto the bathtub floor flashed through Carmen's head, the two continued to stare at one another for over two and a half hours, with not a word said between them.

After all, the situation was pretty clear, what was there to say?

This wasn't about who was right and who was wrong. It was about pride. This was a battle of wills, about who was in charge, about who was going to submit, and about whose tradition and culture would prove to be the best. It was about the hundreds of years of struggle and sacrifice that had lead these two proud warriors, champions of their people, to this moment, to this place, to this desk.

And oh yeah, it was about paying the 25 dollars. And this could have gone on all day, for it was pretty clear that neither one of them was going to budge.

But as the fourth hour of this standoff went by, and as Bellatoro's furious anger and sense of outrage continued to well up inside of him, and just as Carmen was about to break a nail, Bellatoro experienced a moment that can only be described as one of suicidal release, a moment of acceptance that he would sacrifice himself for the greater good and become a martyr.

And as his hot Latin blood began to boil over, and when he could contain himself for not one moment longer, he staunchly and evenly uttered the courageous words that he knew would be the making of his imminent demise. It was the quiet battle cry of martyrdom, a cry whose tone is both sad and glorious at the same time. It was the words that would define his legacy and help to liberate persecuted generations to come.

And it was in this tragic yet glorious moment that Bellatoro began to utter the most elegant, most poetic words and indeed the most powerful words that anyone within earshot had ever heard; words that upon hearing made the Los Federales weep, and which upon hearing pierced Carmen's heart and cut her very soul.

"Ms. Villa Valla Villanova, you are like the mighty palm. You grow quickly and powerfully, as you overshadow and squeeze the life from the sunless trees below you, the fruits of your triumph burgeoning and collecting on your mighty, top heavy, stems. But as your blind ambition and your self-righteous pride leads you to greater and greater heights and add more fruit to the collection of your discontent, like the mighty palm, someday you will crash to the ground under the weight of your own self-importance."

And as tears streamed down the faces of the Los Federales, and as Carmen remembered the almost identical words of her father's assassin and former business partner, she imagined feeling the hands of her murdered family touch her cheek in forgiveness for being the cause of their untimely death.

And while time had stopped in the room for all but Bellatoro, Bellatoro stood up, pulled out his wallet, put 25 dollars on the cherry desk, and said to Carmen, "May God have mercy on your soul, no matta whut!"

And with that, he walked out of the office and was never seen again.

With the Bellatoro incident behind her, and except for a few sleepless, guilt-filled nights of regret and endless weeping, Carmen continued to successfully rule Promontory Pointe with an iron fist and everyone was happy.

The El Paso police department was especially happy since they had not received one call for service in over three months and they could spend their days patrolling Eastwood – hanging out in front of The International House of Pancakes and taking long, syrup-induced naps in the air-conditioned comfort of their patrol cars. With the exception of two gangland style executions, which coincidently happened not on the Promontory Pointe grounds, but on the sidewalk in front of the building, and which Carmen made clear to the FBI that she had absolutely nothing to do with; and a notable citywide increase in cocaine distribution and sales, everything was okie- dokie in the neighborhood, at least for the time being.

Chapter 3.1

Stan Valvo and the Beginning of the End

El Paso, Texas February 2000 – The Boys buy Crestwood

It was the deal of the century and this time Arnie was definitely *in*, probably.

"Don't fuck it up this time," Alan Blaine told Steve as Steve was getting out of the car to go up to the big negotiation.

"I'll try not to, you son-of-a-bitch," Steve told Alan, as he winked his eye to reassure him that this one was in the bag.

The Crestwood Apartments, located in the Eastwood section of El Paso, was on a list of the city's Twelve Most Worst Properties. I believe it was number seven, which is usually considered a lucky number, but it certainly hadn't been lucky for its then-current owner, the Mormon Evangelist Bruce Knapp.

Bruce, and his investor group, The Salt Lake City Boys Back Home, had purchased the building some five years prior, and had had nothing but problems since the day they bought the place, not only having structural issues with the buildings that comprised the complex, but also encountering numerous system malfunctions including the leaky chiller system pipes and faulty electrical wiring.

But even more problematic than that was the fact that they had come under fire from the City of El Paso for hundreds of health and zoning code violations which included, as Shirley Dole had dutifully alerted the City to, leaky roofs, moldy ceilings, cockroach infestation, structurally unsafe stairwells and the biggest one of all, dog shit on the grounds – lots and lots of dog shit!

The complex itself, a 352-unit consisting of 126 two-story duplexes, had been built in 1955 and was spread over 7.8 acres of land, the complex stretching over seven full city blocks.

To its credit, the complex had two distinct features which made it unique in the El Paso real estate market. First, it had a quadruple compressor chiller system which was four times more powerful than the usual single compressor system. Second, the compressor was not powered by electricity as most were, but by natural gas. These two attributes combined, at least on the surface anyway, not only presented the opportunity for optimal cooling capacity but for economy as well, as natural gas was half the price of electricity.

Being that as it may, since the day they had bought the place The Salt Lake City Boys Back Home had been looking to sell it, but there were two major obstacles to overcome before this could happen.

First of all, they owed the bank $4.1 million – this amount being more than the complex was probably worth – and second, and most importantly, there were 1073 health and zoning code violations written up and filed as liens against the property. According to the laws of the State of Texas they couldn't sell the complex until all those violations had been cured and until the four million dollars in fines associated with those violations had been paid. It was quite the predicament. If only Mr. Knapp had donated that $100,000 to the park fund as Shirley had asked him to in the first place, this all could have been avoided, but alas, hindsight is 20/20, Bruce quietly thought to himself.

Now in light of the circumstances surrounding the situation, and in light of the fact that Steve was indeed made aware of the sordid history of the Crestwood complex, why then you might ask, would Steve or anyone else in their right mind want to step into the shoes of the current owners of the place and bear the cross that Mr. Knapp and his Salt Lake City Boys were almost sure to find themselves nailed up to in the not so very distant future.?

Was it ego – the notion that Steve and his buddies were invincible, that they could somehow step into the deepest pile of shit and still come out smelling like a rose?

Was it naivety – the misguided belief that the rules that applied to Bruce Knapp and his buddies didn't apply to Steve and The Boys because they were such good friends of the City?

Or was it simply good business sense – The Boys figuring out that the land value of the 7.8 acres alone was probably worth about $5.6 million, a good $1.5 million more than the $4.1 million Bruce Knapp was looking for to get out of the deal?

Well perhaps it was a little bit of all these things.

But most of all, it was compulsion – the psychological inability that for some reason people in the "deal business" have, to be able to walk away from a deal that seems too good to be true; the deal of a lifetime, the "killer deal," the deal that will put them on the map and prove beyond a shadow of a doubt to their friends and enemies alike, that they are the most clever, adept sons-of-bitches on the planet at negotiating business deals.

And so it was when Steve answered the phone that fateful day in February of 2000.

On the other end of the line was Stan Volvo, Revival Project Coordinator for the City of El Paso.

Stan and Steve had known each other for several years and had worked together on several community projects in the past.

As he began, Stan explained that he had come across some inside info regarding the Crestwood Apartments, that info being that if Steve and The Boys wanted to purchase the property, he could make sure that they could buy the place for the exact amount of the outstanding mortgage of $4.1 million, that mortgage being fully assumable, and the down payment being zero.

It was the "no money down" part that initially piqued Steve's interest, although more prudent thinking led him to ask Stan the 10.1 million-dollar question which was really at the heart of the matter.

How about the four million dollars in fines and the liens on the property which need to be cured at a cost of an additional $2 million before the property can be sold?

And that's where things got really interesting.

"You see it seems that you and your investor group have acquired quite the reputation as being not only excellent businessmen but concerned humanitarians, interested in improving the lives of the citizens of our fine community. And based on the excellent job you and your group have done in the past with renovating and running many of the larger complexes in the Eastwood area, Councilman Jameson has instructed me to tell you that if you were to decide to purchase the complex, the City would be willing to cancel all of the 1073 outstanding violations on the property, forgive the fines and remove all the liens and encumbrances which it recorded on the property. The only stipulation being that when the property was turned over to your hands, you would make the necessary repairs."

And that's where things got really, really, interesting.

"Now the icing on the cake, in this deal," said Stan, "is that, in the end, those repairs aren't going to cost you a dime!"

"Go on," said Steve.

"That's right," said Stan. "But mind you we can't just give you the money flat out. We can however loan it to you through a federally funded 'Inner-City Remodeling Program' which provides interest-free loans for this sort of project and which provides that the amount of the loan be forgiven gradually over a period of five years, as the repairs are made."

"Thus, in the end, for the cost of a few mortgage payments over the years, you can effectively buy the property for almost free."

"WOW!" said Steve. When at the sound of hearing the word "free," he temporarily lost all sense of rational thought.

But as the buzz of the fantasy in his head gradually began to wear off, and as he returned to the world of rational thought, he did for a brief moment entertain a glimpse of skepticism as he wondered how the current owners of Crestwood, the Mormon Evangelist Bruce Knapp and his investor group, The Salt Lake City Boys Back Home, had been induced to make such an arrangement with the city that would allow for the transfer of ownership of the complex to Steve and his Beverly Hills gang. Surely such an arrangement would not be beneficial to Mr. Knapp.

And indeed, beneficial it wasn't. For after considering the one million-dollar down payment Mr. Knapp had initially purchased the complex for, and further considering the additional four million dollars in repairs that Mr. Knapp had put into the complex over the past 5 years, and further, further, considering the fact that Mr. Knapp would be handing the complex over to Steve for nothing, except for Steve's willingness to assume the current mortgage on the place, Mr. Knapp and his group of evangelist investors were going to be out about five million dollars at the end of the day.

Score:
Jewish Guys from Beverly Hills - **1**
Mormon Guys from Salt Lake - **0**

What Steve didn't know, and what he wasn't privy to, was a comment that Stan Valvo had overheard and which he had passed on to Mr. Knapp just a few days before, thereby giving Mr. Knapp a "heads up" that all was not well as far as the Crestwood situation was concerned.

It was a comment he had gleaned from being in the room and overhearing a conversation that had occurred about two weeks before at City Hall between the assistant City Prosecutor and Councilman Jameson of the 13th District regarding those 1073 civil violations that had been on the books for some time now, violations that were only punishable by fines that Knapp had failed to pay.

And as far as he could recall, Stan had overheard that the City Prosecutors Office was considering converting the civil violations to criminal ones, each one a misdemeanor which carried a maximum penalty of $5,000 and six months in jail.

Multiplied by 1073, it was not the $4,865,000 in additional fines that most concerned Mr. Knapp upon receiving

Stan's thoughtful "heads up," but the possible 536 and one-half years in jail he might spend for allowing dog shit – lots and lots of dog shit – to be present on the front lawn of the Crestwood complex.

And in absence of being willing to give up his freedom to assert his constitutional right to accumulate dog shit on his own property, Mr. Knapp, although he was given a full 24 hours to accept or decline the city's offer, graciously accepted Stan's more than gracious proposal to give his property away for nothing and return home to the salt mines of his beloved homeland, in approximately eighteen seconds.

"Let's do this deal," said Bruce.

"Let's do this deal," said Steve.

"Let's do this deal," said Stan.

"And the only catch," as Stan explained, "a minor inconvenience actually, is that in order to get all that free rehab money from the Federal government," The Boys would have to "close on the building first and then apply, since the government couldn't very well loan you money to fix up a property you didn't yet own."

"That makes sense," said Steve.

And so, with little forethought, and after just a five-minute conversation with Morty on the phone, Steve and The Boys decided they were in. And even though they probably suspected that, unlike their other properties, this place truly was a real shit-hole and an actual bona-fide slum, the deal was just too good to pass up.

And besides, Steve trusted the City and wanted to do the right thing, which was to help them and the community to fix up a slum and to make a lot of money doing it.

Yes indeed, Steve liked being a hero.

And so within three short days, after filling out some loan assumption documents with Bank of America, and after personally guaranteeing the loan, and after filing the sales tax permits with the State of Texas, and after setting up a new shell corporation to take title to the property, just like that Steve and the Beverly Hills Boys Back Home were the proud new owners of the city's seventh most worst property, and all was well with the universe.

Chapter 3.2

"Ju Fuching Bish" –
The Fall of the Great Carmen Empire

Crestwood Apartments – El Paso, Texas – February 2000 – Ten Days after Steve and The Boys bought the complex

Now had Carmen Villa Valla Villanova simply been satisfied with controlling the goings on over at Promontory Pointe, well that would have been one thing.

But when she had set up her own management company and taken over the day-to-day operations of the City's seventh most worst property, Crestwood Apartments, well she had gone way too far.

And when Steve had let her remain there as the manager of Crestwood when he and The Boys bought the place; well that was just another example of the out of town slumlords letting the "inmates run the prison".

Those were the very first words that Shirley Dole uttered just ten days after Steve and The Boys took over the ownership of the Crestwood complex, as she spoke to her friend and councilman of the 13th District, Jim Jameson, on the phone.

No! What happened over at Promontory Pointe was simply not going to be allowed to happen at Crestwood. And the real person "in charge" of the neighborhood – community activist and defender of park-less children, Shirley Dole, was going to make sure of that. Yes indeed, she was there to help and she simply was not going to go away. And an almost intolerable situation that was going on in the neighborhood was not going to be allowed to continue.

Sure, under Carmen's "rule" crime in the area had gone down by 73 percent. Sure, under Carmen's management rent collections were up, vandalism was almost non-existent, and sales' tax revenues for the city had nearly tripled. And sure, under Carmen's leadership an anonymous donation of nearly $700,000 had been given to the local school district to fund a hot lunch program, buy computers for the High School computer lab, buy uniforms for all of the junior high school sports teams and build a community playground for the grammar school kids.

But what about "Shirley's Kids?"

And what about the park that Shirley had been raising money for to honor the memory of fallen El Paso Police officer Park Parkinson? And what about all those "settle-ment agreement" donations that Sue-Ann McDonald down at the City Prosecutor's office had been collecting by get-ting all those out-of-town complex owners to give money to Shirley's Eastwood Community Association in lieu of pay-ing City Fines.

And what of Shirley's community task force to stop crime in the neighborhood which she cleverly had named S.T.O. P. E.M. (Social Travesty Obliteration Proliferation Empowerment Movement) and her task force to fight ille-gal immigration which she had named M.I.L.K E.M.(Make Illegals Leave Knowledge Empowerment Movement) and her task force to stop arson fires called F.I.G.H.T.E.M. (Fire Is Going to Hurt Them Empowerment Movement) and her task force to stop rat infestation call R.I.D.E.M.(Rat Infestation is Disgusting Empowerment Movement.)

All these task forces were receiving funding from the budgets of various related city departments and agencies, the police department, the fire department, the sheriff's de-partment, and the department of human services.

But without crime, or illegal immigration, or arson, or rat infestation, how was Shirley going to divert funds to the coffers of her community, or to her own coffers for that matter?

And how was Councilman Jameson's mayoral campaign going to get the political contributions it so desperately needed from the Eastwood Community Association if it, or Shirley, was broke.

No, this Carmen character, this corrupt, criminal, Co-lumbian Kingpin, had to go! And she had to go now, before conditions over at Crestwood got any "worse."

Shirley, the rightful heir to the treasures of Eastwood, had to be returned to her seat of power again and to her position on the throne as the Queen of the neighborhood and the defender of helpless little park-less children (as long as they weren't Mexican.)

And that's why, Shirley told councilman Jameson, that she had organized and chartered her new community task force to fight organized crime in the neighborhood, an organization she had chosen to appoint herself as the Commander in Chief, and an organization she had cleverly named "Friends United-in-fighting Crime Kingdoms Empowerment Movement" or as it came to be popularly known in its abbreviated form, "F.U.C.K.E.M."

In turn, in a phone call to the Mayor of El Paso, Councilman Jameson, in a concerned voice explained to mayor Lanza that certain Columbian elements had infiltrated the fine community of Eastwood and that these "elements," with their cocaine pushing and their kidnapping schemes, were a danger to every citizen of area, especially the children of the area. You know, "Shirley's Kids. Suffer the little children."

"Yes Jim," Mayor Lanza agreed. And with that phone call completed, Mayor Lanza was on the phone with – coincidentally – Morty's wife Nicki Gamble, a staunch supporter of the Democratic Party, whose political foundation had recently given a large donation to the upcoming *Reelect Mayor Lanza* campaign. Nicki was then, in turn, on the phone with her husband Morty, who she knew had just purchased the Crestwood complex and hired Carmen to run the place (although she did not know that she was indeed also a partner in the project), who was then, in turn, on the phone with his brother-in-law and lawyer Martin, who was then on the phone with entrepreneur Steve, who was then on the phone with his wife, who was then on the phone with the soon-to-be-new property manager of the Crestwood complex, Frank's mom Eileen, who had, after being asked by Steve's wife to come back, finally reluctantly agreed, stating that it was only because God, had, in no uncertain terms, commanded her to accept the position as the new Crestwood manager in order that she might "save the neighborhood from the evil doings of Steve and his band of Beverly Hills Christ Killers."

And so in just eight phone calls, more than completing the six degrees of separation that separate and connect everyone in the universe (including Kevin Bacon), the Great Carmen Villa Valla Villanova – the woman who had single-handedly nearly eliminated crime and poverty in Eastwood – was, as Morty loved to put it, "gonna be pounding sand" real soon.

The only real problem was who was going to go over to Crestwood and fire Carmen?

After all, Carmen was a tough character and she could be one serious bitch.

But alas, the responsibility for the unpleasant task fell in Eileen's lap.

And so, armed with a copy of The King James Bible, a mini tape recorder and a can of pepper spray that she had picked up at a garage sale just the day before, Eileen had her son Frank drive her over to the complex to confront and fire Carmen, who was herself armed with an UZI, a hunting knife and a mini-chain saw.

Well, needless to say, Carmen did not take the news graciously and the encounter that ensued came to be known as the:

"Ju Fuching Bish" Incident

When Eileen entered the Crestwood office, Carmen was sitting at her desk and she was on the phone. "Jess, that's right, tell Sosa that the money's on the way, but, en my hoomble upinyone, this Dule karackter needs to tek a permanent vecashun right awey, nu metta whut. Okay? Si."

"Ms. Carmen Villa Valla Villanova?" interrupted Eileen.

"Jes?" asked Carmen.

And then as if she was performing some kind of exorcism or something like that, Eileen began spouting words of a somewhat religious nature, commanding that in the name of Jesus and God, and the Holy Spirit, that Carmen leave the building and the neighborhood she had come to inhabit.

And then, continuing as if reading some kind of royal edict or a search warrant or something like that, Eileen continued to command, "by the power vested in me by the 2033 Monte Verde Avenue Limited Partnership, (always the stealth investors) I hereby relieve you of your duties," proceeding nervously, yet firmly to deliver the news to Carmen that her services were no longer required.

"No lunger required?" asked Carmen in a confused yet challenging tone.

"Yes, that's right; your services are no longer required. Steve has decided to terminate your employment effective immediately," Eileen said in a tone that was a little bit more confident, knowing that Steve and Morty's unquestionable authority was backing her up and was empowering her to take charge of the situation.

"Fuck Esteve, and fuck ju too, ju fuching bish. Who did ju thenk ju are, coming in chere to my office hiding behind Esteve and Señor Morty and telling me that I'm fired from my own complex, ju know with one phun call to Morty I gonna have ju beck on the strit corner, turning tricks like the cheap whore thet ju are, ju fuching cunt!" (Carmen had met Morty when after buying Promontory Pointe he came to see what the place looked like, and Carmen, being the astute politico that she was, realized that Morty was the guy with the money, and having seen *Scarface* herself 22 times, she knew that first ju get the money, then ju get the power, and then ju get the complex, and that was that, no matter what!)

"Ju want to fire something," Carmen said smacking the back of her own right ass cheek, "Ju can fire this, right after you get done kissing it, besa me mucho ju pinchi puta muther fucker bitch whore cunt."

"And ju tell Steve that if he wants to fire me, he can come here himself and tell me to my face and not to send his whore messenger woman. And until then, ju can get the fuck out of my office before I have the Los Federales put ju in the dip freeze until ju nipples break off from those tiny tits of yours, ju fuching bish!"

And then, after fining Eileen $20,000 for "Don't Follow the Rules 180 Times," Carmen dismissed her from the office and got back to planning Shirley Dole's imminent, permanent vacation.

It was a stroke of pure, absolute and coincidental luck that made Eileen look like a miracle-worker or a saint or something like that to Steve and Morty, and which raised the question that maybe she really did personally know God – that just after Eileen had left the office, Carmen's "brother" Victor Villa Valla Villanova, the wealthy Columbian "coffee" plantation owner, called her on the phone and gave her the good news that he had just procured another 1000 acres from a rival "coffee" producer.

As he explained in a jubilant tone, he needed her help in disposing of a bunch of greenish-black Hefty CinchSak Lawn and Leaf Bags that the rival "coffee" producer had left behind. And with this news, Carmen was off, back to Columbia to help her "brother" run his new operation. And that was that, no matter what!

Lucky for Eileen, and Shirley Dole for that matter, that Carmen had bigger "plantains to fry" that fateful day because as she later angrily and boastingly told her "brother," had he not called, she would have definitely needed at least three more Hefty CinchSak Trash Bags for that whore messenger woman. "Ju Fuching Bish!" Carmen thought to herself.

Chapter 3.3

"Oh! What's that I Just Stepped In?" It was Shit, Steve, An Inconceivably Huge Pile of Shit!

El Paso, Texas – March 2000 – The Crestwood Apartments – Twenty-one days after Carmen's departure.

It had been exactly three weeks since Carmen had returned to Columbia to help her brother "dispose of the trash." And by the end of day twenty-one, the section of the Eastwood neighborhood that Carmen had come to control, an almost crime-free, thriving immigrant metropolis, had pretty much returned to the state it had been before the day that Carmen had arrived almost three years earlier – a dilapidated, chaotic infestation of urban blight.

"Something needs to be done!" commanded Shirley Dole at the weekly Eastwood Neighborhood Association meeting. "How did this happen?" she rhetorically asked. "These out-of-town slumlords have only owned this place for thirty-one days and look at it, just look at it!"

As Steve and Morty walked down the parking lot of their newly acquired Crestwood Apartments, and as they witnessed the broken windows, and the buckling stairwells, and the peeling paint, and the falling roof shingles, and the burned out abandoned cars, and the pools of automobile engine fluids which had collected throughout the parking lot, and the broken cinder block walls separating their property line from the complex next door, they couldn't help but wonder if this time they had finally bitten off more than they could chew.

"Did this place look like this before we bought it?" asked Morty.

"Well Carmen was beginning to clean it up but…" said Steve.

And when they walked into some of the apartments to see what the place looked like inside, things seemed even grimmer.

Wet carpet, the smell of cat piss, broken light fixtures, leaking bathtubs, graffiti on the living room walls, water dripping from the ceilings, cockroaches scurrying across the kitchen counters, "Oh my God, what the fuck did we just buy?" asked Morty.

"Don't worry. The city's going to loan us the money to fix this place up," said Steve.

"They'd better, because this time we really stepped in it!" Morty retorted.

Steve said nothing, because there was nothing to say, Morty's perception was correct.

They had indeed stepped in it and stepped in it deep.

At minimum, Morty guessed, it was going to cost at least another $2.136 million just to make the place livable; the biggest and most expensive problems being the chiller system and the stairwells which led to the second floor landings of each of the 177 buildings at the complex.

Because the landings were made of wood, and because they had been the site for countless out-the-front-door homemade barbeque grills, they were full of charred divots and burn holes.

And because the stairs and railings were made of wood as well, they had been on many occasions, when people ran out of charcoal, a source of alternative barbeque fuel. And so pieces, and in some case sections, were torn out and missing.

And this kind of carnage wasn't something that say, a guy like Harold could take care of.

No, replacing stairs and landings on 177 buildings was a "structural" thing that was going to require a licensed contractor and a construction crew and licenses and permits and architects' plans.

And the chiller system, that was going to take an A/C guy and a real plumber, at the very least.

And these were all things that Steve and Morty weren't used to getting involved with because those types of things were not part of "the plan" — also they cost a lot of money. And so far, sticking to the plan, which was to buy stuff cheap, fix it just enough to make it "cosmetically sound," run it for a while, and then sell it had been working out just fine and dandy for Steve and The Boys, thank you very much. "It was a good thing, though," Steve thought to himself, "that Stanton White had put up an extra $2.2 million when he funded the deal," anticipating that perhaps some work might have to be done immediately. And it was also a good thing that Morty was holding those funds in his Fabric Frontier checking account so that the City wouldn't know The Boys didn't really need the rehab money they had been promised by the City, at least right away, anyway. This, Steve reasoned, would motivate the City to move things along and issue that completely forgivable rehab loan immediately and would give Steve and Morty the money they needed to renovate the Crestwood complex and make it at least livable.

And at this stage, as they looked around the Crestwood complex, it was clear that the place was not livable.

So what to do? What to do?

"Well," said Steve, "we can't just do *nothing* – there are people living here in this shit-hole and it makes us look bad that we own the place."

"Well," said Morty, "we need at least two million dollars before we can really do anything so where are we going to get the money?"

"Well, as you know," said Steve, "I made a deal with Stan down at the City Hall before we bought this place and he assured me that the City had Federal Rehab money available to loan us, interest free. Not only that, but he told me that the City would forgive the full amount of the loan if we kept this place for 5 years."

"Well," said Morty, "where's the fucking check?"

"Well," said Steve, "I filled out the loan application weeks ago and left it with Stan's office for processing. I figure it's going to take at least a month for the whole process to go through."

"So in the meantime, we have two choices. We could use the money that Stanton White put aside in the reserve fund to start making repairs or we could wait until the city money comes through and make only minor repairs in the meantime; but most importantly, whatever we do we can't appear to be doing nothing."

Now in fact, the full $2.2 million that Stanton White had given Morty was no longer present in the reserve fund in its entirety. Rather, a much smaller amount, $66,536.78 was left in the account, an amount which when subtracted from $2.2 million, equaled $2,133,440.44, a figure which will become self-explanatory as the story progresses.

And as such, unless Morty, being a multi-multi-multi-millionaire, wanted to kick in the funds himself – like that was going to happen – "Plan A" was really not an option.

Morty's explanation for this was based not on arithmetic, but on a set of beliefs he held regarding the spending of money, that being *not to*, and thus he explained to Steve:

"You see if I were to just fork over the money to the complex, well that would be cheating – it would mean that when we bought the place, we hadn't really gotten a good deal; and since to me, it's all about getting a good deal and making a success of it, ponying up the $2.2 million, whether I have it or not and whether I'm going to get it back or not, is simply not an option that I'm interested in."

So Morty opted for "Plan B," to make only minor repairs in the meantime and wait for the City money to come through.

He was especially intrigued by the part of "Plan B" which called for them to do nothing while *appearing* to be doing something. It was all *secret-agenty* type of stuff and was the kind of clever strategy that that son-of-a-bitch Alan Blaine would think of. "That rapscallion," Morty said to himself.

And so they began to formulate just such a plan to *look busy* and to look like they were spending a lot of money when in actuality they would just be slapping Band-Aids on a patient that had been in a nuclear explosion – painting the buildings, trimming the trees, putting in new landscaping, replacing old carpeting, fixing broken windows and exterminating the apartments.

Now the first thing Steve said they ought to do, before doing any work over at the complex, was to give the place a fresh new image.

After all, Crestwood was already on the city's Twelve Worst Properties list and what better way to freshen things up, than to take the complex off the list by giving it a whole new name and making it appear to be a whole new place.

"Good idea," said Morty. And after bouncing a few names around, one of them, although no one seems to remember who, came up with Woodcrest.

"Now the next thing we ought to do," said Steve, "is to pick someone to head up this 'rehab' project and make it look like a big deal."

By appointing a project czar, it will show the City how serious and dedicated we are at making Woodcrest the crown jewel of Eastwood.

Morty liked the czar concept a lot because it sounded *all political*, like he was the President of the United States appointing an energy czar or something like that.

"We need someone who's good at dealing with bureaucrats and someone who appears sincere, someone who the City will believe is really working diligently to make significant improvements at the property. As a matter of fact, it's best this person, whoever they are, actually believe that we are making *real* repairs, someone who knows a lot about City zoning regulations and very little about actual construction," said Steve.

"But aren't we going to have to pay someone with those qualifications a lot of money to take the job?" asked Morty.

And after thinking about it for a few seconds Steve said, "Not necessarily. I think my wife would be perfect."

Steve's wife had actually worked as a city attorney back in Los Angeles and was quite familiar with both bureaucracy and city politics. And most importantly, the El Paso City folks had gotten to know her while she was accepting a community service award at one of Lieutenant Blumberg's Eastwood Community Award Meetings a few years back, for some rehab work she had supervised over at Pinewood Villas.

And so with their plan *to do nothing* almost completely formulated, Morty had his attorney and brother-in-law file the necessary papers to make Steve's wife, Vice President in Charge of Rehab Construction for The Woodcrest Associates Development Corporation, LLC (always the stealth investors.)

And within two short weeks things were *looking* pretty busy at The Crest.

Sub Chapter 3.3

The Fling, the Ring, and Why Nicki Wouldn't Swallow

The Incident at Moldano's Fine Jewelers

Beverly Hills, California – March 2000 – A couple of days before Morty and Arnie were off to El Paso for their inspection tour of the newly acquired Crestwood Apartments.

Now no one will ever know for sure what happened to the money that Stanton White put aside to fix up the Woodcrest complex, but what is known is this:

When it came to the subject of swallowing, no one on the planet knew less about it, had any less interest in it, or was more repulsed by it, than Nicole Victoria Gamble.

As a matter of fact, all sex, not just oral sex, was of very little interest to her; no, it was seen as something you did every year or so in order to commemorate a special occasion and to give false hope to one's spouse that it might indeed happen again and as such there was no need for him to seek satisfaction outside the marriage.

Yes, Nicki Gamble was a member of a small group of women who simply did not like sex. That fact coupled with another fact, that Nicki's butt was flat, had led Steve's wife, a woman who did indeed enjoy sex and whose butt was not flat, to espouse the *flat-butt-hypothesis* – a postulate in pseudoscience which states that *all* woman with flat butts don't like sex.

It was Steve's wife's uncanny ability to draw definitive and all-encompassing conclusions based on a set of observations of two or less, which had earned her a PhD Degree in pseudoscience, and enabled her to form many such postulates which came to be known in the Schaefer household as *isms*. That coupled with the fact that she was a lawyer, meant that not only were her conclusions sound but that they were always right, 100 percent of the time.

That is why it came as quite a surprise when Steve and his wife learned of the arrangement in place when it came to the celebration of Morty and his wife's wedding anniversary.

The Fling:

Now it was an indisputable fact that Morton Salt and
Nicki Gamble had been married for exactly ten years now,
and it was also a fact that Morton Simon Salt had, at their
wedding, promised his beautiful wife 25 years his junior
that on each and every one of their anniversaries to follow
he would, as a token of his love and appreciation, buy Nicki
a new beautiful diamond engagement ring – an act that
would symbolize a renewal of the *freshness* of their love for
one another – so that each year of their marriage would be
like the first year, over and over and over again.

It was also an indisputable fact that Nicole Victoria
Gamble, in a like-kind gesture on the day of their wedding,
promised her gallant husband that on each and every one of
their anniversaries to follow that she would, as a token of
her love and appreciation, perform fellatio upon Morty and
when he came would finish the act by swallowing his entire
load of semen, no matter how copious the amount, and no
matter how repulsive she found it, an act that would come
to symbolize the renewal of their relationship so that each
anniversary night of their union would be like their first
Honeymoon night, over and over and over again.(Gulp!)

To date, however, neither Morty, nor Nicki had held up
their end of the bargain.

And as anniversary after anniversary came and went,
and as year after year flew by without Nicki being able to
admire a new ring wrapped around her finger, and as every
anniversary came and went and as year after year flew by
with Morty not being able to admire Nicki's lips wrapped
around his size 18EEE throbbing member, (apparently it

was true what they said about guys with big feet), it was clear that the situation had reached an impasse and disillusionment had begun to set in.

"Was this a marriage, a lifelong commitment? Or just a fling," Nicki thought to herself.

"After all, a promise is a promise. Besides shouldn't a woman such as myself, a successful woman of means, and from Beverly Hills no less, have a new diamond ring every year? And not just any ring – no(!) – one befitting my status as the wife of a multi-multi-multi-millionaire businessman! Well of course I should!" Nicki went on thinking to herself in a somewhat insulted tone.

"Besides, all the other wives of the Beverly Hills Boys Back Home got *huge* new diamond rings every year – even Arnie's wife – and Arnie was not even super-wealthy like Morty. I mean you could understand Stanton White's wife getting a new ginormous rock, but Fancy Leventhal? Why those people are practically paupers, why Arnie actually has some kind of job doing some kind of lawyer nonsense or something like that," Nicki rambled on to herself. "This is simply intolerable. No, things cannot be allowed to continue this way! It's humiliating."

Now as to why Morton Salt had not purchased the aforementioned anniversary rings in keeping with his nuptial promise, well there are many possible answers, but as usual, the correct answer is usually the simplest and most obvious one. Morton Simon Salt, although he was a multi-multi-multi-millionaire, was cheap.

And as far as he was concerned, "if it ain't broke, why fix it?"

No, that first one-and-a-half-carat diamond ring with the two baguettes on the side that he had given Nicky on their actual engagement was just fine. "No need to go overboard," he thought to himself. "Besides why buy the cow, when you can get the milk for free?"

But the truth was that Morton Salt was neither going to be getting any milk, nor giving any milk (man milk that is) in the foreseeable future, at least to Nicki anyway, unless he ponied up and delivered unto her, on this their tenth anniversary, a ring that was so grand and so glorious that it would make up for all the other nine anniversary rings that he had failed to deliver in the past.

As to why Nicki hadn't kept up her end of the bargain and had failed to deliver, or more accurately had failed to accept delivery of the outcome of her nuptial promise, is that Nicole Victoria Gamble just thought the whole idea of sex, especially oral sex, was "icky."

She did truly believe in her heart of hearts, however, that for the ring of her dreams she could, on that one extremely rare occasion, participate in an orally gratifying act.

It was this belief that Nicki held, that induced her to issue the "no ring/no sex ever and impending divorce" ultimatum, a proclamation which set this story in motion, and one which presents a possible explanation as to the whereabouts of the 2.2 million dollars that Stanton White had given Morty to make repairs over at the Woodcrest complex.

Now do not think for one instant that Nicki Gamble issued her proclamation lightly. No, Nicole Victoria Gamble was a thorough woman, a scientific woman, and a woman who would not just make demands or issue ultimatums without a great deal of consideration of the matter first. And so, before issuing her "no ring/no sex ever proclamation" she did a little research on the subject to determine the efficacy of her demand and the degree to which the act of swallowing would lend leverage to her ability to induce a successful conclusion to the situation.

And this is what she found:

Hypothesis to be tested: During the act of fellatio, it is found preferential in over 99 percent of all instances that the ejaculate be orally consumed.

She decided to test her hypothesis using a 98 percent confidence interval allowing for two degrees of freedom within three standard deviations of the mean, expecting a slightly skewed bell curve distribution when she plotted the results of her study, after determining the appropriate sample size by applying the rule of large numbers. She then would perform a regression analysis of the sample data to establish the strength of the relationship between the number of men receiving fellatio and the number of men desiring a consumable conclusion and plot the data on a graph, the resulting line of best fit indicating to her whether she should spit or swallow.

Confusing at first, as Nicki began embarking on her research, were the numerous scientific terms used to describe the male ejaculate; cum, semen, sperm, spooge, splooge, spunk, jizz, jism, pecker juice, man root extract, cream of penis, and more!

With so many choices, would Nicki, should she actually receive the ring and actually have to follow through on her promise, be swallowing the correct substance?

And was it absolutely necessary that she swallow to achieve the desired results?

Well further research suggested that it was.

For as she continued to delve into the subject she came across enumerable pornographic publications dedicated solely to the subject of swallowing: Load My Mouth, Swallow This Bitch, Sperm Suckers, Only Swallows, Big Mouthfuls, No Come Dodging Allowed, Swallow Me P.O.V., Cum Drinking Sluts, Swallow My Nut, Gobble My Goo…And these were just the top 10 such publications that she perused, all which suggested to her indeed, as they so crassly put it, that "gulping the goo", "guzzling the gravy" and "chortling the chowder", was an integral and very much desired part of the act that was referred to as the "blowjob," a term which further confused her because it brought up the question in her mind, do you suck it or blow on it?

Confusion aside, it was nevertheless clear to her that men felt strongly about and were likely to be induced to action by the idea of swallowing; and as she reasoned, her husband Morton Salt was more than likely to be no exception.

And thus, the edict was amended and reissued to read, "No ring/no sex, no swallowing, ever."

The Ring:

It was a 12.5-carat, oval shaped diamond engagement ring in a platinum setting with two one-carat baguettes on either side, the total cost of which was to be $2,133,463.22 including tax – where have we seen that number before?

The Incident at Moldano's Fine Jewelers:

Now Moldano's Fine Jewelers was located on Rodeo Drive in Beverly Hills, a three-block long shopping district littered with high-end boutiques, upscale restaurants, designer shops, and lots and lots of jewelry stores – the finest and highest end of which was Moldano's, a three-story Italian palace of a showroom that was host to kings and queens, movie stars, hedge fund managers and oil sheiks.

When the phone rang that fateful day – just two days before Nicki and Morty were to be off on their once a year trip to El Paso for their inspection tour of the great Texas Empire and to see their latest acquisition, the Crestwood Apartments – Morty answered it; it was Gloria Giancana, head "engagement consultant" at Moldano's Fine Jewelers.

Mysteriously, someone – apparently Nicki – had tipped her off as to an impending engagement celebration and a likewise impending need for an engagement ring.

She was calling to invite Morty and Nicki to a private showing of their new winter collection of limited edition engagement pieces which she was sure Nicki was going to love. "Moments like these come along once in a lifetime," Gloria said, and she was there to help see that Nicki and Morty's special moment would always be remembered.

And with Nicki listening to the conversation on the speaker phone in the other room, and with Morty realizing that she was listening, Morty graciously, but begrudgingly, accepted Gloria's invitation.

On the way over in the car Nicki reminded Morty of their nuptial arrangement, reiterated several times that the situation was in need of repair, indicated it was time he remedy the situation, and then reassured him that if he kept of his end of the bargain she would indeed keep up hers. The alternative being, of course, they could get divorced.

When they arrived, Nicki was impressed. Visiting the inside of Moldano's private showroom was like taking a trip to the Vatican. It was decorated like an Italian palace, with marble floors, ornate gold-encrusted furniture, exquisite crystal chandeliers, rare ancient urns resting on cavernlike shelves and at the center of the room – twelve spotlessly glowing, bullet-proof display cases — each containing the most beautiful, the most flawless, and the most expensive diamonds and settings that even Nicki, a woman of substantial means, and for that matter any woman, had ever seen.

Morty however, was notably less excited, and less impressed. Visiting the inside of Moldano's private showroom, for him, was like taking a trip to the dentist, necessary but unpleasant just the same.

There was one thing, however, that Morty did like about it, and that was the limitless supply of ice cold martinis and fancy snacks, particularly the honeydew melon balls, Morty's favorite, that were being passed around by waiters and waitresses, dressed in tuxedos and evening gowns as a recording of Bizet's opera *"Carmen"* ironically played in the background. It was hauntingly surreal and reminded him of Carmen, that nice Columbian lady who Steve had insisted on firing and whose absence had caused the Crestwood, he meant Woodcrest, complex to fall into a state of total disrepair. "And now where were they?" If only she had stayed perhaps he wouldn't need to fix all those Goddamned things wrong with that fucking place.

And while Morty continued to lament to himself the merits and demerits of firing Carmen, and while Nicki and Gloria discussed the merits and demerits of every type and size and shape of every diamond and every setting in the Moldano's showroom, Morty sat in the corner, downing glass after frosty glass of Bombay Sapphire martinis and snacking on delicious bacon-wrapped shrimp, mini-quiches and honeydew melon balls, consuming one of the most expensive *free meals* he was ever going to eat.

Now had he known what he was going to be up against when Gloria first called, he might have just said he was not interested, or he might have just lied and said he had already picked out a ring, or he might have just told her to pound sand and then hung up the phone!

But Morton Salt didn't know what he was up against.

No indeed, what Morty didn't know, was that in the world of fine jewelry, Gloria Giancana was a legend, a master of the deal, her secret being that she had a knack for knowing what people liked and what made them tick, and more importantly, for knowing exactly what to say in exactly the right moment.

Yes, she, just like Steve, was an expert at telling people what they wanted to hear. She also knew how to close the deal. As a matter of fact, she was the best saleswoman, excuse me, *engagement consultant*, that Moldano's had ever had.

So when Morty, a man who desperately *needed* head, and Gloria, a woman adept at *getting into* people's heads, went head to head, that fateful day in March, it truly was no contest.

Having found the perfect ring, a 12.5-carat, oval-shaped diamond engagement ring mounted in a breathtaking platinum setting with two one-carat baguettes on either side, Gloria went for the jugular and in a move that captured the strength and grace of a ballerina and the precision of a surgeon, Gloria slipped the $2,133,463.22 ring on Nicki's finger, uttered the heroin-like words which Nicki so much wanted to hear, "Honey, that looks so beautiful on you, it would be a crime to take it off. Why don't you just wear it home?" and then stared at Morty to see what he was going to do.

It was a move that left Nicki in a state of orgasmic euphoria and one that left Morty in a state of almost nauseous panic, desperately scrambling in his head for a way to wriggle out of the situation. "Oh that clever bitch," he thought to himself.

"Oh my God, I'm going to buy myself a 'Rolls' with the commission I get on this one," Gloria thought to herself.

"Oh my God, it's the most beautiful thing I've ever seen!" Nicki thought to herself.

"Oh my God," Morty thought to himself with nothing much left to say as he considered the situation.

And in a moment of quiet resignation, Morty then rolled his eyes, shook his head in disdain and said to Gloria, "We'll take it," and they were off.

The Anniversary Night

That night, in the penthouse suite of the Four Seasons Biltmore Hotel in downtown Los Angeles, Nicki and Morty began their tenth wedding anniversary celebration with a

champagne toast and a snack from the fruit and cheese bas-
ket which had been delivered up to their room by the Hotel,
"compliments of the house."

A lovely gesture of course, but one nonetheless included
in the weekend wedding package that Morty had booked at
the Hotel, at a substantial discount to boot because the Hotel was undergoing renovations that weekend, and as a result of the noise of the jack-hammers, the Hotel had lowered their rates temporarily to encourage weekend business.

It was after imbibing in the "bubbly" and indeed finishing the entire complimentary bottle of Andre Extra Dry
Sparkling White that Morty started to get romantic.

"Shall we adjourn to the bedroom, Love Chicken?"
asked Morty with a boyish almost-smile and a somewhat-
twinkle in his eye.

"Well, I suppose," said Nicki, "but let me go to the la-
dies' room and prepare."

"I too shall prepare," said Morty as he exited the living
room area of their suite and sauntered off to the bedroom.

And prepare he did, why within two seconds of his being in the bedroom, Morty loosened the belt on his silk
Thurston Howell the Third paisley bathrobe, removed his
ascot, boldly exposing his bare chest – and then proceeded
to almost completely undress, removing not only his silk
pajama bottoms, but his silk boxer shorts as well, the only
vestiges of clothing remaining being his open robe, his ex-
tra-long, extra thin, black nylon socks which completely
covered his calves and extended to just under his knees, and
his size 18EEE Gulliver-Buckle Shoes.

And as he lay down and scooted over to the middle of
the bed, fully opening his robe, and splaying each silky side

of it on either side of the mattress he propped his head up upon a decorative pillow, glanced down at his semi erect member, wondered what was taking Nicki so long, and thought to himself, "I'd better get a head start on this puppy and get things going." It had been quite a while since he had been in touch with his little friend and he thought it might be good if they caught up on things and got reacquainted.

He then proceeded to bring his hands down to his groin, wrap his right hand around the shaft of his penis, and then he began to pump. It felt real good, and it was something he hadn't experienced in a real long time, at least a couple of years.

And as he looked down at his hands wrapped around his manhood, and began to admire its growing size and the way his handiwork was getting the job done so nicely, he happened to glance at his watch which was still fastened around his left wrist and was moving up and down in unison with his stroking hands and making a little shaking sound each time he went up, and then down. Yes indeed, ten minutes had gone by and Nicki was still in the bathroom "getting ready."

"Patience old boy," Morty said to himself. "Pace yourself, it's going to be a long night."

And at this, he heard the bathroom door open, and he heard Nicki walking over from the bathroom towards the bedroom, her silk nightgown making a shuffling sound along the way. And when he looked up, standing in the doorway, there she was, wearing not a nightgown, but a wedding gown, a gown designed by famed Japanese bridal designer Yumi Katsura – a gown so extravagant that the

251

250-yard lace, tulle and ivory silk taffeta gown was adorned with over 10,000 pearls and sequins covering its layers upon layers of fabric and was decked with a five-carat diamond and 1,000 rubies, the ornate gown's cost being estimated at $8.5 million. Nicki had purchased it for herself, to match the beautiful 12.5-carat ring that now adorned her ring finger and represented the holy union that was Nicki and Morty's marriage.

Without saying a word, Nicki shuffled over to the side of the bed, the train of her gown trailing behind her, looked at Morty's already stiff shaft, bent down slightly, and put her left hand on the side of the bed for leverage, her beautiful ring glimmering in the chandelier light. Then she raised her right leg, threw it over Morty's mid-section, and let it come to rest on the other side of the bed. And then she sat there, straddling his groin at the very spot where his penis touched the lips of her vagina. And then she paused.

The head of his penis felt large, very, very large and the entrance to Nicki's vagina felt dry, very, very dry. This is going to hurt, Nicki thought to herself. This is going to hurt, Morty thought to himself. And as she closed her eyes, and let the weight of her body press her pelvis down onto his penis, and as his shaft slowly and dryly scraped its way inside her, inch by inch, until its entire ten-inch length was buried inside her, Nicki cried out in a barely audible tone, "Oooh," shook a little, and then thrust her legs downward towards the bed, thrusting her pelvis upward, and expelling Morty's penis out of her, like a drunk who had just been thrown out of a bar in the old west.

"But it only lasted one stroke," Morty said to Nicki, "Oh, I know, that's all it took," said Nicki. "You were magnificent."

And as Nicki got up off the bed and said she was going to go the bathroom and clean up, Morty looked at her with an almost pathetic "wanting" look on his face, then looked down at his rock hard, pulsing, throbbing, aching to explode cock, looked back at her with an even more pitiful look on his face and whimpered the words, "Could you?"

"Could I what?" asked Nicki.

"You know," said Morty, "help me arrive."

"Arrive where?" said Nicki "Do you have an appointment you need to attend?"

"No," said Morty, "you know….help me……come!"

"You mean with my……..hand?" Nicki asked hesitantly.

"Or? You could, you know….put it in your mouth," Morty edged hesitantly, "or not," Morty then retracted.

Nicki considered the proposition that had just been put before her, considered the ramifications of what might happen if she indeed honor her husband's request, and then in an act of unfathomable generosity, an act totally not in keeping with her personality or her disposition, she leaned back over the bed, took Morty's penis in her right hand and with the very, very, very, very tip of her tongue, ever, ever, ever so slightly licked the underside of his penis' mushroom tip, just once and then recoiled back about one foot away, like someone who had just touched a hot stove.

Well that's all it took to send Morty over the edge, and as he screamed out fearfully, "Oh God, here it comes," and as the semen began to well up inside of his shaft and began to jet its way toward the slit at the top, Nicki quickly swooped back down, gobbled his pulsing spurting cock, and proceeded to swallow every drop of the thick salty man cream that was jetting and pulsing from his member, flooding her mouth for what seemed like almost an eternity.

"She must really love me," thought Morty to himself as he heard her gulp.

"Thank God I didn't get any of that shit on my $8.5 million gown," Nicki thought to herself.

And then she smiled slightly, patted both sides of her lips with her forefinger, and went off to the bathroom to throw up.

Chapter 3.4

"A Tale of Two Cities"

El Paso, Texas – April 2000 – City Hall

It was the best of cities, Beverly Hills, California, and it was the worst of cities, El Paso, Texas – at least that's how Nicki saw it.

Now Beverly Hills is known for three things. First of all, it is probably one of the most exclusive and most expensive areas in the entire country. Second, per capita, it is host to the homes of more movie stars and rock stars than of any other city in the nation, and third, and most importantly, it was the setting for one of the most popular television sitcoms of all time, *The Beverly Hillbillies*, a show whose down-home country music theme song is known worldwide and a song whose simple yet empowering lyrics can be recited word for word by almost every inhabitant of this planet. The lyrics of this anthem have become an American icon, not only embodying the American dream with the story of a poor mountaineer who attains great wealth and social status at the hands of fate, but a story that has become a shared part of our cultural heritage, and in some ways, a national treasure. And being able to live anywhere in the world, where does Jed choose to load up the truck and move to? To the best of cities, Beverly Hills, land of swimming pools, movie stars, and oh yes, land of Morton Salt and his wife Nicole Gamble.

Now El Paso, Texas, the 19th largest city in the United States and sixth largest city in the State of Texas, is neither known for its wealth, its celebrities, nor its television fame, at least not on the same scale as Beverly Hills, anyway.

First of all, the median income for a household in the city is $32,124.

Second, it hosts the homes of only two celebrities that I know of – Robert Englund, of Freddy Krueger of *Nightmare on Elm Street* fame, and Sherman Hemsley – George Jefferson from the TV show *The Jeffersons*.

But third, and most importantly, it has not been, as of yet, the setting for any television sit-com that I know of, let alone an iconic one that embodies the spirit of the American Dream. (It was however the fictional home to the setting of the Two Pines Wedding Chapel Massacre in Quentin Tarantino's movie *Kill Bill 2*, an event which, much like the explosion of Woodcrest, sets a story in motion and has become the stuff of legends.

Now keeping in mind the tales of each of these two cities, and keeping in mind that there may have been a slight feeling of resentment or even jealousy on the part of the El Paso "powers that be" at the time, and keeping in mind also, that there may have been a slight feeling of "we're bigger and better and more important than you," on the part of the Beverly Hills "powers that be" at the time, it was not hard to guess what would happen should the two forces find themselves in, say, a meeting to discuss resolving a problem. As one might guess, the whole thing would probably turn into some kind of pissing match. But for now, let's just stick to the facts, and the facts are these:

In early April of 2000 the Mayor of El Paso invited billionaire heiress and businesswoman-creator of Nicki's Pouches, Nicki Gamble, to a small summit conference to take place on the 18th floor of the El Paso City Hall. The conference was scheduled to be held on April 7, and the subject of the meeting was to be The Woodcrest Apartments.

Now, in retrospect, Nicki thought to herself, perhaps December 7th (Pearl Harbor Day) and not April 7th would have been a more fitting choice for the day of the meeting because it was also a day that a bomb would be dropped on the heads of an unsuspecting group of people, these people being Nicki, Morty, Arnie Leventhal, Steve and Steve's wife.

Now beforehand, and in theory, the meeting seemed like a good idea to all the parties concerned. It would provide an opportunity for Steve and Morty to find out what was happening with their $2.2 million rehab loan, Nicki could make an appearance and get some good press about how she was helping out the City of El Paso, and the City could finally get that shit-hole of a building off their hands and on the right track. The whole thing sounded great and in anticipation of the meeting Nicki had a member of her staff write her a speech about helping the disadvantaged. And since Nicki was going to have a speech, Morty thought it a good idea to prepare a speech of his own, which he entitled, *My Love Affair with The City of El Paso*, which was basically a list of every building that his father Saul T. Salt had owned in the El Paso area over the last forty years.

On the day of the summit it was cloudy in El Paso and a dry wind was blowing down from Utah. Steve went to pick up Morty and Nicki and Arnie from the airport, and at Nicki's request, did not rent the usual Cadillac Deville that Morty and Arnie usually liked to be driven around in when they made their quarterly visits to view the empire. You see it was usually Morty and his college roommate Arnie that made these empire inspection trips by themselves just as they done about a month before. In fact, this was only Nicki's second trip to the fair city and on her first trip she hadn't seen any of the empire's buildings at all, she just had Steve drop her off at a local jewelry store with instructions to just pick her up on their way back to the airport.

And until Mayor Lanza had invited Nicki to the "Tale of Two Cities" summit meeting that was to take place this maudlin day in April, Nicki was not even aware that she was a partner in Woodcrest. Apparently Morty had given her a 25 percent interest in the property as an anniversary present just several days before he became aware that he would be buying her that "God damned ring," and in the excitement of the last month had forgotten to tell her about it. "Well happy anniversary Nicki," said Morty, in a slightly apologetic tone.

When Nicki and Morty pulled up to the parking garage in the back seat of Steve's Silver Chevy 3500 Truck with the Dooley Wheels and the extended cab, they were having a good time. It was like playing trucker, or working guy, or something like that, and it felt good. It was kind of like the reverse of Jed becoming a millionaire, like Nicki loading up the truck and moving to El Paso, it was absurdly funny in an ironic, reverse-Beverly Hillbilly, or even Green Acre-*y* sort of way, at least to Nicki.

And as they pulled up to City Hall, what was this outside the City Hall building? Was it a news truck? And who were they waiting for? Was it Nicki, the world renowned purse designer and founder of Nicki's pouches? Yes, it was! Nicki exclaimed, "Oh this was wonderful, a photo op of me getting out of a working man's car; the folks back home are going to get a real kick out of this." And who were all those people with signs, and banners, and who was that red haired lady with the Marge Simpson hairdo standing at the front of the group of people? Oh, this welcome was way more than Nicki had expected.

Not wanting to make a big scene, Steve decided to drive around back to the garage entrance of the City Hall building and after parking the car, assured Nicki that it would be a better idea to talk to the press after the meeting when she could heroically brief them on the progress made.

Steve and his wife, Nicki and Morty, and Arnie, then exited the truck, walked over to the elevator in the underground parking garage, stepped in and rode it to the 18th floor.

When they stepped off the elevator and walked into the meeting room, the tone was cordial, yet somber. Seated around the giant cherry conference table were about thirty City officials including Mayor Lanza, Councilman Jameson, Sue-Ann, her assistant Enrico, The Police Chief, The Fire Marshall, Lieutenant Blumberg, the City Engineer, the head of the Neighborhood Services Department, and last but not least, Shirley Dole. Notably absent from the meeting was chief building inspector Jake Jacobs, whose absence was explained by Councilman Jameson as merely an oversight.

As everyone sat down, each person at the table introduced themselves, and with the formal introductions complete, Morty began to make his speech that he had so carefully prepared to celebrate this ceremony honoring him and his wife.

"I guess my love affair with El Paso started when I was a boy."

But before Morty could get out his second sentence Councilman Jameson interrupted him and said "I think we need to clear something up here. Now as we all know, you folks have owned Crestwood, I mean Woodcrest for nearly four months, and although you told us that you were going to fix the place up, so far nothing has been done, and conditions over there are deplorable. As a matter of fact the place is a slum. So what's the problem?"

"Well Jim," Steve interrupted, "the problem is that we've been waiting on the 2.2 million dollars that Stan Valvo arranged for us, and as soon as we get the money we'll be ready to completely renovate the place. My wife and Sue-Ann McDonald have been working together to make all the necessary preparations and have gotten bids to do all the major renovation work."

"2.2 million dollars?" Jim inquisitively asked. "What 2.2 million dollars would that be? And who is Stan Valvo?"

"Now to get back to the situation at hand," Jim said dismissively, "we've compiled a few pictures of some of the blighting conditions present at Crestwood, I mean Wood-crest, and we want to know exactly what and when you plan to do something about this slum of yours."

Now "a few pictures" was a bit of an understatement. Over the last 5 and a half years, the neighborhood services department had taken over 30,000 photographs of blighting conditions at Crestwood, I mean Woodcrest – many of which were pictures of dog shit, lots and lots of dog shit. And although Steve and Morty had only owned the place for several months, these photos were now no longer pictures of five-and-a-half-year-old dog shit at Crestwood, they were pictures of Steve and Morty's brand new dog shit at Woodcrest.

Now as soon as Steve, Nicki and Steve's wife had heard Jim's question and had heard the phrase "who is Stan Valvo" coming from Jim's mouth, they realized instantly what was going on. As a matter of fact everyone in the room, except for Morty, immediately figured it out.

But Morty hadn't heard Jim's question because as soon as Morty heard the words "this slum of yours," he had mentally vacated the room, going to his *happy place* in his mind, a place where slums didn't exist, and even if they did he had nothing to do with them. "This is not what I signed up for," he later told Steve after the meeting was over.

And what was it that Steve, Nicki, Steve's wife and everyone else in the room, except Morty, had suddenly realized?

That Steve and The Boys had been set up, of course, that there was no rehab money and that it had been Jim's intention all along to induce Steve and The Boys to buy Crestwood, and then to "wrangle" them into fixing up the place using their own "dime," or twenty million dimes as the case may be.

And as Morty rocked back and forth in his chair thinking happy thoughts and pretending he was back in his office in Beverly Hills, Nicki, who wasn't a happy thoughts sort of gal went into full-on bitch mode and began to explode into a tirade of righteous indignation as she blurted out , "What do you people think I am, an idiot? It's obvious what is going on here."

"Are you so stupid, Jim, as to think you are going to 'shake us down' for $2.2 million? And what kind of crap is this anyway? "Do you think I'm going to let myself become the victim of your little conspiracy?

And what is especially distasteful, Jim, is that it is not some sleazy con-man who is trying to cheat us – I'm used to that – it's a City Councilman, you Jim, a trusted City official using your position of authority, and the City's legal system to advance an agenda that is at best immoral, and at worst, illegal. The whole thing is just perverted."

This is not the way we do business in a **real** city like Beverly Hills. Have you hicks ever heard of a concept called integrity?" she asked.

Well as it turned out, Jim Jameson was not totally concerned with the whole integrity thing but he was concerned with the whole getting-elected-Mayor thing and so far his plan to strong arm out-of-town landlords had been making him very popular among the voters. It was – he hoped – the very ticket that was going to get him elected Mayor in the next election which was coming up soon.

After all, over the last several years, at almost no cost to the city or to the taxpayers, Jim had, with the help of

Shirley Dole, raised over six million dollars to renovate slum properties in the greater El Paso area. His ability to influence out-of-town landlords to "donate" money to these projects, even when it made no economic sense for them to do so, was part of his and Shirley's legacy, and it made him one of the most popular City Councilmen ever.

Indeed, Jim's plan was perfect because it relied on two of the most basic of human instincts, greed and survival.

You see, as far as greed was concerned, Jim had learned that once a landlord – especially one of the little guys – had invested his life savings into buying a building in East-wood, there was no way he was simply going to walk away from his investment, especially if saving the whole thing simply involved throwing a little more good money after bad.

And as far as survival was concerned, no landlord – especially among the little guys – was going to risk going to jail for some zoning or health violations on their properties. Heck, just hiring a lawyer to defend you against such charges was going to cost a small fortune. No it was just easier to kick in some money, sign whatever form of settlement agreement the City wanted you to sign, and live to fight another day.

And as far as Nicki and Morty were concerned, Jim was sure that folks like them, who were *not* little guys and who had shitloads of money already tied up in the neighborhood were not simply going to walk away either. Surely they would make the logical choice to put up another $2.2 million to fix the place up so they wouldn't lose the entire project.

Well Jim couldn't have been more wrong!

You see Nicki and Morty didn't think like most people.

No, Nicki and Morty had their own sense of basic human instincts which didn't, to Jim's dismay, include greed or survival on their "top ten" list. It did, however include:

1. The need to feel important
2. The need to be right
3. The need to tell other people what to do, and
4. The need to get their own way *all* of the time

And as far as Jim trying to strong-arm them into coughing up some cash, well that just didn't address any of those needs on Nicki and Morty's *Top Four Reasons to Get Out of Bed in the Morning*.

No one, and I mean no one, was going to tell Nicki Gamble what to do or how to do it, especially some "two-bit hick politician con-man from some 19th-rate city like El Paso, Texas." No siree Bob!

As far as losing money was concerned, Nicki and Morty had spent more on their anniversary celebration than they had on investing in buildings in Eastwood. Besides, it was for the most part other people's money at stake anyway. And as far as Jim's threats of criminal charges for zoning violations, well Nicki had teams of lawyers on retainer just waiting to get to work fighting that "trumped-up bullshit." And besides, as Nicki was quick to point out, she was just a limited partner. If they wanted to go after someone they should go after Steve, after all "he's in charge."

And so what started out as a simple meeting at City Hall to settle some controversy about some shit real estate deal gone awry and which could have been settled with Nicki writing a check for about the same amount of money Morty had just spent at the jewelry store, the whole ordeal escalated into a gigantic interstate pissing match to see who was going to get their way – a tale of two cities locked in mortal combat, with Steve caught in the middle.

And so as lieutenant Blumberg was showing Steve's wife pictures of dog shit on the Crestwood, I mean Woodcrest, lawn, and as Morty rocked back and forth in his chair saying over and over again "there's no place like home, there's no place like home," and as Arnie continued to point out to anyone in the room who would listen to him that he definitely "was not in the deal," Nicki stood up, grabbed Morty by the ear and said "Jim, keep the fucking place, it's yours, as a matter of fact keep the whole fucking neighborhood."

And with that, Nicki dragged Morty out of the conference room by the ear, with Arnie following them closely behind, led him into the elevator, and down to the first floor lobby, where she told him, "Your days of playing landlord are over. When we get back home tomorrow I'm going to call Martin (their attorney and coincidentally Nicki's brother) and donate every single fucking building we have in El Paso to charity. I'll be damned if I'm going to let this mess up my run for congress."

"Yes, Love Chicken," said Morty. "They can all go pound sand."

"I definitely wasn't in this deal," said Arnie.

"They're fucked, they're going to take it in the shorts," said Scott Brawny, when he read about it in the paper.

"I'd like to take it in your shorts," said Enrico Corleon to Maria Rodriguez Sanders Corleon.

"Does this mean we can start writing up more citations for Crestwood, I mean Woodcrest?" said Sue-Ann McDonald to Steve's wife.

"Where the Hell is Stan Valvo" said Jake Jacobs to Maria Rodriguez Sanders Corleon.

"Where the Hell am I"? said Stan Valvo to himself, wherever he was.

"Don't fuck it up this time," said that son of a bitch Alan Blaine who had just called Steve on his cell phone.

"I love everybody" said the little old lady in Unit Number B back at Spanish Hills.

"HHHHHHHHHHHA HHHHHHHHOOOOOOOOO!" said John Hu as he and Wilbur were stowing tax and stamp-free cigarettes into the trunk of John's new Mercedes back in Hong Kong, which he hadn't made a payment on since he bought it over a year ago.

"Who do I make the check out to?" said Stanton White to his wife.

"Those fucking Slumlords," said Shirley Dole to her husband.

"Ju Fuching Bish," said Carmen to some guy she had just stuffed into a Hefty CinchSak back at her "coffee" plantation in Columbia.

"What is to become of us?" asked Mary back at the M.M. in Las Vegas, which had just been sold by Mr. B for the 39th time in 39 years to some new idiot.

"One more year to go before I can get my back paychecks," said Frank to his sister Jenny who had moved in with him at Pinewood Villas because her husband had just beat the shit out of her yesterday and this time she definitely wasn't going back to him, until he said he was sorry.

"What's that you bought at Eileen's garage sale?" said Harold to Andy.

"It's some kind of sound listening thing, and it might come in handy someday," said Andy to Harold.

"The apocalypse will be coming any day now," said Eileen to Joey Poney.

"Any day now, that's like a really long time like an hour or like even 24 hours," said Joey Poney.

"We only need to sell sixteen more refrigerators before we'll have enough money to pay for little Gabriel's operation, said Victor to his wife Amelia.

"Bend over," said Gabby the Ass Dentist in her new office in another complex just down the block from Woodcrest.

"Shut up and get in the van," said V to one of the new soon-to-be Woodcrest tenants.

"Where's my tools?" said Norris to his wife Anna Belle.

"What did you say?" asked Anna Belle to Norris because she couldn't hear him because she was deaf.

"I'm going to need a new typewriter ribbon," said El Joto to V.

"I'm going to need to sue somebody pretty soon because I'm running out of money," said Harvey Mendel to his new consulting client and then proceeded to spout words of wisdom about guys with beards, and Indians and buffalos, and experts knowing the least and so on and so on and so on.

"I wonder if Steve and Morty are going to buy anymore buildings in El Paso," said broker Bob to himself as he was having lunch at Dave's Famous Barbeque and figuring out how he was going to spend his commission check he had earned from the purchase of Crestwood, he meant Wood-crest.

"Thank God it's not me sitting in that conference room at City Hall," said the previous owner of Crestwood, he meant Crestwood, the Mormon evangelist Bruce Knapp, to his congregation at the LDS Temple back in Utah.

"Looks like we're going to earn some serious legal fees from this one," said Steve's team of Mormon attorneys back in Highland Park.

Only Steve and his wife were left sitting at the table to face the wrath of the entire El Paso City lynch mob that was seated around them back on the 18th floor of City Hall. Morty, Nicki and Arnie had made their way down to the street, hailed a cab, went to the airport, got on a plane, and went back to the decent, civilized world of Beverly Hills, where things like this didn't happen.

And upon touching down at LAX, and feeling the comfort of the warm California ground beneath their feet, they vowed never to return to that hick cowboy wasteland again, swearing to themselves and to the world that the City of El Paso would never see another red cent from the likes of them, and that Woodcrest, or Crestwood, or whatever the fuck it was called, and the whole neighborhood of East-wood could fester and rot in the hot Texas sun, and "Fuck you Jim, fuck you Jim, fuck you!"

And so it was, the Tale of Two Cities – Beverly Hills, California and El Paso, Texas.

"There's no place like home Morty, there's no place like home."

Chapter 3.5

I'm On It

El Paso, Texas – April 8th - The Very Next Day

When the call came in, Jake Jacobs - Chief City Building Inspector, was sitting at his desk, polishing his shiny new silver Inspector's Badge.

"Jake, we need to see what's going on over at that new place *Woodcrest* immediately. I've heard a lot of complaints about code violations over there, especially the dog shit, lots and lots of dog shit," said assistant City Prosecutor Sue-Ann McDonald.

"I'm on it" said Jake as he saluted a picture of his late father, Randy Jacobs, that was hanging on the fabric wall of his 5 x 8 cubicle at El Paso City Hall.

When the call came in, Martin Gamble, Nicki's "big-time big-city" lawyer brother, was sitting at his desk polishing his shiny new gold *Litigator of the Year* plaque.

"Marty, we need to see what's going on over there at Woodcrest immediately. I've heard the City's setting us up to take the fall over some old code violations over there and it's bullshit, lots and lots of bullshit," said Nicki Gamble.

"I'm on it" said Marty, as he saluted a picture of his late father, Leonard Gamble, that was hanging on the cherry paneled wall of his office at Gamble, Tumble and Drye, his extremely prestigious Beverly Hills law firm.

Yes, the machinery of war was in motion, and as Jake set out to begin gathering evidence to help the City prove beyond a shadow of a doubt that Steve and Nicki and the rest of the Beverly Hills clan were indeed slumlords who needed to be taken down, Marty set out to begin gathering evidence to help Nicki prove beyond a shadow of a doubt that not only weren't they slumlords, but they didn't even own any buildings in El Paso in the first place, which thanks to "stealth investing" was, in a convoluted way, true.

"We need to get out of that neighborhood completely, Mart, can't we just donate every single one of the buildings to charity and be done with it?" Nicki rhetorically asked.

"I'll look into it, Nick," replied Martin, and then he began rifling through a list of non-profit organizations that his family foundation had donated money to in the past to see if maybe any of them would be an appropriate recipient for such a glorious gift.

"We need to get them out of that neighborhood completely, Jake, can't we just condemn every single one of their buildings and be done with it?" Sue-Ann McDonald rhetorically inquired.

"I'll look into it, Sue," replied Jake, and then he began rifling through a list of buildings and building owners in Eastwood in order to figure out which complexes in the neighborhood were indeed owned by Steve and Nicki and the Boys.

Now what Jake didn't know, because he was pretty new on the job, was that the City already knew exactly, down to the last piece of dog shit, what was going on not only over at Woodcrest, but at every single other apartment complex in the neighborhood. Yes, they had meticulously compiled evidence of blighting conditions at almost 400 complexes in Eastwood over the last seven years. And 500,000 photographs, 300,000 citations, and 1,250,000 911 calls later, they had come to the same conclusion that all those unfortunate "out-of-town" owners eventually had come to. The neighborhood was an "unruly, uncontrollable beast" that at best you could ride for a couple of seconds before being hurled to the ground and then stomped on.

This was the reality of the situation, and it was scary.

And what was even scarier was the fact that it was beyond the City's resources to really do anything much to improve things. No, the area's problems were like a bleeding wound that required a tourniquet but all the City had to patch it up with were a couple of Band Aids.

The "illusion of control" was the best that the city could hope for and this was a reality that certainly wouldn't sit well with the voters if they were aware of it. Mayor Lanza knew this, Councilman Jameson knew this, Sue-Ann McDonald knew this, Judge McPherson knew this and anyone else on the City's payroll that relied on the electoral process to secure their jobs knew this. The only ones who didn't know this were the 200 or so civil servants like Jake, who worked at the Neighborhood Services Division, who did their jobs day after day, collected their paychecks, and didn't think much about the "big picture", aahh, the bliss in believing that what you're doing actually makes a difference.

So, as far as Jake collecting evidence at Woodcrest, well that was just an "exercise in propriety."

After all, the City had already written up 1073 civil health and safety code violations on the property when it was still called Crestwood, and had been in and out of court with the property's former owner, the Mormon Evangelist Bruce Knapp, for the last five years.

No, the folks down at City Hall knew exactly what was going on and what their next step was, and now it was just a matter of papering the file.

The only one who didn't know this was Jake, and it was no coincidence that nobody happened to mention it to him, because information like this was on a need to know basis only, and at the instruction of Councilman Jameson, Jake didn't need to know.

So when Jake went to research the property history of Woodcrest, as Jake was a thorough inspector and wanted to get all the facts before actually going out to the place, Jake found that the complex was only six months old. Now had Jake looked up the history of Crestwood, and not Woodcrest, Jake would have gotten all the facts. But alas, no one told Jake that there was a Crestwood file.

And now armed with the misinformation that Woodcrest was only six months old, and having *sufficient cause* to inspect the property based on the numerous complaints launched by Shirley Dole, and having been appointed by Sue-Ann McDonald to head up the special investigation into the whole "Beverly Hills Slumlord Situation," Jake headed out in his brand new white Chevy Cavalier inspection vehicle to "get a handle on this puppy," and just in case he brought along eleven citation pads, containing 100 blank citations each, and oh yeah, a picture of his dad which he kept in a small silver badge-shaped picture frame on his desk, just to remind himself that terrible things can happen when code violations exist.

Meanwhile, back in Beverly Hills Nicki's brother Martin had just gotten off the phone with Habitat for Humanity, a non-profit organization that builds or rehabs affordable housing for low-income families; the folks down at Habitat, regrettably informing him that the Woodcrest complex was neither fit to be a habitat for humans, or any other of God's creatures and that they wanted nothing to do with a shithole of a place like it, and that they weren't interested in any other buildings that Nicki and the Boys owned in the Eastwood area either.

It was the 17th similar response that Martin had gotten that morning from a variety of charitable organizations, all of whom suggesting they weren't interested in going near an area like that and wouldn't touch the Woodcrest complex with a 200-mile pole.

When Jake arrived at Woodcrest he had to double-check the address that was listed on the property information sheet he had pulled up on his computer. The place didn't look like it was only six months old. As a matter of fact, it looked like it had been built in the fifties, showing significant signs of wear and tear, and having the same layout and construction style as the rest of the buildings in the neighborhood, which had all been built at about the same time. No, this was the place, 4252 Monte Verde Avenue.

Jake's first thought was that maybe the new owners, since they were from Beverly Hills – "and you know how eccentric those rich people can be – especially Californians," had constructed the place to be an exact replica of a fifties building, you know, so it would fit into the neighborhood more easily. But then why, if the place was new, were there so many obvious code violations? Surely no one would be so eccentric as to build exact replicas of code violations.

Especially exact replicas of dog shit, as there were lots and lots of pieces of dog shit.

But alas, violations were violations – replicas or not – and Jake's job was to write citations for violations that he found. And upon giving the property a quick once-over, he knew there were hundreds, if not thousands, of violations to be found. This was going to take him all week, Jake thought to himself, and that was just for the exterior of the building. No, Jake was going to need some help. Jake was going to need a whole lot of help.

And so Jake got back into his brand new white Chevy Cavalier, and drove back to the office to try and assemble a team of inspectors to go back out with him to Woodcrest the following day.

And oh yeah, he was going to need more ticket books, lots and lots of ticket books.

Chapter 3.6

The Cheese Stands Alone

El Paso City Hall – May 2000

"I've asked you to this meeting to see if we couldn't come to some kind of resolution to the whole Woodcrest situation," said Sue-Ann McDonald to Steve and his wife. "I know you're in a bind and I'm here to help."

But "being in a bind" was a slight understatement that didn't even begin to describe the world of shit that Steve and his wife were in, not to mention the sense of betrayal that Steve was now beginning to feel since Morty and Nicki had "left town never to return."

It had been almost two months since the City and Nicki had declared war on each other at the Tale of Two Cities meeting in April and since then not only had Morty refused to answer any of Steve's phone calls, but he had drained the Woodcrest bank account of all but $10,000, leaving Steve to manage a 352-unit complex – a complex whose water bill alone was $30,000 a month – with petty cash and a skeleton crew of maintenance guys whose paychecks were likely to bounce any day now if Steve didn't get some real money soon, and oh yes, of course, there was the new manager, Frank's mom Eileen.

Eileen had been spending quite a bit of money lately over at Woodcrest on the complex's Home Depot charge account, and news of the bargains that could be had at one of Eileen's Saturday Morning Yard Sale Extravaganzas were reaching as far as Las Cruces, New Mexico some 41 miles north of El Paso.

What with all the excitement and the hustle and bustle of her Saturday morning open air bazaars, tenants' reports of a strange odor seeping up from the ground in the north end of the complex had gone all but unnoticed by Eileen who simply had put the "Maintenance Request Forms" she received on her desk in a big pile that she intended to get to eventually when the "busy season" was over.

Weird comments about a little blue flame that came out of the ground when you held a lighter close to it were also circulating, especially among the maintenance crew, but Eileen didn't have time for that kind of foolishness and simply told Andy, who told her about it, to just mind his own business and get back to work.

Now as Sue-Ann went on to explain to Steve and his wife, she had been trying to locate Morty and Nicki for almost two months but had no success. It was infuriating to her that she had been unable to serve them with the 1073 civil citations that she had had Jake issue on the Woodcrest property and commented that it was very "unsporting" of them to keep dodging her attempts by continually going on vacation out of the country. Even if they had been around in Beverly Hills, and not been on vacation, she probably wouldn't have been able to serve them anyway, since the only address she had for service of process was Morty's office in that non-descript brick office building on Wilshire Blvd. in Beverly Hills, a building which not only had no number markings on the exterior front entrance, but had no markings of any kind on any of the 50 interior office entrance doors that lined the hallways on each of the five floors of the building.

It was for this reason, she apologetically explained, that she had Jake re-issue all of the 1073 civil citations, a list of code violations which carried with it a possible fine of $2,350,000 and a possible mandate of 800,000 hours of community service. And who had Jake reissued the citations to?

"Well I hate to do this, but here you go," said Sue-Ann, "I hope Jake spelled your names correctly."

"But we aren't even the owners of the complex," said Steve's wife defiantly, "How can you name us as the responsible parties?" Steve's wife, an attorney, was pretty sure they really couldn't do that.

"Well, you're probably right, we probably can't do that," said Sue-Ann. "But by the time we sort that out in court it will be another six months, and well, you know six months of legal fees – that's a lot of billing hours that you're going to have to pay for. So why don't we just cut to the chase and find an appropriate solution that will appease all of the parties concerned?"

"Now I have taken the liberty of preparing a draft settlement agreement for your review and approval," Sue-Ann continued. "In return for your signing the agreement, the city will cancel all 1073 citations. By signing, you agree, as the General Partner, to stipulate to certain requirements regarding the maintenance and rehabilitation of all 22 of the complexes which you and your partners have various interests in the State of Texas. This includes, of course, the Woodcrest complex and any other buildings that you or your partners have ever owned in the past or plan to ever own in the future, forever and ever, amen."

It was a deal of biblical proportions and it reminded Steve a lot of a certain consulting agreement he had once signed with a certain poker player named Shmengey Mignone; the reminiscence of which caused him to long for the days when life was simple and he could bask in the comfort of his safe, boring corporate job. But alas, those days were over, and here he was, faced with a hideous dilemma, that not only threatened his financial security, but his very freedom as well.

You see, enumerated in the 420-page settlement agreement that Sue-Ann had given Steve and his wife 24 hours to review and sign, were over 3000 covenants, conditions and restrictions which for the most part required that the Partnerships agree to commit to spend, at the City's discretion, an *as of yet undetermined* sum of money to maintain and rehabilitate each and every one of the 22 properties that Steve, his wife, Nicki and The Boys had anything to do with.

And the penalty for failing to comply, once Steve had agreed on behalf of the partnerships and signed the agreement, was for Steve to be found in contempt of court and thrown in jail until such time that he could convince the Limited Partners to comply with the terms of the agreement and kick in the extra money that the City decided they should kick in; Steve's power as General Partner to do so being non-existent since anybody who knows anything about the law knows that the most fundamental principal of corporate and partnership structure is the concept of limited liability on the part of stockholders, LLC members, or limited partners. It is the bastion of American capitalism and the very concept that investment in our economy is based on.

It was unlikely that the whims of an Assistant City Attorney of a small southwestern city could revamp the workings of the entire American economy as we know it; nor was it likely that the desperate beseechings of a lone General Partner caught in a sea of financial desperation were going to stir the sympathies of his investors (who after realizing the party was over were probably not going to be interested in throwing any more good money after bad.)

No this kind of deal had probably worked for Sue-Ann in the past, on the little guys, but Steve and his group were not the little guys. They were sophisticated investors from Beverly Hills who, above all, knew how to preserve their own wealth and stay anonymous.

And there was no doubt that even if Steve could get Morty on the phone ever again, and were to be able to deliver his futile request that Morty raise more money from the partners for complexes they already owned, there was no doubt in Steve's mind that he would be instructed to "pound sand."

And since, if he signed the agreement, he would be pounding sand at the County Jail, he knew that signing the Settlement Agreement was not an option.

What to do? What to do?

"Sue-Ann," said Steve, "the agreement sounds like an excellent solution but it is 400 pages long, so before I sign it, I think my wife and I should read the whole thing. Can we meet again tomorrow afternoon to finalize the arrangement?"

"Yes, of course, but remember, I must have this signed and on Councilman Jameson's desk by 5:00 p.m. tomorrow before the City's offer expires."

And with this being said, Steve, who had no intention whatsoever of even reading the Agreement, let alone signing it, put the 400-page "Contract with the Devil" in his briefcase, stood up from the conference table, shook Sue-Ann's hand, and walked slowly towards the door with his wife following close behind him.

The stack of 1073 citations remained sitting on the conference table where Steve and his wife had "been given" them just ten minutes before. They had taken great care not to look at, acknowledge, or come into physical contact with the citations in any way, thereby, at least in their minds anyway, creating ambiguity about whether or not they had actually "been served" with the citations, a seemingly unimportant technicality to the lay observer, but an issue of overwhelming importance to the two lawyers in the room, Sue-Ann McDonald and Steve's wife.

Chapter 3.7

The Gunderson Affair

Country Club Estates (the really nice part of El Paso) - June 2000

It had been ten months since Steve had moved with his wife and family from California to Texas and had set up shop in a lovely 3-story 5-bedroom home that he had rented from a fellow named Gary Gunderson.

The house was located in an upscale area of El Paso called Country Club Estates, in a gated community with its own golf course, its own man-made lake, and its own club house. It was very nice, in a *Stepford Wives* sort of way and it was close enough, although not that close, to the neighborhood of Eastwood, so that Steve could effectively manage the burgeoning real estate empire that he was building without having to commute back and forth from California.

And until the day of The Tale of Two Cities Meeting, Country Club Estates was the best of all possible worlds for Steve.

But the winds of change had blown, and as the Woodcrest situation slowly festered, Steve's idyllic life in the utopia of "the Estates" had turned into a relentless existence of sleepless nights, broken dreams and the never ending sound of process servers knocking at his door.

It was clear that this couldn't go on, and most importantly it was also clear that because Steve hadn't signed the City's settlement agreement, things were just going to get worse. It was not clear however whether or not Steve and his wife had ever "been served" with those 1073 citations and as such, Sue-Ann's boss, the Senior Assistant City Attorney, instructed her to "re-serve" them at Steve's home in Country Club Estates.

It had been almost a week since Steve had failed to show up at City Hall with the signed settlement agreement and seeing as that Steve had neglected to return any of Sue-Ann McDonald's phone calls, it was pretty clear to Sue-Ann McDonald that she had been misled and that extreme measures would have to be pursued.

Yes, it was inevitable that the Woodcrest situation was going to escalate, and now it was not a question of *if* but a question of *when* the City would raid the complex and shut it down; and with Steve and his wife being the only "non-anonymous" and "reachable" members of the Beverly Hills Clan since they lived right there in El Paso, the blame for the whole fiasco, not to mention the pound of flesh that would have to be "exacted", would no doubt be coming from them.

There was only one thing to do, at least according to Steve's way of thinking, and that was to leave town. But he couldn't just abandon the entire empire. Apart from Wood-crest, which was definitely a money pit and definitely a slum, the other 21 buildings in The Boys' portfolio were big profit makers, and condition-wise, not that bad. And besides, even though Morty and Nicki had forsaken him, the other members of The Boys were still along for the ride, and Steve felt a sense of duty to them, especially to Alan Blaine, to protect their interests, as well as Steve's own.

The solution seemed simple, to set up shop in Las Cruces, New Mexico, just forty-one miles from the Texas border – near enough to El Paso that Steve could still effectively run things but far enough over the border that the City of El Paso would find themselves out of their jurisdiction, making it difficult, if not impossible, to serve Steve with any more lawsuits or citations.

There was one problem though, actually an extremely small one, that Steve was sure could be easily handled. There were still two months remaining on his lease with Gary Gunderson for his house in Country Club Estates. What ensued from this situation came to be known as:

The Gunderson Affair

The petty tyrannies of self-righteous cowards and the authority they hide behind were to Steve, the worst of all of the evils of mankind. Those petty controlling souls, who seek to enslave others in their miserable little kingdoms were, in Steve's eyes, the true real-life villains.

STEVE O.

We all know them, the section chief, the shop foreman, the assistant principal, the shift commander, the building inspector, the gym teacher; all of them, with their self-serving agendas guised in the righteousness of title.

And it is for this reason, and this reason alone, that even in an especially tumultuous and tense period in Steve's life, when he had real problems to attend to, real dragons to slay, real cities halls to fight, and real families to take care of, that he chose – no, he delighted in – engaging Gary Gunderson in the Gunderson Affair.

Now when you think of an affair, you usually think of a complicated and elaborate situation, like in the movie the *Thomas Crown Affair,* a drama filled with controversy, intriguing relationships and unforeseen twist and turns. But the Gunderson affair contained none of these elements. It was simply a dispute over the early termination of a lease. And if the truth be known, Steve could have ended, if not completely prevented at the outset, the whole affair, by simply cutting Gary a check for twenty-four thousand dollars, which at the time, was not a whole lot of money to Steve.

And if only Gary Gunderson had realized that, before he had escalated the whole thing into "a nefarious conspiracy of a secret society to take over the free world as we know it," he could have saved himself a lot of heartache. But to Gary, it was the affair of the century. And even though looking back he realized that he probably should have just cut a deal with Steve in the first place and let the whole thing go, he secretly knew in his own mind that given the same circumstances again he would be compelled by his very nature to play it out in the very same way.

Yes, Gary was indeed a most inflexible fellow, an odd fellow to say the least, who spent the six warmer months of the year working as a commercial fisherman off the coast of Alaska, an extremely lucrative but dangerous undertaking, and the other six cooler months, working as the assistant City Attorney for Socorro, Texas a small metropolis of about 32,000 people located 20 miles east of El Paso in El Paso County. This undertaking was neither lucrative nor dangerous, but it did give Gary something to do during the fall and winter.

Now what was strange about this employment situation was that positions like Assistant City Attorney are usually considered to be full-time jobs, not part year gigs. It was kind of like being a brain surgeon on the weekdays, and being a plumber on the weekends. It was really odd. But then, Gary was really odd.

Anyway, odd or not, the situation suited him, it gave him control over where and when he would be working, and it gave him a constant structure to his life, a road map, if you will, with every month laid out in the greatest of predictable detail. It made him feel safe and very much in control, and for Gary, being in control was the most important thing in life. This was especially evident in his relationship with his wife Jenny.

Jenny and Gary had met in college at Washington State. Go Huskies! That is what it said on the matching sweatshirts that they both wore on the weekends. Go Huskies! Jenny had been a psychology major and a cheerleader for the Washington State football team and Gary had been a double-major, pre-law and Marine Biology.

When they met, what Gary liked about Jenny the most was her joyful, bubbly personality.

And what Jenny liked about Gary was the way he needed to organize things and take charge. It made her feel safe knowing that he always had a plan and that he could take care of her and provide order and structure to her life. That, and also the fact, that Gary's behavior was so predictable, that when Jenny and Gary were having sex, for example, she knew how long it took Gary to finish – 3 minutes and

14 seconds, and as such she could, if she was tired, take a short 3-minute and 7-second nap, before awaking with an ample seven seconds to spare so she could have enough time to prepare herself to fake a good orgasm.

Now Gary and Jenny had one child together, a two-year-old boy Sven, and Jenny was now five months pregnant with her second child, a girl, Inga. Gary had already named her because, as you might guess, he liked to have things fully planned and worked out to the last detail well in advance.

But the Jenny that Steve and his wife met, the day they went to sign the lease on the house in Country Club Estates some ten months before, was not the Jenny that Gary remembered from his college days. No, this Jenny was a joyless Jenny. A Jenny with no humor left in her life, a Jenny whose face just hung there, like someone who had received electroshock therapy, or a lobotomy.

No, five years of marriage to Gary had taken its toll on her. Much like the petty tyranny of all the overly controlling, it takes its toll on their acquiescent victims, extinguishing their joy and stealing their zest for life.

Now had Steve and his wife not been so distracted by Jenny's obvious traumatic state, and had Steve actually carefully read the lease agreement that he signed with Gary that day, perhaps there would have been no Gunderson Affair at all. But alas, he did not read the document, trusting that Gary was indeed a fair man, being an attorney and all, albeit sensing that he was an odd man, most likely being a wife beater and all.

And so that fateful day in June, when Steve intentionally goaded Gary into the Gunderson affair; perhaps Steve was doing it for Jenny, and all the poor souls of the universe who have ever experienced humiliation and degradation at the hands of a controlling self-righteous bully like Gary

Gunderson. Or perhaps it was just because Gary had really pissed Steve off.

Yes, it all began innocently enough with a phone call in which Steve cordially and apologetically started to explain to Gary that the situation at Woodcrest was making it very difficult for Steve and his family to remain living at Country Club Estates. And as he continued to explain that he would therefore be moving to New Mexico shortly, and that they would be vacating the house they were renting from Gary immediately, Steve nonetheless offered to pay Gary the rent for the remaining two months of the lease, and asked that Gary forward the security deposit, or at least what was left of it after deducting for cleaning and move-out expenses, to Steve's new address in Las Cruces. Steve then made a joke about the real estate business and security deposits, commenting that he didn't know too many land-lords who actually gave them back and then kiddingly re-ferred to his Partners, back in Beverly Hills, specifically Morty and Arnie, as members of the Jewish Mafia.

"What about the *twelve months' notice to terminate* clause of the lease?" Gary accusingly inquired.

"The what?" Steve puzzlingly replied.

"Clause 212.2 clearly states that *the tenant must give the landlord 12 months prior notice before vacating the prem-ises and failure to do so immediately terminates the agree-ment making the full 12 months' rent penalty immediately due and payable."* Gary quoted from the lease.

"12 months prior notice on a 12 month lease – why I would have had to have told you I was moving out the day I moved in – that's completely ridiculous," said Steve in-credulously.

"Well that's what the lease says, and if you didn't agree with it you shouldn't have signed it! But you did."

"Surely Gary you've got to understand, as an attorney, that a clause like this one is onerous and that had I noticed it in the first place, I of course wouldn't have agreed to it. Come on Gary, it's just a technicality and besides, we're both landlords here and we know how this business really works."

But the only thing that Gary understood was that a deal was a deal, and besides, Gary loved situations like this, winning on a technicality made him feel empowered and clever, like he had anticipated something everyone else was sure to miss. And now backed up by the authority of a legal, binding contract, albeit an unfair onerous one, he was not only going to get to stick it to Steve, but he had bettered Steve at his own game. It was sneaky, it was cheating, and it was totally legal.

And Gary was sure, that since he "technically" had Steve and that he "technically" had the law on his side, that Steve, being a man of business and Steve's wife being an attorney, they would abide by the rules of the game and pay Gary his twelve months early move-out rent penalty.

And this is where the story turns "philosophical".

You see, if Steve had been an average nine-to-five guy, Gary would have been exactly right.

Steve would have been initially outraged, planned to argue with Gary about it, maybe even fantasized about suing Gary, mumbled and complained about it to his wife for a couple of days, and then, inevitably, thinking about all the work involved in actually disputing Gary's claim, and thinking about the penalties involved in losing such a dispute and in "not abiding by the rules," even if they were grossly unfair, Steve would have acquiesced and given Gary his pound of flesh.

Think about it, why do most people pay the credit card company the $35 late fee even when they are sure their payment wasn't late? After all, isn't it enough that their initial introductory interest rate of 7% went up to 33% one month after they signed up for the card?

"It's in the terms of the Service Agreement that you signed, says the snippy customer service rep on the phone. Didn't you read the agreement printed on the back of the application? (You know, the one printed in Times New Roman font size .000001.)

"But my payment wasn't late," says the poor credit card holder.

"Our records indicate your payment wasn't posted until a full 14 seconds after the cut-off period," says the snippy customer service rep.

"But I sent it in three weeks before the due date," says the poor credit card holder.

"Well regardless of when you believe you sent it, it wasn't posted until after the cut-off date. Perhaps you should have sent it in four weeks before."

"But I didn't even get the statement until three and a half weeks before it was due, how can I send in a payment before I even get the bill?"

"Well perhaps you should sign up for 'auto-pay' so we can just take money out of your checking account any time we feel like it," says the helpful but still snippy customer service rep. And with that she brings up the fact that with the $35 late fee, the customer's account is now over the

289

limit which unfortunately has now triggered the system to generate an over-the-limit fee of $50, which the customer service rep consolingly tells the customer she would like to be able to remove but since the account is currently delinquent, she is unable to do so. "How would you like to pay, will that be debit card or check-by-phone?"

"Well this is totally unfair," says the poor credit card customer, "and I'm not going to pay."

"Well, O.K. then," says the snippy customer service rep, "but please be aware that your account is now 30 days past due and if it goes to 31 days, this will unfortunately be reported to all three credit reporting agencies and remain on your credit history for the next ten years."

"Check by phone," says the poor credit card customer to the customer rep.

"Go fuck yourself, you petty, small time, self-righteous asshole, says Steve to Gary.

"I'll sue you in court and I'll win, says Gary. Do you really want a "judgment" like this on your credit?" Gary then continues on rhetorically.

"Go fuck yourself," says Steve to Gary again as he starts to add up the outstanding mortgage balances in his head – about $150 million worth – that he had personally guaranteed for Morty and The Boys to be able to buy the 22 complexes that they owned in El Paso, immediately deducing that an extra $24,000 in outstanding debt wasn't going to make much of a difference one way or the other to Steve's credit score.

"Oh yeah," says Gary, who is taken aback by Steve's *doesn't give a shit* attitude and doesn't know what else to say. "I'll see you in court!"

"No you won't you dick-less fuck because I'll be too busy pissing on every floor of your house to show up." And with that Steve hangs up the phone and smiles.

And with that Gary, who doesn't quite know what to make of the whole thing because no one has ever stood up to him before or defiantly told him to go fuck himself, just stands there, slightly in shock, looking out the window for a few seconds and then goes off to scream at his wife for a few minutes because this whole thing is in some way her fault.

And so it begins.

When Steve got the summons and complaint several days later, it was around 10:00 p.m. and Steve and his wife were settling in for bed. It was just as Steve began to peruse the other four lawsuits he had been served with that day that a knock came on their bedroom window. It was Joe Wills, Steve's favorite process server, using the old pizza-box-with-a-lawsuit-in-it trick to cleverly serve Steve with Gary's summons and complaint, Joe having forgotten until it was too late that he had already used that ruse several days before on Steve, but now having made his way all the way through the bushes to Steve's bedroom window, and with no time to change to the old KFC Bucket of Chicken-with-a-lawsuit-in-it trick, he did the very best he could to give an enthusiastic performance, slipping the pizza box through Steve's slightly open bedroom window and waiting for Steve to actually open the box before saying, "You're served".

Steve, not wanting to disappoint Joe, said, "Oh what's this, a pizza?" and then upon opening the box feigned surprise and then shock and then said, "You got me again you clever rascal," and then tipped him $20 for delivering the pizza and wished him a good evening.

"See you tomorrow Joe," said Steve.

"See you tomorrow Steve," said Joe.

And with that, the moment of truth that Gary Gunderson had hoped would be a stunning blow to Steve, turned out to be just another minor annoyance in a long string of annoyances that were becoming part of Steve's everyday life, with one minor exception. Steve got another free pizza and he and his wife were going to have a little fun with this one.

For as they began to look over Gary's Summons and Complaint it became clear that not only was it one of the longest documents they had ever encountered, being 312 pages and containing 192 causes of action, but it was also obviously the ravings of a mad man, which at first seemed hysterically funny and also, at the same time, a little bit scary.

The accusations ranged from fraud, to reliance, to conversion, to destruction of property, to moral turpitude, to bad faith, to conspiracy to commit treason, to a slew of other irrelevant and insane conspiracy theories that would have even made Oliver Stone laugh, finally ending with breach of contract, which was the only cause of action that was actually bona fide; and as Steve and his wife sat on the bed, sharing a slice of peperoni and mushroom pizza they laughed hysterically at the absurdity of the entire thing and joked that the only cause of action that Gary hadn't listed was loss of consortium, but this was probably due to the fact that Gary was not as clever a lawyer as was Norris Finch's attorney and also because there was no consortium to lose, as it was pretty clear there had been no consorting going on in the Gunderson household for quite some time.

Steve then did notice one thing that was different about this lawsuit than the other lawsuits Steve was used to receiving. Steve's wife had been personally named as one of the defendants. And as Steve shared this with his wife, she became noticeably upset. You see, even though she was a lawyer, she had never personally been on the receiving end of a lawsuit before. "That crazy son of a bitch," she said. "Why is he suing me? What did I do?"

Now the first time you receive a law suit, it's kind of like the first time you have sex. It's a big thing. But by your third or fourth law suit, just like by your third or fourth sexual encounter, the impact fades and it becomes just another part of life. But this is something you have to experience and figure out on your own; that law suits are not personal or about emotion, or right and wrong, or justice and injustice, they're just about money.

Lots and lots of money; money for defense attorneys, money for prosecuting attorneys, money for expert witnesses, money for forensic specialists, money for stenographers at depositions, money for court costs, money for legal secretaries to prepare interrogatories, money for office administrators to make copies of those interrogatories and yet even more money for defense attorneys to answer all those interrogatories that those legal secretaries are typing up and those administrators are copying. And oh yeah, even a little money, whatever is left over, for the party or parties, who prevail in the case. Yes indeed, law suits are an industry, and they have very little to do with the people actually suing somebody or the people being sued.

Another thing that became clear as Steve and his wife continued to review Gary's Summons and Complaint was that although it was worded in what were clearly Gary's words, the complaint had been filed on Gary's behalf by a local El Paso law firm, Samson, Delilah & Mertz, Attorneys at Law, a firm Gary was not affiliated with, Steve's wife immediately figuring out that the reason for this was that Gary, as an assistant part-time City Attorney, was an officer of the court in El Paso county, and as such, could not represent either himself, or anyone else but the City of Socorro, in any courtroom in the county.

But Gary hiring a lawyer seemed very unlikely, as Gary was extremely cheap, and the thought of paying someone else to do something he could clearly do for free, would have been abhorrent to him. In Gary's world, money, like everything else, was something that needed to be meticulously controlled, down to the last penny.

So what was going on?

Well, as it turned out, Gary and Stan Samson knew each other because Jenny, Gary's wife worked for Stan as a part-time legal secretary during the months when Gary was off fishing in Alaska.

Sam had a small, but successful practice in town, consisting mostly of real estate related matters; some wills and trusts work and the occasional family law issue involving divorce and child custody.

Seeing as that they were acquaintances and both attorneys, Gary proposed to Stan, that they enter into a gentlemen's agreement whereby Stan would let Gary use Stan's attorney's license number and firm's stationary to conduct his holy crusade against "Steve's evil organized crime syndicate," a world domination conspiracy that Gary had become aware of when Steve had originally called Gary to break the lease and had smugly "boasted" that he was a member of the Jewish Mafia, a declaration that was meant to be a self-deprecating joke that Gary not only didn't get, but took as both a confession and a threat.

The deal was that Gary would do all the work, write up all the pleadings and prepare all the interrogatories behind the scenes, and Stan would be his front man at the depositions and in court. Officially, Stan would be Gary's lawyer, even though, secretly, Gary was Gary's lawyer.

In return, Gary would give Stan 10% of the proceeds of the case. And although the arrangement was somewhat morally questionable, as it skirted the reason Officers of the Court shouldn't be representing themselves in the first place – conflict of interest – it was "technically" legal; and Gary just loved winning on technicalities.

And it was this very *deception* that Gary was trying to perpetrate that not only convinced Steve and his wife to fight Gary's ridiculous lawsuit, but to ruin him in the process. Yes, this "doing of self-serving deeds cloaked behind the mask of authority" was so utterly vile, so utterly wrong, and so utterly detestable to Steve, that he swore not only to ruin Gary financially, but professionally as well. Oh yes, this Gunderson Affair had become much more than just a lease dispute, it had become a "soap-box" on which Steve could stand, a podium from which Steve could speak out not only against Gary and his petty tyrannies, but the tyrannies of all public servants who had used their positions of authority, not for the public good, but to advance their own private agendas. And when Steve referred to "all public servants" what he really meant was "two public servants"— Councilman Jim Jameson and his good friend Shirley Dole.

And so, driven by outrage, the desire for revenge, and an ironic sense of humor, Steve and his wife formulated a plan.

Steve's wife would confront Gary on the surface, technically arguing the merits and demerits of each of his 192 causes of action, while Steve would chip away below the surface – at Gary's mental and emotional stability, mocking him, disrespecting him, publicly humiliating him, and laughing out loud at his absurd accusations and his feeble attempts to discredit Steve and "the Jewish Mafia" (a.k.a. The Beverly Hills Boys Back Home), leading Gary down the path of self-destruction which hopefully would end in a breaking point where his head would explode from the furious anger boiling up inside him.

The plan was a thing of beauty and Gary was totally out of his league; he just didn't know it yet. And if that weren't enough, Steve's wife even had an ace in the hole, but she would wait until the time was just right to unleash it on Gary – that poor, unsuspecting, self-righteous bastard; they almost felt sorry for him.

And so with Steve's wife hot on Gary's self-righteous ass, seriously engaging him in her own self-righteous lawyer sense of moral indignation about each and every one of his 192 causes of action, Steve was freed up to focus most of his time on the real problem at hand, which was how to get Steve and the Beverly Hills Boys Back Home out of the Woodcrest fiasco without losing too much money, and he even put aside a few hours on the weekend just to fuck with Gary and get him riled up. It was the best of all possible situations.

Now in order to assist Steve's wife in seeking her bloody revenge on Gary (how dare he name her personally in his villainous lawsuit!), Steve hired yet another local attorney, Mark Parkinson, a man who was not only one of the few attorneys not working on a case in El Paso County involving Steve on one side or the other, but was also the brother of Park Parkinson, the fallen El Paso Police officer who had been accidentally killed when his Crown Victoria Police Cruiser was rear ended on the 10 Freeway some two years back. Park was the very same officer that Shirley Dole was intending to name her "Shirley's Kids" park after, should it ever come to be built. Not missing the irony of the situation, Steve told Mark Parkinson that he would donate $24,000 to Shirley's Park fund, the very same amount Gary was demanding for the breach of contract portion of his lawsuit, should Mark win the suit. It would be the ultimate

"Fuck You" to Gary, signaling that Steve would rather voluntarily give money to Shirley Dole, a woman he detested and who detested him, rather than give in to Gary's demands. "Take that, you wife beating son of a bitch," Steve's wife thought to herself when Steve told her of the arrangement.

And with Mark Parkinson now acting as Steve's wife's front man, and with Stan Samson acting as Gary's, the lawsuiting began.

And this lead to the interrogatories, a part of the discovery process in which both parties are allowed to ask each other, in writing, a series of *relevant* questions regarding the parties involved in, and the facts of the case. As the process goes, the receiving party is required, by law, to answer the interrogatories, honestly, truthfully, and completely. And it was in this technical rule of the law, that Gary Gunderson so cleverly planned to not only prove beyond a shadow of a doubt that Steve owed him the $24,000, but that Steve was the self-confessed overlord of a subversive group of organized criminals who called themselves the Jewish Mafia, a group who had not only already taken over the financial and media industries, but were now poised to take over the rest of the world as well.

Now upon receiving Gary's interrogatories, it was completely apparent to everyone concerned, except Gary of course, that the questions that Stan Samson had supposedly prepared and sent over to Mark were in fact written and sent over by Gary. The 100 pages of questions that resembled the Inquisition of the House Un-American Activities Committee lead by Senator Joseph McCarthy in the communist witch hunts of the 1950's, were obviously not the work of a humble local real estate and sometimes-divorce attorney. They were the ramblings of a self-absorbed mad man, Gary Gunderson, of course.

The questions were extremely accusatory, extremely personal, extremely irrelevant to the actual case at hand, and extremely insane.

1. Are you now or have you ever been a member of the Jewish Mafia?
2. What is your name?
3. What was your real name before you changed it?
4. What is your religious affiliation?
5. What is your wife's religious affiliation and if it not the same as yours, are you trying to cross-breed?
6. Who are the members of the Jewish Mafia?
7. Have you ever been sued?
8. Have you ever been charged with a crime?
9. Are you a Slumlord?
10. Do you believe in God and if so, which one?
11. You know you owe me the $24,000, don't you?
12. Do you worship the devil?
13. Do you know Frank's mom Eileen because she says you worship the devil?
14. Do you know Shirley Dole because she says you are the Devil?
15. Are you the Devil?
16. What is your sexual preference?
17. Are you having an extra-marital affair?
18. Would you like to have an extra-marital affair with my wife because I saw the way you were looking at her?
19. Would your wife considering having an extra-marital affair with me? If not, why not? Doesn't she know we were destined to be together?
20. Can you provide financial records for each of the 22 properties you own in Texas?

21. Can you provide copies of personal income tax returns for yourself and every one of your business partners for the last 7 years?
22. Can you provide a list of every business partner and business associate you have ever had, ever?
23. List every employer and place of employment for the last thirty years

And so on …and so on… and so on...until:

350. List the top ten reasons why you and your partners want to take over the world?

Now as if reading Gary's questions were not amusing enough, answering them was to be the joke of the century, at least on Gary it was, and as Steve and his wife's secret plan began to unfold, it was apparent to everyone concerned, except Gary of course, that not only was he going to be "toast", but he was going to have to take his lawsuit and pound sand, as Morty would have probably said had he not been incommunicado.

No, there was no doubt that in mockingly answering Gary's inquisitions, Steve's utter lack of respect for Gary's prosecutorial authority would absolutely drive Gary over the edge of reason, a precipice he was already clearly teetering on. Yes, it would just take a tiny little push to help Gary hurl himself into the abyss, to trigger a self-induced nervous breakdown which would leave him rocking back and forth in the corner, sobbing uncontrollably and questioning the very meaning of his miserable little existence. "Was there no sense left in this world?"

Now ordinarily the type of responses that Steve planned to provide in answering Gary's interrogatories would have been cause to charge Steve with contempt of court and probably perjury, but what Steve and his wife knew, that nobody else knew, was that no one in the court system would ever read either Gary's questions or Steve's answers to them.

And why was this?

Well the "this" was Steve and his wife's ace in the hole, because they knew that this case was never going to court.

And how did they know this?

Because Gary's front man attorney Stan Samson was already representing Steve and his wife on another real estate matter and had been for over a year now, but because Gary had filled out all the paperwork himself on the Gunderson matter, Stan had never realized who Gary was suing in the first place.

Well, as any first year law student will tell you, representing both sides in a lawsuit is not only a definite conflict of interest, but cause for disbarment, and Stan –as soon as he found out – would have to fire Gary as his client and the case would have to be dismissed and then re-filed.

And Stan was going to find out for sure, as soon as Steve and his wife were sure that Gary had indeed read the 350 answers to his 350 lunatic questions.

It is perhaps a tragic ending to this little tale of intrigue, this Gunderson affair, that Steve's expectations of sending Gary over the edge did come to fruition. For upon reading Steve's answers, 349 of which were variations on the phrase "Fuck You," he did, as Steve had expected, blow a circuit in his brain, and was so utterly angered and frustrated by Steve's total lack of respect for him, his authority and the legal process in general, that he became completely and inconsolably depressed and utterly disillusioned with his life. Within days of the dismissal of the case, Gary quit his job as Assistant Part-Time City Attorney with the City of Socorro, beat the shit out of his wife, and then moved to Alaska to fish full-time. He was never heard from again. Jenny once again moved back in with her brother Frank over at the Pinewood Villa apartments, and is still, to this day, waiting for Gary to call and apologize.

The one answer to the interrogatories that can be singled out as the straw that broke the camel's back was the answer to question number six – *Who are the members of the Jewish Mafia?* Steve's answer, although not addressing the underlying spirit of the question, was however, "technically" correct and therefore extremely clever. Steve's answer? *Mickey Cohen, Bugsy Siegel and Meyer Lansky; and Fuck You Gary, Fuck You!*

Chapter 3.8

A Midsummer Night's Carol

Las Cruces, New Mexico July 2000

Morty was dead (at least according to his brother-in-law lawyer Martin he was.) There is no doubt whatever about that. The register of his burial was signed by the clergyman, the clerk, the undertaker, and the chief mourner. Steve signed it; and Steve's name was good upon 'Change, for anything he chose to put his hand to. Old Morton Salt was as dead as a door-nail.

Mind! I don't mean to say that I know, of my own knowledge, what there is particularly dead about a door-nail. I might have been inclined myself to regard a coffin-nail as the deadest piece of ironmongery in the trade. But the wisdom of our ancestors is in the simile; and my unhal-lowed hands shall not disturb it, or the Country's done for. You will therefore permit me to repeat, emphatically, that Morty was as dead as a door-nail.

Steve knew he was dead? Of course he did. How could it be otherwise? Steve and he were partners for I don't know how many years. Steve was his sole executor, (at least in Texas he was), his sole administrator, (not including Morty's secretary) his sole assign (not including Nicki of course), his sole residuary legatee, (not including Martin and Nicki's team of 122 lawyers) his sole friend (not in-cluding Arnie who was definitely not in the deal), and sole mourner (seeing as Steve was the only one who was told by Marty that Morty was dead.) And even Steve was not so dreadfully cut up by the sad event, but that he was an excel-lent man of business on the very day of the funeral, and solemnized it with an undoubted bargain. (That K.J. sure could stretch a buck.)

The mention of Morty's funeral, (had it actually taken place), brings me back to the point I started from. There is no doubt that Morty was said to be dead. And if Steve wanted any help at all in getting out of the Woodcrest fias-co from them, that was the story that he'd have to stick to in order for Morty and Nicki to continue funding his opera-tions, the enumerable lawsuits that he was already em-broiled in back in El Paso, and the legal battle that was to ensue over the Woodcrest situation.

It had been almost four months since the Tale of Two Cities meeting back in April and to date Nicki's brother Martin had been completely unsuccessful in giving away to charity Nicki's and Morty's interest in any of the 22 build-

303

ings that comprised the El Paso Empire. As such they were both still on the hook to be charged with the almost certainly coming citations that they had so far avoided being served, but it was just a matter of time now until eventually, some clever process server, perhaps using the old summons-and-complaint-in-a-caviar-tin routine, would find them somewhere in Beverly Hills and break through their corporate veil. Thus, Steve was instructed in no uncertain terms that he "had better make sure that everyone in Texas thought, no, that everyone in Texas knew, that Morty was dead." This must be distinctly understood, or nothing wonderful can come of the story I am going to relate.

Stave I

It was a warm July evening and Steve and his family had just finished moving in to their new home in Las Cruces, New Mexico, a humble four bedroom ranch style house in the beautiful, planned desert community of Buena Vista Sands.

It was not quite the fancy digs they had gotten used to living in back at Country Club Estates in El Paso, but the lower profile dwelling and neighborhood was serving its intended purpose – to keep Steve out of sight and out of reach of the powers that were down at El Paso City Hall. Indeed, to date, neither Steve nor his wife had been successfully served with the 1073 citations that Sue-Ann McDonald had apologetically explained she found necessary to serve them with.

As a matter of fact since moving to the "Sands" that morning, Steve had not only not been accosted once by any process server or any other officer of the court, but had noticed that the usual unmarked police car that was usually surveying the goings on at his home back in El Paso, was noticeably absent.

Also noticeably absent was the broadcast news van with the little satellite dish on top that usually drove by his last home in El Paso several times a day to see if perhaps there was a break in the story regarding Woodcrest or rumors of Morty's untimely demise.

The quiet was kind of nice, but in a way, still a little unsettling. The problems hadn't gone away, Steve was just recluse from them for a while, and as imagined monsters are often much worse than real ones, Steve couldn't help but speculate in his own mind about how the whole Woodcrest situation was going to play itself out in the most hideous of ways.

You see, since the day of the great Tale of Two Cities Summit things had escalated into a full-blown publicity war between El Paso and Beverly Hills, with Steve and his wife caught in the middle and with Councilman Jameson realizing that if he didn't get Woodcrest either fixed up or shut down pretty soon, it was he who was going to look "ineffective" to the voters. And that could cost him the next election.

So rather than risk it (he knew that even if he could "resolve" the situation with Morty and Nicki and get the complex fixed up it would take months or even a year to accomplish), he opted for plan B, shutting the complex down.

Now you couldn't just go and seize the property – no that would be unconstitutional – so Jim had two choices, he could either go "the eminent domain" route, declaring the property necessary for public use and paying the owners the fair market value of the place; or he could go "the criminal activity" route declaring that criminal activity was going on at the property and that as such continued use of the property by its current owners threatened public safety.

Jim, after two seconds of careful consideration, decided to go the "criminal activity" route, because it was the most expedient and least costly; also, it would make him look good.

And so, realizing that he was going to need evidence of criminal activity at the complex, and also realizing that he was pressed for time, he called Sue-Ann McDonald and instructed her to prepare 1073 search warrants which she could have signed by the Environmental Services Court Judge and serve while raiding the complex at such time in the near future when they might have probable cause to do so, and then he also asked her to cancel the original civil citations she had been as of yet unable to serve either Nicki and Morty or Steve and his wife with, and re-issue the same civil citations as criminal ones. Thus, there would be no need to actually gather any new evidence or fill out any new forms. No, those pictures of dog shit over at Woodcrest were no longer pictures of just an unsanitary condition; they were photographs of a crime.

As Steve fell asleep on the couch in the living room that late July evening, he had the weight of the world on his shoulders.

And as he began to drift off to an uneasy slumber, he was suddenly stirred by a gust of wind that blew in through the slightly open glass sliding door that lead to his new desert of a backyard. The gust of wind knocked a Kokopelli

306

lamp off the end table in front of the slightly open door in the living room. And then Steve heard what appeared to be a voice. It was faint at first, but then it grew louder and louder until Steve could clearly make out what it was saying.

"Stevie, my boy.

Stevie my boy, vat are you do-ing chere en the midul ov the de-sert, a niz Jewish buoy like you? Ya shud be beck in the Beverly Hills, playink gulf or shumthing like thet. And vat are you duing shleeping on da couch, shuudint you be upstairs shtupping vith yur vife?"

"Shmuck"!

"Shame on you, it's a shonda(terrible scandal) on your entire mishpucha(family), and your mother must be very disap-pointed".

"Schmuck"!

"This must be a dream" Steve thought to himself, but it seemed so real, and the voice seemed to know him.

And as the voice continued to speak it slowly revealed itself to Steve.

STEVE O.

"And must importantly putzer (well-meaning fuck-up), vat the hell are you duing running around pleying big shot bizness-man landlord with that putz (literally it means limp dick but figuratively it means useless) idiot son of mine, the kid is woithless, a regular Edsel Ford, a vaist of a perfectly good spoim cell. As a matter of fect, ven he vas young, he was so stupid we had to get him buckle-up shoes for those EEE wide feet of his because he couldn't figure out how to tie his shoe laces. And not only that but he's so cheap, he's still veering that very same pair of shoes to this day. Vhat a putz. But eehhhh! Nicht Kefelachkt (let it go, it's a lost cause).

And at that moment Steve sat up and looked at the apparition in front of him and immediately recognized it from a picture he had seen hanging on the wall in Morty's office. It was none other than Saul T. Salt, Morty's father, and the greatest real estate shopping center genius the world had ever known.

"But how can this be"? Steve said. Saul had died in 1971 and this was 2000. "This must be a dream" Steve thought to himself.

And then things started to really get weird.

"Come get yur touchas (ass) off the couch, put your pents on and then you and me gunna take a little ride in my megic 1963 mint condition Thundaboid Convoitable."

"Aren't you the great Saul T. Salt," Steve asked in an amazed tone.

"Salt Shmalt," Saul replied. "Let's take a ride."

Steve and Saul climbed into a cherry-red mint condition 1963 Thunderbird convertible with vanity license plates that read CHUTZPA (balls) and a pair of "fuzzy" shopping center replicas hanging from the rear view mirror. They sped away down the streets of the carbon-copy manufactured Paradise that was Buena Vista Sands in the town of Socorro New Mexico, Steve intently listened to Saul as Saul explained, "You're a good boy putzer (lova-

STEVE O.

*ble fuck-up), but if you're going
to be a real, real estate big shot,
you've still got a few things to
loin."*

*And then in less than two se-
conds flat, Steve and Saul found
themselves sitting in Saul's convertible in a parking lot of an upscale shopping center on Rodeo
Drive in Beverly Hills.
A giant beacon of light was coming from the Vatican Basilica
replica tower atop Moldano's Fine Jewelry Store.*

*Saul turned to Steve and said,
"And now for your fuyst lesson.
Take a look around Stevie, vat do
you see? Do you see any Bud
Light cans lying on the ground?
Do you see any broken vindows?
Do you see anyone woiking on
their cars? Or how about someone fixing any leaks with some
fakakta (crazy rigged) listening
contraption? How about girls
vith rubber gloves insoiting condoms full of heroin into greasy
dirty guys' smelly assholes, do
you see any of that? How about
fake policemen issuing fake $25
tickets for "don't follow the*

*rules," do you see that? How
about guys selling used refrigerators in the parking lot, is any of
that going on? How about any
red-haired mashugina (crazy) la-
dies with picket signs holding
press conferences? No? Are you
sure?" Saul asked rhetorically.*

*"Yes, that's right Stevie, good
boy! You don't see any of that
shit! Now we're getting somewhere. And what do you see Stevie? A couple of fancy restaurants, a gourmet grocery store, a
liquor store with a good wine se-
lection, a health food juice bar
and two jewelry stores, one small
one and one really big one that
looks like the Vatican. Imagine
that, two jewelry stores in the
same shopping area. Who knew?
Now this place Stevie is a good
piece of real estate, a diamond.
And what do we do when we're
walking on the path of investment
and we come across a diamond
Stevie? That's right, we pick it
up. Yes Stevie, when you come
across a property that's a jewel,
you buy it."*

"And now for the second les-son," said Saul, and with that be-ing said, and in a blink of an eye, Steve and Saul found themselves sitting in Saul's Convertible in the parking lot of Woodcrest.

"And now, Stevie, what do you see here?" Saul once again asked rhetorically. "Do you see stair-wells that look like they're going to fall down any minute? Do you see holes in the roofs? Do you see water dripping from the holes? Do you see broken vin-dows and people passing drugs to other people standing outside those broken windows? How about cockroaches, do you see any cockroaches? Oh, there's one, and there's another, and look over there, a whole family of cockroaches, and look they're having a picnic, they're eating a little boy. And who is that lady with the bullhorn chanting vat? Slumlords go home? And look across the street. Do you see a park named after a fallen police officer, because I thought there was supposed to be a park over there but I don't see one."

"All I see is a vacant lot with some broken cars and a lady with a bullhorn trying to collect a lot of money to build a park, but no park. And who's that in front of a microphone holding a press conference vith bums standing behind him? And oh! Listen Stevie, he's singing the song from my favorite TV show about Beverly Hills, but he's not singing the right voids. And what is that he's stepping on? It looks like dog shit, lots and lots of dog shit."

"And finally Stevie, who is that over there in the swimming pool? Why that's you Stevie, your standing in the deep end of the pool and the vater is up to your neck. But wait, that's not water you're standing in, that's shit, a whole swimming pool filled with shit. You're standing neck-deep in a swimming pool filled with shit. And wait, who's that standing on the side of the pool with a bucket of water in their hands trying to throw the water on your head, why that's also you, Stevie, although you look a little younger there. But wait, that's not water

in the bucket, it's vomit. Well Stevie, neck deep in shit and facing a bucket of vomit in the face, I guess your only choice is whether to duck or not. I vunder how you're going to get yourself out of this one? But don't worry Stevie, you're a smart boy, I know you'll do okay."

"But I will say one thing, I pity the poor bastards who own this place, it's a genuine piece of shit, a real slum. The poor schmucks who bought this must have been hoodwinked into thinking they were getting a real bargain, a real deal. Sounds like something my cheap putz son would be taken in by."

"Anyway, Stevie, what have we loined? That when you're walking down the path of life and you come across a pile of shit in the middle of the road, you don't have to step in it, you can simply go around it. And one thing's for sure, you certainly don't have to buy it. No, you can get all the shit you can handle in life for absolutely free."

314

*"Get the message, Stevie? I
thought that you would."*

*"Now go clean yourself off
and go make me proud! And oh
yeah, nice job on that Gunderson
schmuck."*

*And with those words being
said, and in the blink of an eye,
Saul was gone.*

When Steve opened his eyes, he was back laying on the couch in his new living room. But somehow, things were different, he felt different, like a new man.

The crushing worries that had weighed on him these last six months since buying Woodcrest didn't seem so overwhelming anymore and somehow he had this renewed sense of confidence, knowing somehow that the ability to clean up this whole mess was one that he had possessed all along.

But what of his visit from Saul? Had it all been a dream or had it actually happened?

And then suddenly he thought of the Little Old Lady from Unit #B and how whether she actually ever existed wasn't really important, that it was his memories of her and what he had learned from the memories of his adventures with her that was important.

And so dream or not, Steve felt truly lucky to have met his idol, the inventor of "Stealth Investing" and the greatest shopping center developer of all times, the legendary Saul T. Salt.

And then it was there, plain as day in Steve's head, the answer to all his problems, "Stealth Investing."

Chapter 3.9

Harold and Andy Save the Day

El Paso, Texas – August 2000 – Just an hour and 45 minutes to go!

At exactly 10:31, only seconds after Eileen had finished praying, Harold and Andy pulled up to the hissing spot on the grass in front of unit 14.

Andy stepped out of the truck first, ten-pound sledge hammer slung over his right shoulder, and a huge roll of silver duct tape balanced around his left upper arm. Harold followed behind carrying a shovel; a large steel spike and one of those 36-container refrigerator packs of ice cold Miller Lite in the 12-ounce cans. Apparently the store was out of Bud Light, and Harold didn't have the time to go to the other market to get his first choice which, of course would have been Bud Light. But emergency situations call for emergency measures and as Harold had learned from the

Marine Corps, often the difference between success and failure is the ability to "adapt, improvise, and overcome." Not that Harold had been in the Marines, but he had seen their new recruiting commercial on TV and what they were saying seemed to make a whole lot of sense. So Harold figured he'd just make do with the Miller until he could get this damn chiller thing resolved.

To mark the spot of the leak, the place the hissing sound was coming from, Harold carried the large red steel spike over to where Andy had left his half-full beer can. Andy walked over with the sledgehammer and while Harold held the large red steel spike, Andy pounded it about five feet into the ground to make sure it was nice and tight and firmly planted. The last couple of inches were the hardest because there was a rock or something that kept making a metallic clunking sound every time Andy hit the top of the spike. But with two or three really hard swings, the spike finally went right in and coincidently, as Andy banged the spike for the last time, the hissing noise coming from the ground got a whole lot louder. "Eureka," Andy said, "I definitely think we found our leak, I can hear it as plain as day."

And now they were ready to dig. Harold started digging around the spike and lasted about a minute until he started to get winded. Most guys would have lasted about two minutes before needing to stop, but Harold, as you know, had only one lung so it took him half the time to get winded and run out of steam. So while Harold recovered and took a cigarette break, Andy continued to dig the 6'x 6' x 6' trench they would need to get at that leaky water pipe.

After about twenty minutes, and while Harold was still taking a smoke break, Andy had dug down about two feet when he too became exhausted. So Harold stepped in to give Andy a hand. About two minutes after that, and after Andy and Harold had removed the steel spike from where they had first put it about 22 minutes before, and moved it to the second half-full beer can location, they began taking turns digging the second 6' x 6' x 6' trench they would need to get at that leaky pipe. The reason they took turns digging was that the shovels over at the plumbing supply warehouse were "like super-expensive" and after buying the duct tape and the pipe and the rest of the stuff they needed, they only had enough money left to get one shovel. Also as Harold was quick to point out, Miller cost way more than Bud so when he went to pay for the plumbing supplies he had way less money in his pocket to begin with.

At exactly 11:45 a.m., Harold and Andy were standing at the bottom of a 6'x 6' x 6' trench, one that looked very similar to the trench that existed exactly forty years, thirty-five hours and forty-five minutes earlier. Just next to their knees and between their legs were, to their surprise, two pipes. A black pipe on top and a red pipe directly, horizontally, beneath it. The red pipe, which was hard to see because it was on the bottom, had some kind of sticker on it that in yellow ink, made a circle with a line through it. And underneath that line was what looked like a picture of a shovel. And there was some partially scratched out writing on the bottom that said something like *Dang* or *anger* or something like that. Andy figured that must have been the name of the company that originally manufactured the pipe.

But now, with there being two pipes and all, and not the one pipe that Harold and Andy had figured on, Harold and Andy faced a dilemma. There were two pipes, not one, and neither Harold nor Andy was sure which one was the chiller pipe and for that matter, what the second pipe was at all. So, seeing as that there were two pipes, both of which had a few small aspirin sized holes in them, and since they weren't sure which one was the chiller pipe, they figured they'd better patch both.

But then a problem arose. It seems the large silver roll of duct tape they had purchased at the plumbing supply warehouse was not large enough to patch both pipes. They had unfortunately discovered this after they were finished wrapping the black pipe that was on top and were about half-way finished wrapping the red pipe underneath. But seeing as that Harold had this kind of intuitive feeling that the top pipe was indeed the chiller, and seeing as that they had wrapped **most** of the holes in the red bottom pipe anyway, Harold made the decision to fill back in the trench, and to go send Andy to test the chiller system to see if it were working.

If it was, they could then return the shovel back to the plumbing supply warehouse so they could get their money back, and use the refund to get a twelve-pack of Bud Light and one of those really large boxes of Slim Jims that they sell over at the Sam's Club.

At 11:52 a.m., just as Harold and Andy were almost finished filling in the 6'x 6x 6' trench they had worked so hard to dig, something interrupted them.

"We interrupt this program for a special news bulletin!"

"This is Christine Marshall, Channel 5 Eyewitness News, live, here in El Paso's Eastwood Neighborhood at the Woodcrest Apartment Complex where we have breaking news."

"The City of El Paso has just launched a massive raid on the complex, responding to complaints of a down chiller system and of blighting conditions which have been said to have existed for months now. Apartments without electricity, leaking water pipes, cockroach infestation, broken windows and raw sewage just among the thousands of apparent code and safety violations being allowed to exist here at Woodcrest."

"And in what may be the most scandalous and shocking part of this incident, according to State records, the complex is owned, in part, by billionaire purse tycoon and heiress Nicole Gamble and her husband, billionaire businessman Morton Salt."

"According to City documents filed earlier this morning, the chiller system at the complex has been down for 24 hours and as such, the City has probable cause to conduct this raid. The owners of the complex were, over the past several months, continually warned by the City that the place was in dire need of repair but despite numerous attempts by the Neighborhood Services Department to assist the current owners in renovating the complex and fixing the numerous code violations present at the property, they have refused to cooperate. Further, the current owners, Ms. Gamble and her husband, have reportedly refused to make any improvements to the property or contribute any additional funds to remedy the situation and have turned a blind eye towards the problems of the people who reside in their complex, continuing to allow them to live among deplorable conditions and in constant peril from disease, vermin and other unsafe conditions without any regard for their safety or well-being. It's just shameful."

"Let's listen in on the live press conference currently getting underway."

And with a crowd of about one hundred people assembled directly behind and around him, and standing in front of building Unit 1 North, in the east parking lot of the complex, Councilman Jim Jameson, of the Eastwood District, walked up to the make-shift podium, a podium dramatically constructed of eleven bags of garbage which he had had his staff bring with them from his office downtown, leaned closer to the microphone, and began to speak.

Standing next to him was Shirley Dole, local community activist and defender of park-less children and the head of the Eastwood Community Association, the non-profit group of concerned citizens who were working with the City to help improve conditions there in El Paso's Eastwood Neighborhood, and rid the area of the evil influences of out-of-town landlords, especially Jewish ones.

And then, to the surprise of the crowd, and a local television audience of about 2 million people, rather than begin to make a speech, Councilman Jameson, after giving the usual acknowledgements and introductions, began driving his point home in a much more creative fashion, a clever approach that would not only deliver a message to the out-of-town landlords he had come there to admonish but would show the good citizens of El Paso and the general voting public what a dynamic and effective leader he was and could be. After all, City elections were only one year away and Jim had his eye on the Mayor's seat.

Cleverly sung to the tune of *The Beverly Hillbillies* theme song, Jim began and Shirley joined in to perform their own version of this most popular television theme song.

> *"Come and listen to my story 'bout*
> *Nicki and her beau,*
> *Who bought a lot of buildings 'cause*
> *they had a lot of dough,*
> *But when it came to fixing things*
> *they really didn't care,*
> *Until the City stepped in and said it*
> *wasn't fair.*
>
> *Slums they were, buildings manifest-*
> *ing an array of numerous blighting*
> *conditions, that is.*
>
> *Well the first thing you know, ole*
> *Nicki skipped town,*

Left their buildings back in Texas –
said they wouldn't be around
To make conditions better for the
folks who can't afford,
To live in better places than the ones
owned by Slumlords!

They're back in Beverly Hills now-
that is, driving Rolls Royces, swim-
ming in swimming pools, hanging
out with movie stars."

Well Nicki, you just stay there, and
y'all don't come back now, ya
hear!"

And as Jim and Shirley were finishing up their little song for all the country to hear, (as the story was picked up by all of the national news networks) a caravan of nearly 200 City vehicles, which stretched all the way down Monte Verde Avenue – including ambulances, police cars, S.W.A.T. vans, fire trucks, building inspector sedans, a mobile command center bus and even a helicopter – raced up and into the east parking lot of the Woodcrest Complex, screeched on the breaks, and came to an abrupt, and immediate halt.

And within seconds of their arrival, and from within this assortment of various landing craft and personnel carriers, an army of almost 500 El Paso City employees stormed into the parking lot, and ran frantically and erratically toward the Complex Office in a maneuver that resembled the D-day invasion on the beaches of Normandy.

The only difference being that on this day there was no one there to return fire. The only people outside to receive Councilman Jameson's invasion forces were Harold and

Andy, as it was 132 degrees in the parking lot by then, and everyone else with any sense had gone inside.

Nevertheless, as the deafening sound of helicopters whirled above them, and the sounds of sirens screamed and the sound of protesters chanted and the sounds of illegal alien tenants pulling the blinds of their apartment windows smacked shut, Sue-Ann McDonald, assistant City Prosecutor and her assistant, the former and once assistant City Prosecutor Enrico Corleon, stepped out of their vehicle and walked slowly towards the complex office preparing to arrest the owners of the complex for not fixing the chiller system in time and to the serve the complex's manager Eileen with the search warrants they were there to serve that day.

At the tail end of the caravan that had come to rest in the Woodcrest parking lot, sitting and waiting in a white Ford Escort was none other than Jake Jacobs, Lead Building Inspector for the City of El Paso, and with a slew of papers spread out on the grey vinyl front seat next to him, Jake had already used up most of the citation forms left in his 100-citation form booklet even before he had turned the corner into the driveway.

And as he watched Sue-Ann and Enrico walk slowly towards the Woodcrest office, he being the true professional that he was and realizing the gravity of the situation, put in an emergency call for help, which went out over the walkie-talkie system as a code 9 – officer needs assistance – Jake frantically summoning his assistant, Maria Lopez Corleon (she had recently married her one time lover, the unintentional killer of her first husband Tom, in a civil ceremony while at a law enforcement convention in Downtown Las Vegas. Although the magic was pretty much gone and the sex with Enrico was getting routine and predictable, she needed the security of having a husband with a steady government paycheck and a good health plan.)

"Maria, Jake said, "I'm going to need at least ten more citation booklets, and if you can, grab a few pens off my desk and maybe bring a water bottle or two. I think we're going to be here for a long time and I don't want to get de-hydrated."

And as the Channel 5 Eyewitness News van turned the corner into the driveway it immediately took notice of the 6' x 6' x 6' ditch that had been almost completely filled in by then. Driving up on the lawn between the first and se-cond row of buildings just 200 feet from the spot where Harold and Andy had started searching just 23 hours and 52 minutes before, Harold and Andy stood – exhausted, pant-ing and pretty well smashed from all those Miller Lites they were drinking to quench their Texas-sized thirsts as they sweated and dug in the almost-noon day sun.

"And who would you be?" asked Carol Baker, Consum-er Affairs Correspondent at Channel 5 Eyewitness News as she put the microphone up to Harold's mouth and then backed up a little because Harold was really dripping sweat. Some of it had already gotten on Carol's beige pant suit that she had picked up over at Stein-Mart when they had that big "Middle of Summer Sale" the weekend before. She was planning to return it and wanted to make sure that Harold didn't sweat on it any more than he already had.

"Harold Bittlehauser, Lead Maintenance Engineer here at Woodcrest Apartments," Harold declared.

"And what seems to be the problem?" asked Carol.

"No problem now," replied Harold. "I think we got this puppy pretty much up and running, although it's going to take a couple of hours for the system to be running at max-imum efficiency. "Go check her out Andy," said Harold.

And as Andy went to the compressor room to check the chiller system Harold continued the interview for about five minutes as he explained to a growing audience of what was now about fourteen million people, in great detail, what it was like to have only one lung and how he had been unjustly convicted on several occasions for DUI and how he was only drinking Miller Lite this morning because the store was out of Bud-Light and how if anyone else out there needed some plumbing work done he and Andy were available on the weekends "cause he really needed to get his cable bill paid."

And just as the digital numbers on the clock on the dashboard of Jakes Ford Escort struck 11:59 a.m., Andy came running out from the compressor room, screaming at the top of his lungs, "she's working, the chiller is working, son-of-a-bitch! We did it Harold! We saved the day. We did it." It was the moment of a lifetime and it also meant, Harold and Andy were going to finally make some big bucks. And it had all been memorialized right there on, what was by this point, national TV.

For Jake Jacob's however, and indeed for every member of the 500-man raid assault team, especially councilman Jameson, it was a moment of great disappointment.

Why with the chiller back up, and fourteen million people knowing it was back up, the City had no probable cause to search the complex, and without a search they couldn't issue those 1073 new Criminal Citations. It was back to the drawing board as far as running these out-of-town owners out of town and it might be back to getting a real job for Councilman Jameson because this was going to make him look bad, real bad.

The disappointment, however, came especially hard for Jake. As a matter of fact Jake had quite a dilemma. It seems he had already written up, prematurely, about 100 citations for a broken chiller system that was in fact, *not broken*.

And once you used the pre-printed citation forms from the sequentially numbered citation booklets with the carbon-copies, you couldn't simply just tear up the tickets. No, the City Auditor's Office kept track of those sorts of things and once a citation number had been assigned, it had to either be disposed of through the court system or it had to be cancelled by the inspector who wrote up the citation, which required filling out a separate "Citation Cancellation Form" for each of the citations originally and erroneously written.

Further, for each citation to be cancelled, the inspector would have to give a written explanation for the reason for the cancellation from a list of eight acceptable reasons which were listed in section 11B of the Citation Cancellation Form. And to Jake's dismay, nowhere in section 11B was listed a reason even resembling "Fucked Up and Jumped the Gun." Indeed, Jake was in a bit of a pickle and it was going to be a long night un-ticketing all those tickets.

Now in the glory and excitement of the moment that was shared by fifty million people, a great secret that was only known by one person had eluded all; because what Andy didn't know, what Harold didn't know, what Carol Baker of the Channel 5 Eyewitness News Team didn't know, what the Neighborhood Services Department didn't know and what the entire viewing audience in the Southwestern United States didn't know, was that Harold and Andy in fact had not fixed the chiller system at all.

What only Steve knew was that 22 hours earlier, just about two hours after the system had first gone down, Steve had received a phone call from Joey the picker-upper guy at Woodcrest. Joey, who was stoned as usual, told Steve that his apartment was "kinda warm" and when Steve asked how long it had been that way, Joey replied that he thought it had been about 100 hours. Upon hearing this, Steve recalculated Joey's "stoned time" estimate into real time and determined that the chiller had been down for about two hours.

Steve then had immediately called Roto-Rooter who, without Harold and Andy realizing, had located the leak on the other side of the property, excavated the pipe, and repaired the chiller system by about 11:00 that morning – almost a full hour before Harold and Andy had duct-taped what they thought was a leaky chiller pipe and, as they had believed, saved the day.

Now it will never truly be known if the spike that Harold and Andy drove into the ground that day actually ruptured the gas pipe or not, nor will it be known whether the pipe that Harold and Andy actually wrapped with duct tape was the gas line or the electric line, nor will it be known whether or not the unearthing of the trench in some way broke a natural pressure seal which had kept the gas line from leaking significantly for the past forty years.

But what *is* known is this – the inevitable gas explosion that was to take place this unusually hot day in August was only a matter of minutes away from happening, and there wasn't anybody, anywhere, who was going to be able to do anything to stop it.

And had Sue-Ann McDonald and Enrico Corleon and Shirley Dole and Jake Jacobs known this at the time, perhaps they would have "high-tailed it out of there" and gone back to the office or gone out to lunch or something. But alas, hindsight is 20-20. And besides, they were there anyway and even though they were the only four members of the "raid" team left at the property, and even though it was 12:11 p.m. and definitely time for lunch, Sue-Ann, Shirley, Jake, and Enrico decided that despite the fact that the chiller had been back up for nearly an hour before the 24-hour deadline, and despite the fact that no dangerous or unhealthful condition now actually existed at the apartments, there was no reason, at least in their mind, to call off the raid which had just been organized and mobilized.

No! Probable cause or not, they simply were not going to go away. And seeing as that Shirley and Sue-Ann both agreed that the chiller system, working or not, was most definitely just the tip of the iceberg, what this situation called for was a preemptive strike.

Shirley justified this preemptive measure based on her detailed knowledge of the Old Testament, which in the book of Isaiah, defines Beelzebub as "Lord of Flies" making a reference to the connection that flies, (pronounced *Jews*, by Shirley) and other vermin, were in biblical times associated with the spread of disease and other pestilence. Thus, to Sue-Ann, having learned from Shirley's announcement at the last Eastwood Community Association meeting, that Steve was in fact Beelzebub, it logically followed that a preemptive strike against the spread of vermin and disease was not only justified, but was necessary.(Sort of like the policies of the Bush Administration in Iraq, but on a slightly smaller scale.)

And luckily, Sue-Ann, who had seen that Marine recruiting commercial that Harold had seen as well, was prepared. You see, before leaving her office that day, she had instructed Jake to "write up" and hand to Sue-Ann the 1073 Criminal citations for a multitude of health and safety violations that had nothing to do with the chiller system being down – Sue-Ann figuring that while they were there she could kill two birds with one stone. So at exactly 12:12 p.m., after discussing whether "Shirley's kids" would rather have a water slide or a skating area in their new park, Shirley and Sue-Ann decided to conduct the "raid" by themselves, without back-up.

And as they walked together slowly towards the office to serve the 1073 citations in Sue-Ann's hand , Eileen, inside the office, who had seen them coming from the bathroom window she was peeking out from, began frantically destroying unattended-to maintenance request forms, that second set of books in which she kept track of exactly how much money she was stealing from Steve for his own good, and most significantly – a message pad of tenant phone calls complaining of a strange gas-like odor that was coming from the ground right in front of unit #1 where Joey the groundskeeper resided and where Harold had first discovered that he could light the ground on fire and see that little blue flame which flickered and then went out.

Speaking of the "little blue flame," oddly enough, although Harold and Andy had *not* fixed the chiller system, it *appeared* upon filling in the trench tightly they had sealed a gas pipe leak that had been fueling the little blue flame.

But appearances aside, the pipe leaked on. And as pressure began to build underground, and as the gas that was leaking out was unable to travel to the surface and escape as it had done for the last forty years, it took a new path and began to travel along the space between the gas and electric pipes, the one that Barney Wolcott, a Construction Foreman for the El Paso Electric Company had filled in with dirt just forty years, one month and thirty-six hours before.

The gas continued to travel along the pipes for about twenty-five feet until it reached the gas intake valve on the stove in unit #1, Joey's apartment, where through a small crack in the valve it finally escaped into the kitchen.

And as the gas from the pipe that Harold had just "fixed" continued to travel underground and slowly escape into Joey's kitchen, and as Joey the groundskeeper was returning to his apartment for lunch, Sue-Ann McDonald was carrying her stack of 1073 citations up to the front door of the Woodcrest office.

And as Joey the groundskeeper was walking into his apartment and closing the door behind him, Sue-Ann was knocking on the door of the Woodcrest office.

And as Joey was failing to notice (because he had no sense of smell) a gas odor coming from the kitchen in his apartment, Eileen was opening the door of the office to let Sue-Ann and Shirley in.

And as Joey was reaching for a marijuana cigarette and getting ready to fire up one of those disposable lighters that Harold had bought at the 7-Eleven, Sue-Ann was explaining to Eileen that she was being served with 1073 health code citations, and saying "Don't be alarmed! We're here to help."

And at exactly 12:14 p.m., as Sue-Ann was finishing pronouncing the "p" in the word help, Joey was staring at the flame which erupted up from his blue plastic lighter.

And as Joey momentarily realized that everything had suddenly gone black and was commenting to himself that "this must be some really good shit," Shirley and Sue-Ann and Eileen heard a deafening *boom* and felt the ground rumble and then shake.

And as Joey found himself floating peacefully in the air upwards towards a beautiful white light, Shirley, Sue-Ann and Eileen stared in awe at the giant fire-ball that rose 300 feet into the air all cherry-red and lemon-yellow and or-ange-orange.

And then they felt the shock wave that followed, which literally stopped time for a brief instant and then sent a shower of over a million pieces of glass and debris, raining down over what just five short seconds before had been the North End of the Woodcrest Apartments.

And as Eileen immediately concluded that "The moment of judgment was at hand," Joey, mangled, charred, but alive(!), fell out of the sky and landed in the front seat of Shirley Dole's orange Jeep, setting off the alarm and completely ruining the fake bearskin seat covers she had just bought and had installed over at Stylus Chevrolet the day before.

"Praise Be the Lord! The moment is at hand," said Eileen, and then she got down on her knees to pray.

And as Eileen's knees were hitting the floor in the office, Steve and his real estate broker, Bob, the man who had brokered the Woodcrest deal and sold the complex to Steve and The Boys in the first place, were just sitting down to lunch at Myoto's, a trendy sushi restaurant in the fancy part of El Paso, about eleven miles from the complex.

And as Steve was ordering the spicy tuna roll and the octopus salad, and as Bob was ordering the California roll and a bowl of soup, the entire emergency crew that had just left Woodcrest just seventeen minutes before when the raid had been called off, was returning to the complex to combat the ensuing fire that was set off by the thunderous gas explosion.

And as the Channel 5 Eyewitness News truck up-linked its satellite feed of the goings-on at Woodcrest, and as Harold and Andy were hunting through the aisles of Office Depot trying to find a blank invoice book so they could write up a fake Roto-Rooter bill for $5,000 to give to Eileen to give to Steve so they could get paid for fixing the chiller, Steve and Broker Bob were watching the TV which was behind the sushi bar counter at Myoto's.

On it was a live news broadcast of an explosion which had just taken place somewhere in the El Paso area. Steve took a bite of his tuna roll and turned to Bob and commented on how the fire was probably a result of some crackhead free-basing in his apartment. Bob took a sip of his miso soup and then told Steve that Bob's ex-wife used to freebase cocaine but unfortunately, she had never blown up.

And as Steve said to Bob, "I pity the poor bastards who own that fucking place," and as Bob agreed, the camera from the Channel 5 Eyewitness News van panned in on the green wooden carved sign in front of the complex that was on TV.

The sign said, **WOODCREST APARTMENTS** and on the ground just below the sign, was an old job completion ticket, charred and crinkled and worn with age. And on the bottom of the ticket appeared a name and a signature,

Barney Wolcott, Construction Supervisor, El Paso Electric Company.

Sub-Chapter 3.9 to the Negative 50

What Was That Little Blue Flame?

Crestwood Apartments Construction Site – El Paso, Texas 1955

On Thursday July 7th, 1955 the construction of the Crestwood Apartments was about one month away from completion. It was an unusually hot summer day and the Southwestern Gas Company had just finished digging a series of six-foot deep trenches and laying the four thousand feet or so of underground gas piping that would, for the many years to come, provide natural gas service to the complex.

Seeing as that it was almost 4:30 p.m. and all the piping was already in, the foreman on the job site decided to call it a day and send his crew home a little early so that those of them who owned television sets could catch the broadcast of the Milwaukee Braves - Chicago Cubs baseball game being played at Wrigley Field in Chicago that evening.

The gas company foreman himself had bet $10 on the Braves and he really wanted to get home as soon as possible so he would have time to adjust the antenna on his television set.

He and the crew were scheduled to return to Crestwood the following Monday morning to fill in the trenches. They would have normally been scheduled to return the very next day to complete the job but they had been assigned to attend a "safety" meeting in Highland Park that Friday morning and wouldn't make it back to El Paso in time to get any work done.

The very next day, on Friday at exactly 8:00 a.m., while the gas company crew arrived at the safety meeting, the El Paso Electric Company construction crew arrived at Crestwood to begin their installation of the electric lines. They weren't scheduled to begin work over at the complex until the following Tuesday but they were running ahead of schedule and figured they might as well get a jump on things before the weekend.

Barney Wolcott, the foreman of the Electric Company crew was unaware that the gas crew was attending that safety meeting in San Antonio that day and he assumed that since they weren't at the job site, they were done with their end of the installation, although why they hadn't filled in the trenches was a bit of a mystery to Barney.

Barney was also unaware, because he had failed to notice the memo back at the Electric Company, that he and his crew were also scheduled to attend the very same safety meeting that Friday, thus explaining why he and his crew were for some reason one day ahead of schedule.

The subject of the meeting was *"The proper procedures for the trenching and spacing of sub-terrain gas and electric lines,"* and had he and his crew known about and attended the meeting that day, they would have been made aware of the new State Code Regulation that required electric and gas lines to be spaced at least 36 inches from one another.

But alas, they hadn't, and besides, Barney had other things on his mind.

The All-Star Game was coming up that following Tuesday and Barney had promised his crew that if they could get the Crestwood project done early, they could all take that day off before coming to Barney's house that evening to watch the game on his new Bryn Mar television set. It was to be played in Milwaukee and was likely to be a hell of a game; the American League team roster including Mickey Mantle, Yogi Berra and Ted Williams and the National League roster including Ernie Banks, Roy Campanella and Stan Musial. Being a big Mantle fan, Barney had bet $45 on the side of the American League.

And so seizing upon the opportunity at hand, to finish the job a day ahead of schedule, Barney decided to utilize the already existing gas trenches and to lay his electric lines in those very same trenches that the gas lines were already laying in.

Not being an idiot, of course, he realized that it would not be safe for the gas and electric lines to touch, and as he was accustomed to burying his electric lines about four feet below the surface of the ground, Barney instructed his crew to first fill in the 6-foot deep gas trenches with about 24 inches of dirt before laying the electric lines over them.

And so, on that fateful hot Friday morning in El Paso, the electric construction crew carried out Barney's instructions and laid the electric lines two feet above and parallel to the gas lines, filling the two feet between the gas pipes and the electric cable with dirt and then filling in the trenches over the electric lines, also with dirt.

It was a brilliant idea and one which saved the electric company about 100 man-hours of work, bringing the installation of the electric lines at the complex not only in ahead of schedule but well under budget, not only insuring that Barney would probably get a promotion but also that he and his crew could take not only Tuesday off to see the All-Star game, but they could take Monday off as well.

After about nine hours on the job, the trenches were filled in, and the job was completed.

Accordingly, the crew left Crestwood at 5:07 p.m. and returned back to the El Paso Project Office, where Barney filled out the necessary project completion paperwork and signed off on the seven minutes of overtime that the crew had accumulated getting the project fully completed ahead of schedule.

At exactly 5:25 p.m., as Barney was calling his wife to see what they were having for dinner, a freak electrical storm that produced grapefruit-sized hail stones and winds in excess of sixty MPH, suddenly developed in the greater El Paso area and raged furiously and uncontrollably for about four minutes until it suddenly and abruptly stopped.

The storm was centered on the western edge of the city in a brand new neighborhood which was to become known, in the years ahead, as Eastwood.

At exactly 5:35 p.m., and completely unaware that the storm had even occurred because there were no windows in the Electric Project Office, Barney left headquarters and returned home for dinner.

Having just bought one of those brand new Zenith Black and White "Bryn Mar" 21" portable television sets with the silver and maroon metal stand, and after adjusting the antenna so the picture came in almost perfectly, he sat down on the couch in the living room with one of those metal TV trays in front of him to eat and to relax with his wife and watch a summer rerun of his favorite TV show *I Love Lucy*. It was the classic episode which was originally broadcast on May 9, 1955, just about two months before – the one in which Harpo Marx appeared on the show and re-enacted the famous mirror scene from the Marx Brothers movie *Duck Soup*.

At about 10:00 p.m.; after watching *Lucy,* the *$64,000 Question* show, and a brand new show called *The Lawrence Welk Show* which had premiered on ABC just one week earlier, and after finishing a six-pack of Bud, he went down to the liquor store a few blocks from his house, to get some more beer and a pack of Marlboros. He also wanted to check the latest copy of TV guide to find out when the up-coming Rocky Marciano/Archie Moore fight was going to take place and to see if it was going to be broadcast on tele-vision.

To his disappointment, it was not. But he did find out that you could actually see the fight at the Highland Park Drive-In; as the heavyweight bout was to be screened ex-clusively for "theatre-television" and was to be viewed in 133 theatres and drive-ins in ninety-two cities across the U.S.

The fight was scheduled for September 21st and would take place in Yankee stadium, and having been an Archie Moore fan for quite some time, he decided to spend the ten bucks, which was a lot of money at the time, to get a ticket for the live theatre broadcast. He also bet fifty dollars on Moore to win.

At 10:25 p.m., on his way back home, as he passed by what was soon to be the front lawn of the Crestwood Com-plex, he decided, even though he was off the clock, to stop and take a look at the filled-in trench to see if the dirt had properly settled yet.

It looked just fine with the exception of a downed tree branch which was lying on the ground near the trench. The tree was split in two down the center, and it looked like it had been struck by lightning, the section that was on the ground appearing to have recently caught on fire, as it was charred and all mangled up.

But the trench seemed to be just fine. And so after taking one last drag of his Marlboro cigarette, at exactly 10:29 p.m., he tossed the still-lit butt on the ground, turned around, and walked slowly back to his truck, getting in, starting the engine and slowly driving away.

As he began heading down the street, in the very spot where he had flicked his cigarette butt just about a minute before, a little blue flame mysteriously ignited, flickered up from the ground for just a brief second, danced around playfully, and then just as mysteriously as it had ignited, went out.

Post *Mort*em
Chapter 3.1415926535

Much Ado about Nothing

Austin, Texas -2002 – In regards to the explosion at Woodcrest

Ironically, in a two-year investigation conducted by the State Fire Marshall's office in conjunction with the Federal Aviation Administration (it seems Joey's body had been blown high enough to enter Federal Air Space and as such was subject to the agency's jurisdiction), it was determined with almost 100 percent certainty that the gas explosion that had occurred at Woodcrest that hot summer day in August was indeed, just as Eileen had thought, caused by an act of God.

The official report, which was 18,000 pages long and cost the Texas taxpayers seventeen million dollars to complete, recorded the official cause of the gas explosion as a "lightning strike" which had caused a surge in the electric line, which had in turn burned the outer coating of the gas line, causing a slow leak which eventually led to the explosion. The report did not give credit to either Harold or Andy for temporarily patching the leak nor did it give credit to Joey Poney for discovering it.

As for the El Paso Electric Company and the late Barney Wolcott, who had illegally installed the electric line over the gas line in the first place, no criminal wrong-doings were ever acknowledged.

The electric company did write Joey a formal letter of apology, however, and in a gesture of kindness awarded him the sum of $300,000 in compensatory damages. After paying his hospital bills and 40 percent lawyer's fees plus the costs of the lawsuit, Joey was left with just over $250 which he promptly spent on some of that "really good shit" that he had gotten from that new Columbian lady manager over at Woodcrest.

As for Shirley Dole, who did *not* want to wait for the results of the "official" investigation, she conducted her own investigation into the cause of the gas explosion two days after it had occurred and after carefully interviewing one person, Bill in unit #15, who had seen Harold light the little blue flame with those Bic lighters, she, within two seconds, concluded that the actual cause of the explosion and the fire that followed was exactly the opposite of what the Fire Marshall, the FAA, and Eileen would come to conclude 2 years later; Shirley declaring the official cause of the incident to be not "an act of God," but "an act of Satan," and explaining that the little blue flame that came up were simply the fires of hell overflowing into Woodcrest because it was owned by Steve and his ungodly crew.

As for Jake, who within the 24-hour time limit successfully cancelled all one hundred of the erroneous citations he had written for the "not down" chiller system, and the additional 1073 citations for the various criminal zoning violations, he had to take a two-month leave of absence to have surgery on his right hand due to nerve damage which was caused by severe cramping of his palm when he refused to let his wife help him in writing out all those cancellation forms.

As for Harold and Andy, they are to this day still waiting for their check.

For although in return for being dead, Morty had promised Steve to continue funding the Woodcrest operation until such time as they could get rid of it, when Steve and Morty got together to review all the invoices, a problem arose.

As Steve, Morty, and Dolores (Morty's secretary) curiously wondered why they had received two separate invoices from Roto-Rooter, and as they compared the two Roto-Rooter invoices, both for the sum of $5,000 and both covering the work done diagnosing the leak and repairing the chiller system at Woodcrest that fateful day, they immediately noticed that one of the invoices had the red *Roto-Rooter* logo printed on the upper left hand corner and the invoice number printed on the upper right hand corner reading Invoice#58479.

They further noticed that the other invoice had the red *Roto-Rooter* Logo on the upper left hand corner but this one was drawn with a red magic marker and read *Rota-Rewter*, this invoice being numbered #*wun*.

Easily spotting the second invoice as a fake, Morty instructed Steve not to pay it, and then not wanting to take any chances, he instructed Steve not to pay the first invoice either, just to be safe. And then reveling in the moment he said, "Let them pound sand Steve, let them all pound sand."

In the end, the Slumlord case of the century turned out to be a case of much ado about nothing. It was an event which ended both with a bang and then a whimper, the bang being the explosion that rocked the neighborhood for a few seconds that hot August day which then, with the next day's disaster, was quickly forgotten; the whimper being a settlement which was finally reached between the City and the parties concerned, a paper tiger of an agreement meant to save face for the City Officials who so vehemently prosecuted the case to no avail and an agreement to seemingly punish Steve and the Beverly Hills Boys for letting their ambitions get the better of them.

In the final analysis, it was Stealth Investing that saved the day and a dream that Steve had once had that turned out to be both his and The Boys' salvation.

Being unable to prove with any reasonable certainty who actually owned Woodcrest, or any other of the 22 properties The Boys were supposedly affiliated with, the City had no choice but to throw in the towel; and in return for Steve and the Boys agreeing to a small list of meaningless concessions, the City agreed to drop all 1073 criminal citations and offset all of the $8,550,000 in fines which had been levied.

The concessions were as follows: The Boys agreed to stop buying property in El Paso for a period of 5 years, The Boys agreed to disclose which properties they actually had interests in, The Boys agreed to donate $10,000 to Shirley's Kids' Park, and finally the Boys agreed that Steve would, on their behalf, be required to make a public apology to the City and the citizens of Eastwood at the next Eastwood Community Association Meeting.

It was a Tuesday afternoon at around 5:00 P.M. when the "apology meeting" convened in the auditorium at Eastwood Elementary School. In attendance were a handful of employees from the City's Neighborhood Services Department, Sue-Ann McDonald from the Prosecutor's office, a smattering of local tenants who had come mostly for the free doughnuts and coffee, and of course Shirley Dole. Noticeable absent were Councilman Jameson and Mayor Lanza, whom upon hearing there was no news coverage scheduled for the event, didn't see the point in attending.

As Steve walked up the stairs of the stage in the auditorium and approached the podium, the chattering going on in the room continued unabated and as he stepped up to the podium and began to speak, no one in the room, including Shirley Dole, seemed to pay very much attention.

The pockets of conversation in the audience, from what Steve could overhear from the stage, were centered on two subjects. First, comments on how good the coffee and doughnuts were, and second, rumors of what was going on at a complex in the neighborhood that had just been named the 3rd worst property in El Paso. The property had recently been purchased by a group of wealthy investors from Chicago and was being managed for them by a guy named Andrew Gold.

Even though they had owned the place for a full two months now, nothing had been done to improve the deplorable conditions of the property at all and the group, Andy and the Chicago Boys Back Home were apparently stalling, claiming they were waiting for a rehab loan they had been promised by a guy down at City Hall named Stan Valvo.

"On behalf of myself and my partners, I would like to take this opportunity to apologize for getting involved in the neighborhood of Eastwood in the first place, for investing any money in the community and for not giving Shirley Dole the kind of donation she originally asked for so she could build her Shirley's Kids' Park right away. And as a gesture of our remorse, we are hereby donating our entire interest in the Woodcrest complex to Shirley Dole, personally, so that she can own and run the place, the way it should have been owned and run in the first place. Surely Shirley will do a better job than we did and it is with the

344

most humble of intentions that we sincerely wish her all the luck in the world in her new endeavor. Thank You!"

Exactly one year later to the day, Shirley Dole was indicted on 1073 counts of criminal zoning violations at the Woodcrest complex, mostly dog-shit. She is still to this day awaiting trial.

www.ingramcontent.com/pod-product-compliance
Lightning Source LLC
Chambersburg PA
CBHW051440170526
45166CB00001B/58